DATE DUE			

D1261037

Noam Chomsky

Twayne's United States Authors Series

Frank Day, Editor

Clemson University

TUSAS 634

NOAM CHOMSKY
Photograph by M. Scott Moon.

Noam Chomsky

By Michael C. Haley
University of Alaska Anchorage

Ronald F. Lunsford
University of North Carolina Charlotte

Twayne Publishers • New York
Maxwell Macmillan Canada • Toronto
Maxwell Macmillan International • New York   Oxford   Singapore   Sydney

Twayne's United States Authors Series No. 634

Noam Chomsky

Michael C. Haley and Ronald F. Lunsford

Twayne Publishers   Maxwell Macmillan Canada, Inc.
Macmillan Publishing Company   1200 Eglinton Avenue East
866 Third Avenue   Suite 200
New York, New York 10022   Don Mills, Ontario M3C 3N1

Library of Congress Cataloging-in-Publication Data

Haley, Michael C.
    Noam Chomsky / by Michael C. Haley and Ronald F. Lunsford.
        p.   cm.
    Includes bibliographical references and index.
    ISBN 0-8057-4013-9
    1. Chomsky, Noam.   2. Generative grammar.   I. Lunsford, Ronald F.
    II. Title.
    P85.C47H27   1993
    410'.92—dc20   93-26570
                                                              CIP

The paper used in this publication meets the minimum requirements of American National Standard for Information Sciences—Permanence of Paper for Printed Library Materials. ANSI Z3948-1984. ∞™

10 9 8 7 6 5 4 3 2 1 (hc)

Printed in the United States of America

To Our Parents
John and Margaret Haley
Chester and Reba Lunsford

Contents

Preface

Late one afternoon in December of 1989, we found ourselves standing in the hallway outside Noam Chomsky's office at the Massachusetts Institute of Technology (MIT), waiting for what was to be the climax of a very stimulating and rewarding visit in Cambridge. Most of that week we had spent just down the hall, inside Chomsky's private library (to which he had kindly entrusted us with a key), studying the careful chronological collection there of his hundreds of publications on language, philosophy, and politics. Now we were waiting for an interview with Chomsky himself. Naturally, we were excited and not a little nervous about the prospects of conversing with the world's premier linguist.

We were nervous even though this interview was actually to be our third talk with Chomsky. Our first—arranged (with the help of Larry Rottmann) more than a year in advance, on account of the enormous demands on Chomsky's time—had been held on Friday (1 December) of the previous week. Chomsky's answers to our questions then had been helpful, but when it was obvious that there were many more questions we needed to ask, he had somehow managed to work us into his busy agenda for a second interview on Monday (4 December)—at the conclusion of which we of course still had a long list of unanswered questions, now including many new ones. So Chomsky had volunteered to meet with us for yet a third interview at the end of his rather long day of classes and appointments on Thursday, 7 December, which also happened to have been his sixty-first birthday.

Around 5:30 p.m., while we fidgeted outside Chomsky's office with our notes and tape recorder, worrying that perhaps he had forgotten all about us in the hectic rush of his schedule, there suddenly arose from the far end of the hallway an animated confusion of voices. A moment later Chomsky appeared there, surrounded by at least a half dozen of his students as he made his way back to his office. Apparently, we were not the only ones with just a few final questions for the day.

After he had satisfied (or at least placated) most of the students reasonably well, Chomsky led the two of us through the office complex he shares with Morris Halle and into his inner office, closing the door

ix

behind us. Right away he said, "Excuse me for just one minute." Sitting down behind his desk, he took up a pen and note pad and began to write. We went on about our business, setting up and testing the tape recorder, then took our seats and waited in silence for Chomsky to finish what he was doing. Whatever it was, it certainly took him longer than "just one minute." For a good four or five minutes he continued to stare intently at the note pad, even when he was not writing on it. He seemed absolutely oblivious to everything else.

Finally, with a little start, he appeared to remember that someone else was in the office with him. He put the note pad away with an apology for making us wait, explaining that one of the students in his last class had suggested an interesting new idea that he had wanted to write down for more careful consideration later on. This seemingly trivial little episode impressed us both as one of the most revealing moments of our meetings with Noam Chomsky.

It also illustrates something that poses no small challenge for a book of this sort. Throughout his career, the growth of Chomsky's own ideas has been bound almost inextricably with the birth of new ideas among his colleagues, and it is clear that he always numbers his students rather high on the list of his colleagues. Thus many of the theoretical innovations of "Chomskyan linguistics" have not come exclusively from the mind of Noam Chomsky. Chomsky often makes a point of mentioning the names of various students and other associates to whom he attributes specific and sometimes major innovations in the development of his theory of language. However, if other people have made important contributions to his theory of language, it is no accident that these people have most often arisen from the ranks of his own students and associates. Indeed, perhaps no other single fact about the whole history of Chomskyan linguistics more convincingly demonstrates Chomsky's own status as a truly seminal thinker.

With regard to this book's primary focus on Chomsky's theory of language, then, the main goal has been to give an overall general sense of what that theory is, of how it was born, and of how it has developed over the years. This necessarily involves talking about certain key figures who have played important roles in the growth of Chomsky's thought, but we have made no systematic effort in every case to sort out which ideas came specifically from Chomsky, which from his students or other colleagues, and which from the creative interaction that always seems to be going on between them.

For instance, while chapter one devotes a good deal of attention to the people and circumstances in Chomsky's life during the 1950s, when he formulated an early version of his revolutionary theory of language, chapter two concentrates almost entirely on some basic principles of that early theory itself. Chapter three gives some slight attention to the contributions of Chomsky's MIT associates during the 1960s, when he developed his first significant revisions of the theory, but here again the emphasis is upon the principal themes of the theory itself, especially as it evolved through the 1970s. By the early 1980s, it had become increasingly clear that a major conceptual shift—no mere revision—was occurring within Chomskyan theory, and that a radically new model of language was emerging from this conceptual shift. Chapter four attempts to describe a few components of this new model, as well as how these components interact; it is here that the challenge of describing the theory itself has necessitated an almost complete neglect of the contributions by other linguists (particularly by linguists in Europe). Furthermore, in none of these chapters has it been possible to give a thorough, in-depth analysis of Chomsky's more technical material; for that—although of course not only for that— nothing can equal Chomsky's own original writings.

The same is true of chapter five, which is largely concerned with Chomsky's social/political thought. With space for only a single chapter on this important topic, it has not been possible to provide a detailed examination of Chomsky's positions on the various political issues about which he has in fact written and spoken volumes—more than a score of volumes. The goals therefore have been to present an overview of the general character of Chomsky's political thought (taking representative cases as illustrations of this), to develop a sense of Chomsky's unique style as a political analyst, and to explore in greater depth some possible connections between his social theories and his philosophy of language and mind. Again, however, whether in politics or in linguistics, there is no substitute for Chomsky's original and inimitable writings.

We want to express our gratitude to Noam Chomsky for his help. He made time and extra time for us in an incredibly busy schedule. He answered our questions freely, patiently, and expansively. He opened the door of his private library to us. He even spent several late-night sessions carefully going over the long transcripts of our interviews, making corrections and offering valuable amplifications.

We did refrain, however, from asking him to read the manuscript of this book (though there is little doubt he would have been willing to do it), and so his helpfulness with our research should not, in any way, be construed as his endorsement of our final product. The interpretations and evaluations of Chomsky's work as represented in this book are strictly our own.

Note: Michael Haley drafted chapters one through four, and Ronald Lunsford drafted chapter five; the research, the planning, and the three interviews with Chomsky were a collaborative effort.

Chronology

1928   Avram Noam Chomsky born 7 December in Philadelphia, Pennsylvania, to William and Elsie (Simonofsky) Chomsky.

1930   Enrolls in experimental progressive school.

1939   Publishes first political editorial (on the fall of Barcelona).

1945   Enrolls at the University of Pennsylvania.

1947   Discovers modern linguistics via *Methods in Structural Linguistics* by Zellig Harris.

1949   Receives B.A., University of Pennsylvania. Marries Carol Doris Schatz.

1951   Receives M.A., University of Pennsylvania. Begins 4-year term (1951–55) as Junior Fellow, Society of Fellows, at Harvard University; meets Morris Halle.

1952   First begins working on generative grammar of English.

1953   First article appears ("Systems of Syntactic Analysis" in the *Journal of Symbolic Logic*). Takes a few months' leave from Harvard and travels to Israel to live on a kibbutz.

1955   Completes first version of *The Logical Structure of Linguistic Theory* (unpublished until 1975). Receives Ph.D. from the University of Pennsylvania. Begins teaching at MIT.

1956   Presents seminal paper, "Three Models for the Description of Language," at MIT Symposium.

1957   *Syntactic Structures.*

1958   Appointed member of the Institute for Advanced Study, Princeton. Invited to present "A Transformational Approach to Syntax" at the Third Texas Conference on Problems of Linguistic Analysis in English.

1959   Publishes important review of B. F. Skinner's *Verbal Behavior.*

1961   Appointed full Professor of Modern Languages, MIT.

1962   Invited as a featured speaker to the Ninth International Congress of Linguists.

1964 *Current Issues in Linguistic Theory.*

1965 *Aspects of the Theory of Syntax.*

1966 Named Ferrari P. Ward Professor of Modern Languages and Linguistics, MIT. Named Visiting Beckman Professor of English, University of California-Berkeley. *Cartesian Linguistics* and *Topics in the Theory of Generative Grammar.*

1967 Awarded D.H.L., University of Chicago, and D.Litt., University of London.

1968 *Sound Pattern of English* (with Morris Halle) and *Language and Mind.*

1969 *American Power and the New Mandarins.*

1970 Awarded D.H.L., Loyola University, and D.H.L., Swarthmore College. *At War with Asia.*

1971 Awarded D.H.L., Bard College. *Problems of Knowledge and Freedom.*

1972 Awarded D.Litt., Delhi (India) University. *Studies on Semantics in Generative Grammar.*

1975 *The Logical Structure of Linguistic Theory* is finally published (Plenum), 20 years after completion. *Reflections on Language.*

1976 Appointed Institute Professor, MIT.

1977 *Essays on Form and Interpretation.*

1978 *Human Rights and American Foreign Policy.*

1979 *Language and Responsibility.* Gives a seminar (later known as the Pisa Lectures) at the GLOW Conference in Italy.

1980 Awarded D.Litt., Visva-Bharati University, Santiniketan, West Bengal. *Rules and Representations.*

1981 *Lectures on Government and Binding: The Pisa Lectures.*

1982 *Some Concepts and Consequences of the Theory of Government and Binding, Towards a New Cold War,* and *Noam Chomsky on The Generative Enterprise, A Discussion with Riny Huybregts and Henk van Riemsdijk.*

1984 Awarded D.H.L., University of Pennsylvania. Receives the Distinguished Scientific Contribution Award, American Psychological Association. *Modular Approaches to the Study of the Mind.*

1985   *Turning the Tide.*

1986   *Knowledge of Language, Barriers,* and *Pirates and Emperors.*

1987   *On Power and Ideology, Language and Problems of Knowledge,* and *Language in a Psychological Setting.* Receives the George Orwell Award of NCTE.

1988   Awarded the Kyoto Prize (ca. $350,000) in Basic Sciences. *Generative Grammar: Its Basis, Development and Prospects, The Culture of Terrorism,* and *Manufacturing Consent* (with Edward Herman).

1989   *Necessary Illusions.*

1991   *Deterring Democracy* and *What Uncle Sam Really Wants.*

Chapter One

Noam Chomsky: Idealist of the Cognitive Revolution

Outside Agitator

The date was 11 September 1956, second day of the special Symposium on Information Theory being held at the Massachusetts Institute of Technology. One of two featured papers for the day was being presented by a young and relatively unknown linguist who was just beginning his second year as an instructor at MIT. Many leading figures in communication theory and related sciences were in the audience, listening intently. One of them was the psychologist George Miller, who would later recall this exact day as the birthday of the cognitive revolution.[1]

What exactly was this "cognitive revolution"? There is no simple answer to this question, because the movement is still growing fast, changing every day, continually redefining its shape and direction as it spreads deeper and wider through many different fields of human inquiry—especially psychology, anthropology, philosophy, artificial intelligence, neuroscience, education, and of course linguistics and communication. The people involved in this movement, having been drawn into it from so many different disciplines, have infused it with an equal number and diversity of philosophical agendas, to the effect that there are now warring factions within it, all trying to march under the banner of "cognitivism" while each tries to wrest that banner away from the others. At least from its earliest stages, however, the cognitive revolution can be seen as a concerted movement to resurrect some rather ancient issues in philosophy as the specific concerns of a modern science—what Howard Gardner calls "cognitive science," or an "empirically based effort to answer long-standing epistemological questions" having to do with "the nature of [human] knowledge, its components, its sources, and its deployment" (Gardner, 6).

Further, no matter how many diverse directions the cognitive revolution may have taken since its beginning, its modern genesis is surely and inextricably linked to the seminal ideas in that young linguist's paper of 1956, which so impressed George Miller and others at the MIT symposium. The paper was entitled "Three Models for the Description of Language," and it was written by Noam Chomsky.[2]

For Chomsky himself, of course, it was a somewhat crude beginning. After all, he was only twenty-seven years old when he presented the paper. He could not have foreseen all the revolutionary developments that would arise from the "generative-transformational"[3] model of human language his paper proposed, let alone all the drastic changes he himself would make in that model over the next thirty-five years. So the paper was only a start, but it was a good start. Because human language is perhaps the core system of human cognition, the worldwide cognitive revolution in the human sciences today still owes much of its impetus to the "Chomskyan revolution" in linguistics.[4]

In one way at least, Chomsky was and is the prototypical revolutionary. From our very first short interview with him (a few days before his sixty-first birthday),[5] my strongest and most lasting impression was of his unabashed and uncompromising idealism. This, after four decades of out-and-out linguistic war with the reigning establishment in the behavioral sciences, a war in which many of his most ardent early comrades (including many of his own students) have turned against him. He himself does not see it that way, though. While he does not suffer opposition to his ideas gladly, it simply is not in Noam Chomsky to look upon such events as defections or disloyalty, or to view the endless and sometimes solitary character of his life's work as an unreasonable burden. To him, such matters are all in the nature of science, in the nature of all human inquiry—indeed, in the very nature of the human mind itself, the incorrigible creativity of which continues to fascinate him all the more even as it defies each new orthodoxy thrown up to capture it.

This outlook endures, too, after five decades of bitter political dissidence and agitation against practically every great governmental power on earth and most especially against the government of his own country. Having published his first political editorial at the age of ten, and having held steadfastly to his basic libertarian principles since age twelve, Noam Chomsky was and is—at least with respect to his tenacious idealism—the prototypical revolutionary.

In any case, his strong idealism probably made him well suited for his particular role in the cognitive revolution. This in part was because the theory of language with which Chomsky helped to launch that revolution is explicitly predicated upon an open appeal to a kind of "scientific idealism"—namely, the idealization of language as an abstract cognitive system to be studied in isolation from certain pragmatic factors of social context, which would prevent one from doing what Chomsky sees as "linguistic science." As Chomsky is quick to point out, there is really nothing "new," in the larger history of science, about the use of theoretical and methodological abstractions and idealizations of this sort. In fact, he thinks, this ought not even be controversial, let alone "revolutionary." All true scientists must be guided by certain abstractions and idealizations in both theory and method, whether or not they admit it, or whether or not they even know it. Given the prevailing mind-set in the fields of linguistics and behavioral science when Noam Chomsky arrived on the scene, however, his open and candid reliance on certain key idealizations about language was truly revolutionary, and it remains controversial even today.

Chomsky is often criticized, for instance, for assuming the ideal of a "homogeneous speech community" in his investigations of language. The criticism continues despite the fact that he always makes this assumption explicit as an idealization and often takes time to argue (quite persuasively) that it is in fact a necessary idealization—necessary, at least as a preliminary step, even for those sociolinguistic or cross-linguistic studies whose target is the linguistic diversity to be found in actual speech communities. The controversy surrounding this particular idealization, however, is a relatively minor one compared to the near "scandal" created (in some circles) by Chomsky's heavy reliance on abstract, quasimathematical linguistic schemata, a kind of idealization that itself springs from the radical core of Chomsky's revolutionary theories about language: namely, his view of the grammar of language as an idealized system, a set of exceedingly abstract, precise, universal, and biologically innate cognitive principles that determine the very structure of all linguistic knowledge. Indeed, Chomsky's key idealization is his view of language *as* knowledge, language as an unconscious form of knowledge that is both distinct from and fundamental to actual linguistic behavior.

While this idealization is of course a central topic in this book, it by no means contains the whole story of Chomsky's revolutionary idealism, nor does it fully explain what about this idealism so naturally suited the man to his role as one of the founders of the cognitive revolution. No, there is something more, something that is perhaps basic to his character. As already suggested above, Chomsky's idealism has another side to it, an inherently dangerous side perhaps, but one that I believe is key to his emergence as a truly visionary thinker in intellectual history. It is by virtue of this aspect of his idealism that Noam Chomsky is deeply—and perhaps cynically—suspicious of most forms of authority, all established traditions of orthodoxy and power. The most obvious manifestation of this is the decidedly anarchistic character of his libertarian socialist political views. I believe that it may also at least help to explain how Chomsky came to be the father of generative-transformational grammar as well, and thus to emerge as the founder and leader of a worldwide revolution in linguistics during the 1950s and 1960s.

What leads me to this belief, above all, is the fact that Chomsky has led a new vanguard of linguists on yet a second revolution in language theory, a revolution during the 1980s and nineties that has all but overturned what was widely known as the "standard theory" of transformational grammar. As the standard theory, of course, this was nothing less than another orthodoxy, the new orthodoxy established by the first Chomskyan revolution of the 1950s and sixties. Chomsky's unforgiving idealism in the search for truth simply holds nothing to be sacrosanct, even if such intellectual commitment means he must tear down much of the theoretical superstructure (sparing only the foundation) of that abstract edifice which, for at least a quarter of a century, stood as a monument to his own remarkable early achievements.

That second revolution is in itself a story for another chapter. Just the background to the first revolution is more than enough for this chapter. It is, after all, a rather curious story, and perhaps the single most curious thing about it is the unconventional (even unlikely) route by which Chomsky came to be its central character. While the idealism that marked his personality from early childhood generally suited him for his role as a revolutionary thinker, the course of his academic career would not have made many people expect that Noam Chomsky would revolutionize the world of professional linguistics.

Yet, perhaps even that is part of what uniquely qualified him for this role: Like many other revolutionaries, Chomsky arose suddenly from outside his own field, with no pretensions to it. And so, with an ease that flows perhaps from having nothing to lose, he just walked right up to the podium that September day in 1956 and calmly stepped out to the leading edge of a revolution that was ready to happen.

The time was ripe, as he himself (downplaying his own role) often has observed in retrospect. The entire intellectual world of Cambridge was ready to burst wide open with new ideas. However, if (as George Miller says) Chomsky's "Three Models" paper is part of what caused this bursting of new ideas, the instrument Chomsky used in the paper to accomplish this feat was a rather long, sharp needle. The content of his paper itself, that is, probably was not at all what some of the most prominent figures at the MIT Symposium were so eagerly anticipating. In fact, Chomsky's ideas flew directly in the face of the prevailing optimism and enthusiasm about some of the latest models of communication theory at the time.

A curious story indeed when you look at the setting more closely: At this time in the 1950s, recent advances in electronics, particularly in the development of computers, and the growth of mathematical theories of communication and information had led to an unprecedented aura of excitement, a palpable sense that science and technology would at long last be successfully connected to studies of the human brain and human behavior. One of the big buzzwords was "cybernetics," coined in 1948 for a new science dealing with the comparison of electronic computers to the human nervous system. With growing pressure to establish such interdisciplinary connections, the central position of human language, too, already had been clearly anticipated. Only the year before (1955), for instance, the well-known linguist C. F. Hockett had published a theory of language structure modeled on a Markov finite-state machine.[6] Breakthroughs in automatic speech recognition and even in machine translation were widely believed to be imminent. All of these and related matters were being discussed with great exuberance, no doubt, at the MIT Symposium on Information Theory in 1956. Truly, the stage was set for revolution.

And then, just imagine: Up to the microphone stepped a twenty-seven-year-old instructor beginning his second year of teaching undergraduate linguistics and logic, along with some courses in Scientific French and German (in which he was, admittedly, barely competent). He had three degrees to his credit, all earned in highly unconventional ways. His doctoral dissertation, word had it, was only one chapter from a huge, audacious book that nobody (not even MIT Press) wanted to publish. Still, he already had published five or six articles in linguistics, and he was reported by some to be a rising star. No less than the linguist Zelling Harris and the philosopher Nelson Goodman had spoken highly of him. Even the great linguist Roman Jakobson had been impressed with him, helping him in fact to get the position at MIT. And maybe, at least as far as this audience was concerned, he had something else going for him: He held a joint appointment in MIT's Research Laboratory of Electronics—working (at least in principle) on a research project in machine translation. What would this bright young researcher have to say about progress at the Laboratory?

Machine translation was not even the topic of his paper, of course, but its clear implication was that such a thing simply could not be done! Human language would not submit to the likes of any linear machine. It was too complex, too creative, to be generated with any simplistic finite-state process. On the other hand, he suggested, what a truly generative model of language needed were transformations.

Suddenly, at least in the minds of a few key figures like George Miller, the cognitive revolution was underway. Given the intellectual climate that had set the stage for it, Noam Chomsky—despite his visionary idealism—may have been one of the least likely candidates to lead it. Not only were his credentials as a linguist suspect, but he had already openly abandoned the long-established scientific methodologies of the standard European and American structuralist tradition, the scientific approach to language that was a cornerstone of the behavioral sciences. Most importantly, Noam Chomsky (ever true to form as an outsider) was decidedly unenthusiastic about—and almost flippantly dismissive of—some of the key language-technology developments that almost everybody else was so excited about.

To the surprise of many, though, that was exactly what was needed in order to get the movement started on the proper track. Chomsky's ideas about language were novel, fresh, radical, but still exceedingly precise, and there can be little doubt that much of their appeal in 1956 was the explicit mathematical notation in which he formalized these ideas. But if the time was ripe for his contribution, the time was also out of joint in certain crucial respects. It needed not only a precise thinker but an idealistic visionary and an unconventional outsider like Noam Chomsky to set it right.

Unconventional Origins

Avram Noam Chomsky was born in Philadelphia, Pennsylvania, on 7 December 1928 to William and Elsie (Simonofsky) Chomsky. His father, who had left Russia in 1913 to avoid being drafted into the Czarist army, was a scholar of medieval Hebrew grammar.[7] His mother was a teacher of Hebrew at the experimental progressive school in Philadelphia where her husband was now the school principal.

Noam was enrolled in this school before the age of two and was to remain there until about the age of twelve. The school certainly was progressive and unconventional, especially for those times, in that its emphasis was on personal creativity and expression and the pursuit of individual interests. Instead of the traditional forms of classroom regimentation, students often worked by themselves or in small groups, without competition between one another or ranking of the students by their teachers. In these respects, the experimental progressive school contrasted sharply in Chomsky's mind with the highly competitive, success-oriented public high school he later attended in Philadelphia. In his revealing interview with James Peck, Chomsky leaves no doubt as to which approach to education he preferred at the time, and which he would recommend today; while the progressive experimental school clearly had a profound impact on him, he told Peck he remembers "virtually nothing" from his high school education.[8]

In our own (second) interview with him, when he was asked how the experimental progressive school may have shaped his ideas, Chomsky replied in part, "For one thing, I think one should be suspicious of any form of arbitrary power and hierarchy and authority."[9] Clearly, the unconventional character of his first school experience helped to foster his own special brand of idealism, a kind of idealism that also seems to have made him very much the outsider even in high school during the early 1940s. In that same interview with us, Chomsky made another remark I thought was telling, especially with regard to his attitude about what might be called group loyalty to tradition:

I remember when I was in high school, and I was all excited, passionate, about the high school football team. And I remember asking myself, Why do I care? I couldn't say one word to any of these guys. And I don't want to sit at the same table with them, and they don't want to sit at the same table with me, and they're no different than the guys at the other [high] school, and what do I care whether they win a game or they lose a game? All that this does is enhance blind and foolish loyalties, which is extremely dangerous, because that carries over into chauvinism for the state and others; it's extremely dangerous. (Interview2)

The remark not only exhibits the idealism about individual freedom of thought that animates Chomsky's political views; it also portends, rather poignantly I think, something of the disenchantment and personal alienation which that same idealism made Chomsky's lot, often leaving him isolated on the "fringe" of the American educational and academic establishment.

When he graduated from high school and enrolled in the University of Pennsylvania, as he told Peck many years later, Chomsky had high hopes that things might be different in college (*Reader*, 6–7). With only a few notable exceptions, however, he found life at the university to be only a disappointing extension of his high school experience. He felt so alienated from it that he resolved to drop out of college altogether at the end of his sophomore year, in order to pursue his personal interests (mainly political). The reason he did not actually go through with this resolve was one of those few notable exceptions—his contact with Zellig Harris, a professor at the University of Pennsylvania and a leading figure in modern structural linguistics. It was not Harris's reputation as a linguist, however, that first drew Chomsky to him; it was rather Harris's political ideas. Their mutual involvement in political issues of the time brought them together in a chance meeting, and Chomsky was so impressed with Harris's understanding of social questions that he began to take some of Harris's courses.

The year was 1947. Noam Chomsky was eighteen years old. Though still an undergraduate, in only his sophomore year, he now began to take Zellig Harris's graduate courses in linguistics, and at last he was challenged, fascinated, by a subject of some importance within the traditional world of academe.

Of course much of the appeal to Chomsky must have been Harris's decidedly unconventional methods of teaching. The small group of students who comprised the professor's closest circle felt "quite alienated" from the larger campus life of the university; they were drawn together around their mentor by political and other intellectual interests besides linguistics (*Reader*, 8). Harris would lead them in day-long sessions in his home, sessions that apparently covered politics, linguistics, and other topics. Harris apparently took note of Chomsky's growing curiosity about linguistics and related topics, for he used this as an opportunity to urge that Chomsky take some more formal course work. At his suggestion, Chomsky thus began to attend graduate courses in philosophy with Nelson Goodman, among others, and in mathematics with Nathan Fine. Perhaps most importantly of all, Harris gave Chomsky the page proofs of his forthcoming book, *Methods in Structural Linguistics.*[10]

Chomsky found the book intriguing. He has since often credited it, in various places throughout his own writings, as having provided him with his formal introduction to the field of linguistics. Having read the proofs of his own father's work in medieval Hebrew grammar many years earlier, he had some prior informal acquaintance with historical linguistics, and he had even at that time been struck by the explanatory power of certain diachronic principles of language change. But Chomsky saw in Harris's *Methods* something new and exciting to him, something that was ultimately even beyond the book's own vision or scope—the possibilities for a "synchronic" model of language, a kind of model that might capture the distribution of linguistic elements at any given moment of time with the same explanatory power sometimes achieved by diachronic models in historical linguistics (which capture the distribution of similar elements across whole periods of time).[11] In any case, Chomsky had never formally studied the kind of material he found in Harris's book. After some stimulating discussions with Harris about it, he resolved to finish his undergraduate degree after all, with a major in linguistics.

It must have gratified the professor immensely to discover that his own research work had exerted such a strong motivating influence on his brilliant student. What Harris could not have known at the time was that Chomsky had seen something more in *Methods in Structural Linguistics* than methods of structural linguistics. Beyond even his own knowing, he had in fact begun to see the makings of a new theory, a theory that would someday supplant structural linguistics as the dominant school—namely, generative theory.

Harris set Chomsky right to work on a project he must have thought would be challenging enough to keep the young man's interest: the goal of producing a systematic structural grammar of some language. Chomsky chose Hebrew, with which he already had some acquaintance, and set about the task of constructing a taxonomic grammar by applying the rigorous methods of structural linguistics as he had understood them from Harris's book. It was not long, however, before Chomsky began to have difficulty with these methods. As will be explained in greater detail in the next section, the methods involve a strict discipline of rules for scientific induction—rules known as "discovery procedures"—for the linguist to follow in extracting and classifying data from an "informant" (ideally, a native speaker of the particular language under investigation). So Chomsky got himself an informant in Hebrew and slavishly followed all the procedural rules for a while, but the early results he obtained, he would later say, seemed "rather dull and unsatisfying" to him. (I imagine that he also found the regimen of the informant-data-gathering method itself to be rather tedious and cramped for his style.) And so he simply abandoned these efforts, he says, and "did what seemed natural": He recast the formal devices in Harris's *Methods* for an entirely new purpose, discovering (on his own) "a system of rules" for actually "generating," not just extracting and classifying, certain language structures found in modern Hebrew (*LSLT,* 25).

The result was a temporary solution to Chomsky's difficulties with the structuralist discovery procedures. It at least permitted him to complete his undergraduate thesis in 1949, *Morphophonemics of Modern Hebrew,* an altered and more extensive version of which (under the same title) was also to become his 1951 master's thesis. This work was actually the first modern generative (though pretransformational) model of language. It allowed Chomsky to earn his bachelor's and master's degrees from the University of Pennsylvania—albeit in his characteristically unconventional way—but the treatise hardly turned the world of professional linguistics on its head, perhaps in part because the work was not published until some thirty years later.[12] On the other hand, this long delay in its publication was probably more of a symptom than a cause of its negligible impact. The real cause lay deeper in the nature of the discipline of linguistics itself as a scientific establishment: Chomsky's sort of "generative" work was simply not "real linguistics" as it was construed in the early 1950s.

This limited reception of his work did not bother Chomsky at all, however, for the simple reason that he himself did not even believe it was real linguistics at the time. He still thought real linguistics was what Harris was doing—using the strictly inductive discovery procedures of the established structuralist tradition for the strictly inductive purposes of gathering and classifying data. While Chomsky had already confronted, in his own mind, the less than satisfying quality of the results obtained by following such a regimen, he still thought the discovery procedures were, in principle, quite correct, and that the problems he had with them could be "fixed" so as to give richer results. He knew that he had not, in his undergraduate and master's theses, really fixed these procedures; he had merely borrowed some of their formal devices for an altogether different purpose, a purpose which he still thought was extraneous to real linguistics. And so it was that Chomsky had found, in his thesis work, only a temporary solution to his difficulty with the discovery procedures, and this difficulty continued to trouble him.

It troubled him deeply for the next several years, in fact, because it turned out to be a fundamental difficulty in theory, rather than a superficial difficulty in method. It must have saddened him somewhat to discover that he could not therefore resolve this difficulty within the theoretical framework of his mentor, Zellig Harris. But then, Noam Chomsky has never been one to be either held back or driven on by blind loyalties; a higher idealism informs his mind—an idealism that Harris himself had helped to inculcate.

So it was that out of his honest struggle to resolve the difficulty he had found in what for Harris was only a "method" would arise Chomsky's own revolutionary new theory, a theory which (unlike his thesis work) would not be merely generative but "transformational" as well. In this respect, there could have been some solace for Harris (though it is doubtful that any was needed) in the knowledge that he, not Chomsky, was actually the inventor of the transformation. On the other hand, in the mind of Harris the transformation—like the discovery procedures themselves—was only another method of the old linguistics; in the new linguistics of Noam Chomsky, the transformation was to become a central concept of theory, a theory that would change the definition of real linguistics (at least in Chomsky's mind) by altering its fundamental goals as a discipline, thereby according it a position at center stage of the cognitive revolution. In 1951, all that obscured these exciting new goals in the vision of Noam Chomsky were the old and well-established discovery procedures of the man who had brought him to linguistics—Zellig Harris.

Discovery Procedures vs Discovery

Another of Chomsky's teachers who clearly was impressed with him was Nelson Goodman, with whom Chomsky took some graduate courses in philosophy at the University of Pennsylvania. Goodman was one of the few who encouraged Chomsky to work further in the direction suggested by his undergraduate and master's theses. Chomsky was very impressed with Goodman, too, particularly by his work on "simplicity" in "constructional systems." A set of "simplicity measures" was something Chomsky was trying to achieve in his emerging system of generative grammar. More importantly, Chomsky found in Goodman's ideas a suggestive "critique of induction," which came close to the

heart of Chomsky's own growing dissatisfaction with the strictly inductive character of Harris's discovery procedures. Goodman's notions
thus fortified Chomsky in his quest for a generative, rather than a
merely taxonomic, linguistic theory, even though Chomsky himself
still thought of this quest as something of a "private hobby" (*LSLT,*
29, 33).

Perhaps the most important practical thing Goodman did to help
Chomsky along was to nominate him for a fellowship in the Society of
Fellows at Harvard University. As Goodman was influential, the nom-
ination succeeded, and Chomsky was appointed as a Junior Fellow at
Harvard in 1951, an appointment he held until 1955. These four years
were surely among the most important and productive of Chomsky's
life. With the stipend that went along with the fellowship, he was able
(for the first time in his academic career) to live at a university without
having to work on the side. And this was not just any university, of
course; it was Harvard. While I suspect that Harvard's tradition and
prestige meant little or nothing to Noam Chomsky, he made full use
of the wonderful facilities and resources that were available to him
there. With no official responsibilities, he was free to do as he pleased,
attending courses or seminars and engaging in discussions, mainly
with the philosophers of language—people such as John Austin,
W. V. O. Quine, Eric Lenneberg, and Roman Jakobson.

One of the most important people he met (and had endless discussions with) was a graduate student there: Morris Halle. Halle was
studying under Jakobson at Harvard and at the same time teaching at
MIT. It was in fact Halle who (along with Jakobson) was later to help
Chomsky get his first position at MIT. Chomsky met Halle shortly
after arriving at Harvard in 1951; they became close friends and were
to become close collaborators on a number of important research works
in generative linguistics over the years to come.[13]

Among the first important things they did together at Harvard,
though, was argue. Interestingly, what they argued about were those
structuralist discovery procedures that had been bothering Chomsky
ever since his first attempt to experiment with them at the University
of Pennsylvania. In the discussions with Halle on this subject, however, it was Halle who said the discovery procedures made no sense and
Chomsky who defended them. Halle thought Chomsky was on to
something powerful with the generative approach to language and
urged him to give up the structuralist discovery procedures. But
Chomsky still believed they were basically correct, still believed he

could work out his problems with them, and that he must do so, since these were the procedures of real linguistics. At the same time, spurred on by Halle's interest and encouragement, he continued to work on his private hobby of generative grammar, and he was coming more and more to see the explanatory possibilities in it. Yet these explanatory possibilities were quite different than what the discovery procedures implied was a goal of linguistic "explanation." The tension that arose in Chomsky's mind about the whole notion of explanation—not only what was being explained, but how—is so important to an understanding of his generative-transformational grammar that the question of the discovery procedures calls for a closer look.

As suggested earlier, Harris's discovery procedures were (in the tradition of structural linguistics) just an inductive method for use by the linguist in extracting data (ideally from an informant) and organizing it into categories. Essentially, this is accomplished through a substitution test: If one element can be substituted for another in the same test frame or linguistic environment, then those two elements may be said to belong to the same "substitution class." The procedure, being inductive, is performed "from the bottom up"; that is, it begins by isolating phones (sounds) and performing the substitution test on them so as to create classes of phones, then at the next higher level to isolate whole sequences of phones, performing substitution tests so as to discover classes of these sequences, and so forth, all the way up to the sentence level, where whole syntactic constituents are isolated and classified by the same procedure. While the discovery procedures were thus a sophisticated and elaborate method for organizing the data of language into categories at every level, for our purposes the method is most easily illustrated at the sentence level. Consider the following two sentences in English, for instance:

> The dog ran up the hill
> The cat ran up the hill

Once we determine (perhaps from an informant's acceptability judgment) that both sentences are in fact grammatical sentences of English, we may say that *dog* and *cat* belong to the same substitution class— because one can be grammatically substituted for the other in the same test frame or environment ("The _____ ran up the hill"). We might even use this same test frame to establish (for purposes of this theoretical taxonomy only) that many other words belong to the same substi-tution class: *lion, tiger, boy, girl,* for instance. As we continue to perform many different tests of this same general sort, adding different words to different substitution classes, we are "inductively" building up the categories of our provisional grammar, which is essentially tax-onomic in character.

Under its most strictly conservative interpretation, such a taxonomic grammar makes no claim at all as to the reality or even "psychological reality" (mental actuality) of the categories, subcategories, and supra-categories it will of course ultimately contain (if, unlike Chomsky, we have the patience to keep testing and cross-testing long enough). The goal is simply to derive a descriptively compact classification system. What further purpose, if any, such a process may have served was often left unclear, for under this most conservative interpretation, the tax-onomy itself was somehow construed as the goal of linguistic science (in much the same way that a field worker in entomology might be concerned only with gathering and classifying insects according to var-ious parametric criteria). Furthermore, linguists were supposed to maintain strict scientific objectivity throughout this enterprise, ap-proaching their task without any preconceptions as to what the cate-gories might turn out to be. After all, the categories themselves were not to be thought of as psychologically real structures that were already somehow "in the mind"; rather, they were only theoretical constructs, built up inductively from scratch, and linguists were supposed to re-member that the best of these classification schemes were only "fic-tions," albeit useful ones (at least for purposes of elegant and compact organization of an often huge corpus of seemingly chaotic data—no small achievement in itself, especially for an anthropological linguist studying a previously unstudied language).

Perhaps most important of all, the discovery procedures that create these categories were to be thought of only as inductive linguistic methods, as tools that were suitable and convenient devices within linguistic theory in general, but which in themselves implied no par-ticular theory about language (even though they did in fact imply a theory—one that Chomsky would ultimately decide was wrong). That is, the discovery procedures meant only to define the steps a linguist follows to describe a language; these steps in themselves represented nothing about language per se. For instance, the steps to discovery they delineated for a linguist were certainly not intended to represent the actual process or cognitive system through which the grammar of a language is unconsciously organized or constructed by an ordinary native speaker of that language. The discovery procedures could no more "mimic" the actual system of language acquisition than they could claim (under the so-called conservative view) to reveal anything at all about the actual cognitive linguistic structures acquired.

And yet, from very early on, these were precisely the possibilities towards which Harris's discovery procedures pointed the theory-making mind of Noam Chomsky. If what he was trying to do as a linguist was worth doing at all, Chomsky felt, it must at least offer the hope of discovering something about the mental reality of language. While the linguist is often and necessarily engaged in the construction of hypothetical models, these models must be something more than mere fictions, useful only to other professional linguists within some narrow and self-referential world of their own model-making; rather, the models must be construed as empirical hypotheses about something real in the mind/brain—hypotheses that can really be confirmed or disconfirmed. And if they can be confirmed or disconfirmed by the linguist's procedures, then why might not these same procedures themselves be construed as empirical hypotheses—hypotheses that model, in principle at least, the actual cognitive system by which language is initially realized in the minds of ordinary native speakers?

After all, native speakers face, as children, the same task the linguist faces: From the linguistic data presented to them, which is often chaotic or impoverished, they must discover the rules of the language. Of course native speakers do this informally and unconsciously, for the most part, whereas the linguist wishes to construct a formal and precise grammar to facilitate conscious understanding of the language. But in this undertaking, the linguist often uses native speakers as informants. If the linguist wants to "discover" what the informants (unconsciously) "know," why should the linguist's method of discovery not be at least roughly analogous to the cognitive processes by which the informants themselves came to know it? (See "Induction vs Abduction" below.)

While this latter question seems a natural one for Chomsky to have asked, it suggested a radical departure from what was thought of in those days as linguistic science. After all, language was not "knowledge"; it was "behavior" or "habit" or some such thing. Against that background, Chomsky's query, while still something he pondered only "on the side" in those early days at Harvard, may well have been the most revolutionary step of all in his thinking, for it started him on a course that would soon lead him to abandon any concern whatever for the structuralist discovery procedures—the very procedures, oddly enough, that had provoked him to this query in the first place. The discovery procedures had pointed him in the right direction, but the further he went in this new direction, the more convinced he became that the old discovery procedures themselves were wrong in principle. They discovered results that Chomsky often found were empirically wrong (not representative of *what* the native speaker knows), at least in part because the method of discovery itself was wrong (not representative of *how* the native speaker knows).

In short, they were wrong because they are inherently inductive. Induction, while important in science as a method of testing new hypotheses, is simply not the process by which new hypotheses (scientific or otherwise) are actually discovered. It is not a process by which the child can discover the principles of language, and it is not a process by which the linguist can discover the content and nature of the child's discovery. To understand the extraordinary process and content of this discovery, Chomsky would come to believe, must be a real and central explanatory goal of linguistics, a goal that requires abandoning the inductive discovery procedures of structural linguistics in favor of a very different method—in fact, a different theory—of discovery.

Induction vs Abduction

Some years later, well after he had already formulated his own ideas about it, Chomsky would find a philosophical precedent for this new theory of discovery in what the American mathematician, scientist, and semiotician Charles Sanders Peirce (1839–1914) had called *abduction* (as opposed to *induction*).[14] In fact, Chomsky would ultimately come to see generative grammar itself as one "manifestation" of an initiative to develop something like a "Peircean logic of abduction."[15] Chomsky's development of this seminal theme thus will be a central topic of this book, but for now, a rather shortened (and perhaps oversimplified) discussion will have to suffice: Abduction is the mind's recourse to a highly specialized, biologically innate faculty (it might be called a "genetic guessing instinct") in order to discover some hypothesis that would make sense of the evidence presented to it—evidence that is often chaotic, contradictory, degraded, or impoverished. A strikingly confusing and incomplete body of evidence about language is exactly the situation, Chomsky believes, facing the child in its early linguistic environment. It is also of course the same situation

that faces all linguists. In fact, it perpetually haunts and tantalizes them, especially as they contemplate the child's amazingly rapid and unconscious mastery of a linguistic system whose complexity is forever taxing the most elaborate and studied descriptions of modern linguistics. How does the child perform this "miracle"? How can linguists, in turn, even come close to comprehending the mechanisms and results of this miracle? In order to discover the principles of language that a child discovers, must linguists approach the task of discovery in the same way the child approaches it?

Strange as it may sound, Chomsky's novel thinking in this area has in fact suggested, a number of times, a provocative analogy (with certain important qualifications) between the cognitive process of language acquisition and the scientific process of theory construction— particularly linguistic theory construction. At a minimum, the two processes share the same basic cognitive character in Chomsky's view: They are not inductive, but abductive.[16]

The abductive faculty is not "general intelligence," but neither is it "special intuition," in the sense that there is nothing mystical or transcendental about it, remarkable though it is. Like Peirce, Chomsky holds that any abductive faculty is merely the function of certain biologically fixed limits, limits that define the "instincts" peculiar to any given species. Birds do not discover how to build their distinctive and species-specific nests, nor spiders how to spin their amazingly intricate and efficient webs, by general intelligence or inductive reasoning; these special kinds of knowledge—reflected in finished products that in many respects are marvels of engineering—far exceed whatever levels of general intelligence or inductive reasoning may be found among birds and spiders. Nor do they "learn" these structures from some sort of instruction or evidence that has been presented to them. With extremely little exposure to illustrative examples (and sometimes none at all), they discover these structures, essentially from within themselves, instinctively. And it is in fact a discovery. Some minimal exposure to adult "models" is sometimes needed to trigger the instinct, and a little trial and error is almost always required. But the process of discovery is strikingly rapid and efficient and uniform within a given species, a fact that of course obtains primarily from the special anatomical and neurological structures that are innate to that species.

Why, ask Chomsky and Peirce, should we believe that the human species is somehow exempt from this principle of instinct-driven discovery through biological specialization, expounded as that principle

is throughout the animal world? As Chomsky in particular would ask, to what sorts of discovery or to what sorts of knowledge or to what sorts of structures are the children of our species more uniquely or more irresistibly disposed—and thus more likely predisposed by specialized innate faculties—than to language? Why should it be considered strange, Chomsky came to wonder, that linguistic theory must be centrally concerned with these matters, in both its goals and methods? After all, acquisition of language, he says, "is not unlike theory construction of the most abstract sort" (*LangMind*, 90). Nevertheless, according to at least one student of the philosophy of science, Chomsky stands almost entirely alone (except for Peirce) in believing that the human "logic of discovery" is founded, not on general intelligence or inductive reasoning, but on certain highly specialized abductive faculties in human biology.[17]

When he first went to Harvard in 1951, however, Chomsky knew nothing of Peirce's abduction, nor had he completely worked out the concept in his own mind yet, for he was still struggling with Harris's purely inductive discovery procedures, trying futilely to re-formulate them so as to obtain more satisfying results with them. In fact, his very first published article (in the *Journal of Symbolic Logic*) was an effort to formulate a syntactic discovery procedure that would really yield a productive insight if strictly applied.[18]

It was not the only sort of research with syntax he was doing, of course; he still had his private hobby, which was occupying more and more of his mental life. In fact, as early as 1952 he began his first serious work on a generative grammar of English, obtaining results which (like those he had obtained in his earlier generative work on Hebrew) he found "quite exciting" (*LSLT*, 30). Morris Halle, too, was excited by this approach and encouraged Chomsky to work on it even more. Stimulated by Halle's encouragement, Chomsky worked even harder on it, but he could see that it was taking him farther and farther away from structural linguistics, mainly because it was driving him to consider "more abstract underlying structures that were far removed" from anything obtainable by Harris's discovery procedures (*LSLT*, 31). The conflict was sharpening in Chomsky's mind: The method of structural linguistics created grammars inductively whereas the method that Chomsky's instincts naturally drove him to, and that seemed to produce the most exciting results, was clearly an abductive approach. That is, he was (abductively) hypothesizing "abstract underlying structures" for empirical trial and evaluation against the data of language, instead

of (inductively) synthesizing categories step by step upward from the data. The conflict was sharpening, but it was not being resolved.

Perhaps what Chomsky needed was a "break" from this academic confusion. He took about six weeks' leave of absence from the Society of Fellows at Harvard in 1953, during which he went to live and work on a kibbutz in Israel. It was something that he had first dreamt of doing back in 1947, when he had resolved to drop out of college after his sophomore year at Penn in order to pursue his political interests. Chomsky was deeply concerned about the situation in the Middle East, as he is to this day; going to live on the kibbutz, he hoped, would give him an opportunity to work in a very direct way for Arab-Jewish cooperation. It may also have given him an opportunity to work (perhaps unconsciously) on his theoretical problems with language. The physical labor on the kibbutz was hard, and there was very little food, but in many ways it was a fulfilling experience for him. In other ways, it was not all he had hoped it would be. Ever true to his idealism, he was particularly uneasy with some of the "ideology" and "general conformism" he encountered on the kibbutz (*Reader,* 8–9).

Though it was only a short break, the trip itself seems to have provided the occasion for a major turning point in Chomsky's thought about language and linguistics: It was apparently during the ocean crossing that he decided at last to abandon the structuralist discovery procedures and to turn his full attention to the sort of intellectual work he really wanted and felt driven to do—generative grammar. Many years later, he still recalled the exact moment when he made this decision. It was, he remembers, "On board ship in mid-Atlantic, aided by a bout of seasickness, on a rickety tub that was listing noticeably . . ." (*LangResp,* 131).

In view of all the revolutionary developments that would follow in course from this decision, perhaps the old "rickety tub that was listing noticeably" provides a fairly accurate metaphor for the situation in which American structural linguistics was shortly to find itself. At that particular moment in 1953 when Noam Chomsky abandoned the ship, however, it was hardly "listing noticeably." It was rather sailing proudly on its own inexorable course; as a matter of fact, almost everyone—perhaps even Chomsky himself at that moment—believed that the ship was absolutely unsinkable. The only person in the world who had always believed Chomsky should abandon it altogether, leave it behind and get on with his real work, was Morris Halle. And now at last Chomsky himself had decided to do so, for reasons of his own.

Whatever all these reasons may have been, they surely could not have been pragmatic career considerations. Chomsky had no prospects at all for an academic post in 1953, and his appointment as a Junior Fellow in Harvard's Society of Fellows was due to terminate very soon. Striking out on his own into the uncharted and strange waters of generative grammar was hardly a way to improve his job prospects at the time. But Chomsky the idealist just wanted to understand human language. Structuralism was on a different course. He probably had no particular intentions of sending it to the bottom of the Atlantic Ocean, but when he "jumped ship," he made some waves.

Jumped indeed. It was perhaps, after all, really something of an abductive leap—a bold and heady plunge, but one that was guided by an instinctive sense of where the waters were deep enough. In any case, when he surfaced again at Harvard and set his own course, Chomsky's progress with the new theory was astonishingly rapid. In the next year and a half, while completing his tenure at the Society of Fellows, he wrote a very long book (about 1,000 typed pages) called *The Logical Structure of Linguistic Theory* (completed in 1955), the first thorough, formal, generative, and transformational model of language. Before he completed his final revisions, the manuscript was already gaining some interested attention. Harvard Libraries put it on microfilm, and it was otherwise duplicated and circulated. When he first submitted it for publication, it was rejected, but when the book was finally published in 1975 by popular demand, the microfilm and duplicated copies already numbered in the hundreds. Perhaps most important of all, at least insofar as Chomsky's immediate career prospects were concerned, was the ninth chapter of the book, entitled "Transformational Analysis." It earned Chomsky his Ph. D. in 1955 (awarded by the University of Pennsylvania, even though most of the work was done at Harvard). His entire doctoral dissertation consisted of that one chapter, which was perhaps the most innovative of all.

In the autumn of 1955, through the initiative of Morris Halle, who was teaching at MIT, Chomsky also was appointed to the faculty there, to teach undergraduate linguistics, logic, and philosophy of language in the Modern Language Department with a joint appointment in the Research Lab of Electronics. Thus he came to be in the right place at the right time to present his seminal "Three Models" paper at the MIT Symposium on Information Theory of 1956. The rest, as they say, is history.

However, while George Miller had good reason to believe that this was where the cognitive revolution began in psychology, the Chomskyan revolution within linguistics proper actually did not catch fire until somewhat later. The entrenched academic establishment of contemporary linguistics was still (understandably) resistant to such dangerously radical new ideas as Chomsky's. When he submitted a revised version of *The Logical Structure of Linguistic Theory* to the MIT Press in 1956, for instance, it was promptly rejected—with the telling admonition that an "unknown author" undertaking such an "unconventional approach" should not be trying to publish such a long, audacious book without first having published articles on the topic in the professional journals. Chomsky thought this was "not unreasonable," but neither did he find it easy. The one article he had submitted of this sort to a linguistics journal was rejected, "virtually by return mail" (*LSLT,* 3). He had tried the lecture circuit too—at Georgetown, at a summer Linguistics Institute in Chicago, and of course at the MIT Symposium—and his talks were published in the conference proceedings. There was some lively interest from specialists in other disciplines, but most professional linguists simply ignored Chomsky's early work (or had not yet encountered it).

He may have been discouraged about his prospects for publishing his new ideas, but Chomsky found very good use for them in his teaching. As noted in the Preface, one of the most striking qualities of the whole theoretical nexus of Chomskyan linguistics is the extent to which, throughout Chomsky's career, his innovations have been bound almost inextricably with his teaching, often making it exceedingly difficult for an analyst to sort out which ideas came specifically from Chomsky, which from his students, and which from what might be called the "abductive magic" that always seems to be happening between them. In any case, Chomsky threw himself into his teaching at MIT in the mid-1950s, incorporating his notions about generative grammar into his class lectures and trying to adapt his presentations to the particular interests of his students. In one of his undergraduate classes, for instance, there seems to have been a rather strong interest in some of the latest models of "automata theory," which were all the rage at the time. Seeing in this a good teaching opportunity, no doubt, as well as a chance to explore his own ideas further at the same time, Chomsky developed his class notes by incorporating some of his materials on generative grammar into the context of automata theory.[19]

When Morris Halle saw these class notes, he suggested that Chomsky show them to Cornelis Van Schooneveld, editor of the *Janua Linguarum* series at Mouton. Van Schooneveld was interested, so interested in fact that he offered to publish the notes. The result was *Syntactic Structures,*[20] the monograph that is generally credited with having begun the generative-transformational revolution in linguistics.

As far as Chomsky was concerned, however, this little book was only "a sketchy and informal outline" of some of the material from his (as yet) unpublished big book, *The Logical Structure of Linguistic Theory.* In fact, he still doubts there would have been much notice paid to his little book at all, had it not been for a "provocative and extensive review article by Robert Lees," which was published almost simultaneously with the monograph itself (*LSLT,* 3).

So, if his first big rock went right over Goliath's head, David would get his attention with a smooth little stone. "Sketchy and informal outline" or not, *Syntactic Structures* represents an important achievement, as Lees makes clear in his review.[21] It is at least a very accessible introduction to Chomskyan linguistics (it was in fact my own, when I first read it during the early 1970s in a class conducted by another great teacher, Kellogg Hunt), and so it seems a natural place to begin again, in the next chapter. Its technical and theoretical achievements aside, there is something else that I think recommends it: It came out of a classroom, a classroom in which the seminal ideas of a visionary thinker were brought into dynamic relief against the background of his students' special interests. Chomsky's introduction of the material on finite automata theory—material that was totally absent from his longer work on generative grammar *(LSLT)*—might thus be called something of a pedagogical afterthought. It was something he introduced only in order to engage the minds of his pupils. In the final analysis, however, this may very well have been a critical part of what made the book hit home.

At the least, Noam Chomsky's attitude of vital involvement with the minds of his students is surely part of what made the book famous. After all, Robert Lees was Noam Chomsky's first graduate student at MIT—"though in reality," says Chomsky, "a colleague" (*LangResp,* 135).

Chapter Two

The Foundations of Generative-Transformational Grammar: *Syntactic Structures*

In comparison to the much more elaborate technical virtuosity of *The Logical Structure of Linguistic Theory,* Chomsky's *Syntactic Structures* presents only a "sketchy" model, as he calls it, a model that is also rather narrow in scope compared to the much broader conceptual range of his *Aspects of the Theory of Syntax* published some eight years later.[1] Nevertheless, Chomsky's first short monograph did at least clearly establish the notion of "generative-transformational grammar" in contemporary linguistics. The more comprehensive *Aspects* model built upon the almost purely syntactic findings of *Syntactic Structures,* altering some technical details of its formal devices while preserving its theoretical foundations intact; at the same time, *Aspects* broadened and deepened these foundations by extending the new theory beyond syntax into the domain of semantics. As will be discussed in Chapter Three, the "standard theory" of this *Aspects* model has, in turn, undergone further and more radical changes during the 1980s and 1990s—a fact not at all surprising in view of the revolutionary character of Chomsky's mind and basic approach. On the other hand, the single most startling discovery I have made in my research for this book is the degree to which some of Chomsky's most far-reaching themes and fundamental concepts are already clearly apparent (though often nascent) in the framework of his first short monograph. As Howard Gardner, the noted psychologist and historian of the "cognitive revolution," has observed, one of the most remarkable things about Noam Chomsky is his adherence to the basic conceptual agenda he first proposed to the scholarly community in *Syntactic Structures* (Gardner, 213).

Gardner's observation, the accuracy and astuteness of which I have discovered and rediscovered, perhaps suggests that altogether too much has been made of Noam Chomsky the "revolutionary," after all, just as he himself has often said (e.g., *GenPrize,* 40–43). While he has cer-

tainly exerted a revolutionary impact, Chomsky is nonetheless a thoroughly systematic and "evolutionary" thinker, as well (Leiber, 111). In
the growth to each new species of his theory, no matter how violent or
radical a mutation may have triggered it, there is in Chomsky an un-
canny yet natural sense of selection, a meticulous, focussed, almost
teleological sense of preservation, ensuring the survival of all that was
essential and best from the old species of theory within the design of
the new.

Noam Chomsky as "evolutionary revolutionary"? There is just no
appropriate label, and it is hard even to find a good metaphor for the
way his ideas have developed. "Growth from the seed of the early theory" is too vegetative and slow; throughout his career, Chomsky's ideas
have rather seemed to reach a sort of "critical mass" from time to time,
resulting in something much more like a "nuclear explosion" than mere
"growth." But this metaphor will not work, either, because an explosion of this sort does not preserve enough (if anything at all) of the
atomic structure that basically accounts for it. Conversely, Chomsky's
quantum leaps, while often abandoning substantial parts of the old
theoretical apparatus in favor of drastically new designs, always seem
to arrive at a reconfiguration (usually on a broader or more abstract
level) of some primary essence in the original conception. To account
for this fact, we might borrow one of Chomsky's own metaphors for
something different (but perhaps not altogether different): He once
described the growth of language itself in the child as a "successive
maturation of specialized hardware."[2] He was of course talking about
a kind of "hardware" whose basic laws of organization he believes are
genetically encoded in the child from the beginning, and about a kind
of "maturation" that nevertheless passes through strikingly distinct
stages with remarkable rapidity. In these same two respects, then,
"successive maturation of specialized hardware" (though we might substitute "software" for hardware) does seem a rather appropriate analogy
for the development of Chomsky's own linguistic models, as well.
There is an almost fractal-like replication of the same driving theoretical principle, albeit in radically different models and at dramatically
different scales; from this perspective (not only but especially in the
larger context of Chomsky's more recent and more sophisticated work),
the tightly focussed central vision of *Syntactic Structures* acquires a peculiar and growing significance—like that strangely familiar little
bud-studded image that keeps reappearing in a Mandelbrot set.[3]

It is not just that Chomsky's broader theory developed from his original model of syntax and thus naturally exhibits similar features of design; it is rather that the whole abstract essence of the overall design itself almost seems to have been there all along—in miniature as it were—within that original and skeletal component of syntax, whose most salient implications simply went unnoticed until they were allowed to play themselves out on a grander scale. After all, while frequently noting mistakes in his earliest models, Chomsky has often said (e.g., *LangResp*, 113) that he views his ongoing work as being very much within the framework of his very earliest work in generative grammar. I simply never took such statements very seriously until I sat down and read *Syntactic Structures* again.

Further, as noted in Chapter One, much of the detailed superstructure of the standard theory (as represented by the *Aspects* model) has been torn down and abandoned in the second "Chomskyan revolution." Strange as it may sound, I think these developments actually bring the earlier work, *Syntactic Structures*, into a more favorable light: As narrow in scope and spare in frame as it was, it might be viewed as embodying a sort of "rarefied essence" of the concepts "generative" and "transformational." Without meaning to minimize the important achievements of *Aspects*, whose more thorough and explicit arguments fleshed out some of the most profound implications of the earlier model (at the same time it filtered out a very few superfluous ones), I think *Syntactic Structures* deserves to be reassessed in this new light. The value of doing so, I believe, is two-fold. First, it reveals what a remarkably systematic thinker Chomsky has been throughout his career, at least with respect to the basic substance of his concepts. Second, it provides an opportunity to rectify some common misconceptions about his theory, misconceptions that seem to have compounded themselves even as his theory has developed greater complexity. *Syntactic Structures* may have firmly established the notion of generative-transformational grammar, but thirty-five years after it was first published, there is still much confusion and controversy over just what is meant by generative, by transformational, and even by "grammar." *Syntactic Structures* may even be partly responsible for some of this confusion and controversy, but even in this respect it is still an invaluable asset to understanding, if only because of the simple purity with which it defined the critical issues at controversy. Spare and sketchy though it is, it reanimated age-old debates about the nature of language by basing the study of lan-

guage on new foundations—foundations in mathematics and cognitive
psychology.

The Mathematical Foundations

Only very recently, looking back over the whole history of the two
revolutions in linguistics that have sprung from his work, Chomsky
remarked, "Modern generative grammar, in fact, can be regarded in
part as the confluence of the conceptual tools of modern logic and
mathematics and the traditional idea, inevitably left vague and unformed, that language is a system that makes infinite use of finite
means" (*Kyoto*, 6–7). This "traditional" albeit "vague" idea—which
Chomsky attributes to Wilhelm von Humboldt[4]—of language as "a
system that makes infinite use of finite means" obviously has to do
with a very important cognitive principle underlying human linguistic
creativity; generative grammar uses the tools of mathematics merely to
give explicit form to the principle underlying this important phenomenon of linguistic creativity. Nevertheless, many people in the humanities have reacted very unfavorably to Chomsky's "confluence" between
mathematics and the study of natural language—a fact that may help
to explain why Chomsky has often felt more fairly and openly received
by mathematicians (*LangResp*, 6–7). On the other hand, Chomsky fully
understands the dangers of applying mathematics to language; in that
same lecture at Kyoto University, he went on to say that the analogy
between natural language and "formal languages such as formalized
arithmetic" is "profoundly misleading" (*Kyoto*, 46). Elsewhere, he has
blamed a certain critical "misleading choice of terms" (having specifically to do with his own early use of the terms *grammar* and *language*)
on this same confluence between the study of natural language and
certain formal systems of mathematics—a convergence of different intellectual traditions that he calls a "historical accident" (*KnowLang*,
29–30).

Truly, it was something of a historical accident, as the previous
chapter chronicled. Part of it has to do with the unconventional nature
of Chomsky's own training. At the suggestion of Zellig Harris, he
formally studied the foundations of mathematics at Penn and at Harvard (*LSLT*, 33), though he considers himself basically "self-taught" in
mathematics—and "not very well taught," he adds (*LangResp*, 6). Even
today, as he told us in an interview, when he wants to understand
something in advanced mathematics, he often has to ask a mathema-

tician or "sort of figure out" on his own what he needs to know.[5] Some students in the humanities might wonder why Chomsky, if his interest really is in natural human language, ever wanted to know all this mathematics in the first place. While the full answer to that question is quite far-reaching, its immediate effect is to take us right back to the circumstances surrounding the historical accident that gave birth to generative grammar, or at least to that version of generative grammar that helped to start the cognitive revolution.

In the 1950s, there was a new model afoot termed the "mathematical theory of communication," otherwise known as "information theory."[6] (Recall that it was at the 1956 MIT Symposium on Information Theory that Chomsky presented his seminal "Three Models" paper.) There was also something called "automata theory"—a topic of special interest to Chomsky's students in an undergraduate course (Chomsky's notes for which were the origin of *Syntactic Structures*). While recognizing that the excitement about these particular mathematical theories might be "quite justified" for some applications, Chomsky was very skeptical of their applicability to human language from the very first (*LangResp* 125–27; *LangMind*, 3–4; *LSLT*, 7), in part because he thought they had dangerous political implications, in that they seemed "connected with behaviorist concepts of human nature" that might be used for "manipulative" political purposes (*LangResp*, 128). Thus Chomsky became involved with the mathematics relevant specifically to these theories precisely because he wanted to show that they were inappropriate for human language.

In view of these circumstances, it seems somewhat ironic that Chomsky's effort to establish generative grammar in a context that allowed him to address his concerns about the danger of any "mechanistic" treatment of human language should now have led to the common misconception that his theory of language is itself somehow mechanistic. Nothing could be further from the truth. As John Lyons has observed in his lucid and helpful book on Chomsky's early writings, one theme that runs very deep throughout Chomsky's life and work is his "conviction that human beings are different from animals or machines and that this difference should be respected both in science and in government; and it is this conviction that underlies and unifies his politics, his linguistics, and his philosophy."[7] Thus Chomsky's use in *Syntactic Structures* of material from the contemporary mathematical theory of communication was not an endorsement but a compelling refutation of such approaches to human language.

This, however, certainly does not tell the whole story. When Chomsky adopted a formal (some would say "mathematical") frame of reference for generative theory, he was not merely fighting fire with fire. The "conceptual tools" of contemporary mathematics to be found in generative theory are not limited to those of the mathematical theory of communication; as we will see, generative-transformational theory also uses something known as "recursive function theory," which Chomsky says provides a "quasi-mathematical mode of expression" for linguistic rules (*LangResp*, 125). Indeed, Chomsky had used this same quasi-mathematical mode of expression throughout *The Logical Structure of Linguistic Theory* (long before he had any thought of *Syntactic Structures*) and in fact even in his undergraduate and master's theses on Hebrew—the very birth of generative grammar. In calling it a quasi-mathematical mode of expression Chomsky intends to imply (and in fact he goes on to insist) that his adaptation of recursive function theory to linguistic rules is not to be construed as "mathematics" proper or even as "mathematical linguistics" (*LangResp*, 125, 127)—a separate discipline that is now a small branch of mathematics, and to which (interestingly) Chomsky has made significant independent contributions.[8] However, while it is true that mathematical linguistics is a separate discipline, it clearly had its birth in Chomsky's quasi-mathematical approach to the formulation of strictly linguistic rules; mathematical linguistics in fact constitutes the abstract study of such generative rule systems, just as these rule systems themselves constitute the abstract study of human language (*LangMind*, 71–72). Situated between pure mathematical linguistics and the study of the very special and particular structures of natural human language, then, Chomsky's quasi-mathematical approach makes a significant contribution to both. Indeed, as Lyons suggests, one of Chomsky's most revolutionary and enduring contributions to linguistics—not just to mathematical linguistics, but to linguistics proper—is his achievement of a rapprochement between these two disciplines in ways that illuminate (through both similarity and contrast) many of the most problematic and/or previously unnoticed structural principles of human language (Lyons, 43, 69–70).

Thus to call Chomsky's generative rules a quasi-mathematical mode of expression does not mean that Chomsky was merely adopting some convenient "code" that allowed him to speak in the argot of his day. The quasi-mathematical character of his theory was largely responsible for its strong appeal to many technology-minded scientists of the cognitive revolution. There is, however, a much more important reason for this than just the fact that mathematical approaches happened to have been in vogue during the 1950s. There is a much deeper reason for the appeal, one that is fundamental, not only to the cognitive revolution in general but to Chomsky's theory in particular, and it is crucial for anyone who wishes to understand his theory to consider this reason carefully. As George Miller put it in thinking about Chomsky's "Three Models" paper (the one that helped to start the cognitive revolution), "Other linguists had said language has all the formal precision of mathematics, but Chomsky was the first linguist to make good on the claim. I think that was what excited all of us" (Gardner, 28).

People are entitled to think that the terms *formal precision* and *quasi-mathematical* necessarily mean "mechanistic" and "automatic," but as long as they persist in this way of thinking, they have little hope of understanding Noam Chomsky's extraordinary achievements in the study of human language. It is perhaps worth mentioning at this point that I am certainly no mathematician. In fact, my background is in the traditional humanities. I therefore appreciate that many people (myself included) may not have a sufficient background in mathematics and logic to follow some of Chomsky's formal proofs in the "Three Models" paper, and that some people may even need a little preliminary help (as I did) with the much simpler notation in *Syntactic Structures*. But to suppose that Chomsky's mathematical or quasi-mathematical approach is somehow inimical to human language—to the infinite creativity and freedom of human language—portrays an extremely shallow view of human cognition. The structural principles of language that are brought dramatically to light by Chomsky's formalizations are clearly fundamental to the boundless productivity of the human language faculty itself. This is especially true of Chomsky's transformational formulations, which he conceived of (even in *Syntactic Structures*) as a "natural algebra" (*SS*, 44). There is nothing about formalizing such principles as explicit and precise rules that is hostile to creativity. Quite to the contrary, as Chomsky himself would later reflect, "Creativity is predicated on a system of rules and forms, in part determined by intrinsic human capacities. Without such constraints, we have arbitrary and random behavior, not creative acts."[9]

Even assuming this answer is accepted, however, it still leaves the question of why the rules need to be formalized in a way that is even quasi-mathematical. It is a fair question, and perhaps the rules do not need to be formalized in this particular way, after all. In fact, I suspect

Chomsky would be equally happy with any formal notation that possesses the sort of explicitness and precision he finds in math and logic. But if we are to study the principles underlying human linguistic creativity with any degree of clarity and rigor (instead of relying on vague and wistful musings), then we will need some means of making these principles explicit, as Chomsky argues eloquently in the very first paragraph of the Preface to his first book (*SS*, 5). Furthermore, it is just possible—intriguingly possible—that Chomsky has found in the conceptual tools of mathematics something far beyond just the best means of making the creative principles of human language explicit. Specifically, it is just possible that the human mathematical faculty itself may have developed—in the actual evolution of the human species—as an "abstract by-product" of the human language faculty (*Managua* 168–69, 183). Some of Chomsky's most recent and most provocative speculations (which he is careful to call speculations) are precisely along this line of thought.[10] If these speculations are correct, Chomsky's dramatic success in formalizing principles of language by using the conceptual tools of mathematics might be an indication of something far more profound than his own cross-disciplinary ingenuity. But even if these speculations are not correct, it already seems abundantly clear that at least one aspect of the human mathematical faculty—namely, the capacity to make "infinite use of finite means"—is deeply rooted in the nature of human language as well. These considerations lead right to the heart of what is meant by generative grammar.

The Quasi-Math of Generative Grammar.   Chomsky gave his first clues as to what he originally meant by the terms *generative* and *grammar* in the first two sentences of his Introduction to *Syntactic Structures*. There he defined syntax (the monograph's restricted focus) as "the study of the principles and processes by which sentences are constructed," a study whose goal is itself to construct "a grammar that can be viewed as a device of some sort for producing the sentences of the language under analysis" (*SS*, 11). The sort of device for producing sentences that Chomsky had in mind is not a physical machine (like a computer); it is a grammar (a set of rules) that generates sequences of elements in a language (*SS*, 13). Thus, in its most primitive sense (with certain complications to follow, of course!), a generative grammar can be viewed as a set of rules for "producing" sentences. Simple as this may seem, it was quite an innovative and controversial approach in 1957 (and still is today). As suggested in the previous chapter, the idea of a linguistic model that can actually generate linguistic expressions—as opposed to a linguistic "method" that merely segments and classifies linguistic elements—is exactly what originally and most dramatically separated Chomsky's approach to language from that of the reigning American structuralist tradition.

Even in *Syntactic Structures,* however, the matter is not so simple as it seems at first; it is a spare foundation, but there is depth and weight to it. In the first place—even though Chomsky does say his goal is a grammar that can be viewed as a device for producing sentences—his use of the more precise term *generative* has a more abstract sense. As Lyons has pointed out, the use of the term *generate* in *Syntactic Structures* is derived from a mathematical usage (Lyons, 43–45). In Chomsky's application, a grammar that can generate is one that can abstractly "project" (*SS,* 15), with explicit formal rules or descriptions, though it does not necessarily produce. What the grammar projects is a complete "set" of utterances; what it projects this set from is an incomplete "corpus" of utterances. That is, the grammar uses an incomplete collection (corpus) of utterances as the basis for its projection of what the complete (though presumably infinite) set of utterances must be.

This complete set of utterances projected by the grammar is what Chomsky defines, in *Syntactic Structures,* as a "language" (*SS,* 13). In his later work, however, he would decide that this definition of language was misleading. The faulty definition was suggested to him, he now believes, by a "misleading and inappropriate analogy to formal languages" (like arithmetic). That is, the notion of a set suggests a collection of actual things—a set of objects or a set of real numbers, for instance—and this does not do justice to the true sense of language Chomsky was striving to formulate. Specifically, he would later come to define language more clearly as the "internalized system of knowledge" that underlies the production of actual utterances. The set of actual utterances made possible by this knowledge he would later call an "E-language" (or "external language"), whereas the real object of his study is the internal system of linguistic knowledge itself—what he calls "I-language" ("internal language") to differentiate it sharply from the E-language concept (*Sophia,* 36–37; *KnowLang,* 29–30). Here, then, is one point upon which the original mathematical foundations of generative grammar may have led to some confusion over the central concept of language. It also affects how we understand the term *generate*: If we think of a language as an external set of sentences, then we might misconstrue Chomsky's goal of having the grammar generate sentences as necessarily meaning to actually produce sentences. On the other hand, if the term *generate* is properly understood in its abstract quasi-mathematical sense, then I think it actually prefigures or fore-shadows Chomsky's ultimate conception of language as I-language or "knowledge."

In order to get a preliminary sense of this quasi-mathematical use of the term *generate,* consider (first) the following simplistic analogy of how it might work in a case involving ordinary numbers. Suppose you overhear me in the next room talking to myself; wondering what I am up to, you begin to listen intently. Suddenly, you realize that what I am actually doing is counting aloud for some reason (maybe I need some practice with my numbers), and you are curious to know just what sort of little exercise in arithmetic this might be. But you can hear only muted snatches of my actual string of numbers through the wall: ". . . six, eight, . . . fourteen, sixteen, eighteen, . . . twenty-four, . . . thirty, thirty-two, thirty-four, thirty-six . . . forty-two, forty-four, . . ." and so forth. You might hypothesize (rightly or wrongly) that I am counting only the even numbers, or counting by twos. If you thought it was worth it, you could write your hypothesis down in a formal algorithm (say, $x \rightarrow x + 2$) that would project my complete set of numbers from the fragmented and incomplete corpus of numbers you have actually heard me speak. Assuming a positive and even number as the initial value of $x,$ that is, your algorithm abstractly generates (in the mathematical sense) the complete, albeit infinite, set of positive even numbers. But does it actually produce even one of these numbers? Not really. (True, you could put your rule to that use with a computer, but you will probably want to leave the actual pro-duction end of things to me . . . in the next room!)

As already indicated above, the analogy to formal languages like arithmetic can be misleading as to what is meant by language. My counting analogy is therefore intended only to clarify the abstract sense of *generate,* not to describe Chomsky's generative model of human lan-guage in particular. After all, human language is far more complex than counting. In Chomsky's view, the human number faculty and the human language faculty do share one very interesting feature (the fea-ture of "digital infinity," or the capacity to generate an infinite set of expressions from a finite set of elements or "digits"), but there are many other features of human language not to be found in ordinary counting exercises like that above. One of these features is the pervasive phenomenon in human language of "nonadjacent dependency"—de-pendency between linguistic elements not immediately adjacent to one another (*SS*, 22–23). For instance, in the sentence *The woman who speaks rapidly is my cousin,* we say there is a "dependency" between *woman* and *is* (subject-verb agreement), even though the two words are not adjacent to one another in the sentence, being separated by some intervening words (*who speaks rapidly*). In my counting analogy above, note that this is not the case; at least if the algorithm accurately projects the real system of numbers I am using in my little counting exercise, the value of each new number depends only on the value of the number immediately preceding it (i.e., $x \rightarrow x + 2$ simply means that you take each number and add two in order to get the next number). In view of this difference between human language and counting, Chomsky's goal in *Syntactic Structures* is very ambitious: He wants a grammar that will abstractly generate (project) the full and infinite set of sentences in a human language (construed here as an E-language) with the same formal precision achieved by generative rules in mathematics—this, despite the fact that human language has complex, noncontiguous dependencies that are unlike some of the ordinary linear operations in math (e.g., counting, which of course is only the simplest math). Despite how ambitious the goal is, Chomsky's remarkable progress towards reaching it in his "Three Models" paper, which gives formal proofs to some of the propositions repeated in *Syntactic Structures,* is clearly what excited many of the early leaders of the cognitive revolution (Gardner, 28), and this aspect of his work as a whole may in fact represent his "most original" and "most enduring" contribution to linguistics (Lyons, 43).

Chomsky approaches this goal in *Syntactic Structures* with a sensitive understanding of its difficulty. The difference between human language and ordinary counting, for instance, highlights a principle of language that Chomsky shows (in a much more rigorous way than here) cannot possibly be accommodated by the sort of device many linguists and mathematical communication specialists were so excited about in the 1950s: the Markov finite-state machine (*SS*, 18–25). Basically, Chomsky shows that a finite-state grammar of this sort would have to produce sentences in linear order from left to right (somewhat like counting, though he does not draw that analogy). That is, given an "initial state" or first word, such a device would have a built-in set of choices for an appropriate second word; the second word would then dictate the options for the third word, and so on. Such a device could therefore generate a subset of sentences like *The woman speaks rapidly* or *The woman is my cousin,* for in these cases the choice of each new word might be said to depend on the immediately preceding word (e.g., *woman* is a grammatical choice after *The,* and *speaks* is a grammatical choice after *woman,* and *rapidly* is a grammatical choice after *speaks,* etc.) But how would such a model handle sentences like *The woman who speaks rapidly is my cousin?* As already noted above, in this case there is a clear nonadjacent dependency between *woman* and *is*; you could leave out the intervening words *(who speaks rapidly),* and this dependency between *woman* and *is* would still be precisely the same sort of dependency (i.e., subject-verb agreement); the intervening words do not affect it at all. Thus, the choice of the word *is* in the full sentence above does not depend—not even partially—on the immediately preceding word, *rapidly*; and yet that is exactly what a "finite-state grammar" would (by definition) have to stipulate.

A finite-state grammar is one of the most powerful devices to emerge from the mathematical theory of communication in the 1950s; it can in fact produce a huge corpus of sentences. It can even be modified with the insertion of a "loop" (*SS,* 19), so that it acquires the capability of producing a potentially infinite set of sentences. That is, with a loop in the finite-state chain, a word or group of words could be repeated any number of times, so that the device could produce not only *The woman speaks very rapidly,* but also (with a loop at *very*), *The woman speaks very, very rapidly* and *The woman speaks very, very, very rapidly,* and so forth. But when applied to natural language as a generative device, it makes a false projection about the full set of sentences possible in the language. Namely, it projects that every sentence is a simple, linear, left-to-right, word-by-word chain, with each new word dependent on what the last word was (somewhat like counting). Strange as it may sound, even if this chain is made potentially infinite with a loop, it still leaves out of its projection the majority of sentences that make up the set of sentences possible in natural language—namely, all those sentences that (unlike linear processes such as counting) exhibit complex noncontiguous dependencies.

Does this difference between human language and ordinary counting (noncontiguous vs contiguous dependency) mean that Chomsky is on the wrong track to borrow the concept of generative from mathematics? After all, someone might reason, math seems to generate numbers abstractly, whereas human beings actually produce language in some other, more complicated way; if these mathematically generative rules cannot really tell us anything about how language is actually produced (or so this reasoning goes), what good are they? That is a fair question. The answer, if it is to be convincing at all, must ultimately rest on Chomsky's demonstration of how certain much more powerful generative and transformational rules can in fact reveal—in actual linguistic examples—something important about the nature of human language. Some of Chomsky's demonstrations of this will be sketched later on, but the question of precisely WHAT Chomsky's grammar intends to reveal about human language is so bound up with the notion of generative—especially as distinguished from producing—that I would like to consider some other nonlinguistic analogies before leaving this crucial point about the quasi-mathematical use of generative.

Suppose I give you the following formal description of a geometric shape: "A plane figure consisting of four straight sides, each of length x, and four right angles." The description or formula explicitly or precisely projects (in a quasi-mathematical sense, generates) a square—in fact, it projects an infinitude of squares (because the value of x can vary). But does it actually produce even one square? Not really. Of course you might decide to put my formula to that use, but then it would be you who produces the square. If you decide you would like to use my formula to draw a square, but you make a mistake in applying the formula, the formula itself still projects a square—what you were trying to draw. If you decide you are in no mood to draw even one square at the moment, the formal description still projects an infinitude of squares—what you might draw, given world enough and time. If, realizing this, you are now suddenly very much in the mood to draw, and you decide to produce 100,000 squares of different sizes, my particular formal description—considered as a generative rule in the quasi-math sense—does not even really tell you where to begin in producing your first square; it does not, for instance, tell you to "Draw Right one inch, then Down one inch, then Left one inch," and so forth. You might just as well begin by drawing a ten-inch vertical line, then (at a distance of ten inches from your first line) draw another ten-inch vertical line, and only then connect the two vertical lines at the bottom with a ten-inch horizontal line, and so forth. The actual steps are up to you. In fact, realizing this, you might even discover that you can actually produce squares more easily and quickly without any (conscious) reference at all to my explicit formula for a square.

Well then, if we really want to get on with the business of doing geometry, surely we can dispense altogether with such clumsy, formal, abstract, and "explicit" (i.e., generative) formulas, right? If what you mean by doing geometry is simply "producing geometric shapes," the answer is yes. But if what you mean by doing geometry is "studying geometry," the answer is emphatically no—or so I believe Noam Chomsky would answer. You can draw squares all day long without any (conscious) reference to my explicit formula (or anybody else's explicit formula) for a square; but my formula is not, for all that, irrelevant to the study of squares, nor even to the study of what you are doing when you produce a square. Indeed, this formula (or some other) is absolutely indispensable to such a study. The reason is simple: Unless my formula is wrong, every geometric figure you draw, if it is really a square, will have to satisfy the formula, whether or not you are consciously thinking of the formula. Even if the formula is wrong (and it may be), it is still not, for that reason, irrelevant to the study of squares. It is in fact one hypothesis about the structure of a square, and as such, it is also relevant to at least one crucial aspect of what you are doing when you draw a square. That is, it hypothesizes something about the "logical" conception you are trying to give birth to when you draw a square, though not the "chronological" steps you must follow in doing so. It does not prescribe any particular sequence for producing any square, but it projects the necessary general character of every square. It does not describe the specific mechanics of square production, but only the general laws to which square production must conform. In the same way, Chomsky's generative-transformational formulas do not describe the actual mechanics or mental steps you go through to produce (or to interpret) a sentence, but only the "formal relations" of those sentences that are "structurally possible" in a given language (SS, 48).

On the other hand, there is a limited sense—just as Chomsky directly states in the Introduction to *Syntactic Structures* (SS, 11)—in which a generative grammar "can be viewed as" a device for actually producing sentences. As we will see below, Chomsky's early generative model of language definitely does present ordered steps for deriving sentences. In this respect, it stands in obvious contrast to my square formula in the geometry analogy above; my formula for a square, if it can be construed as generative in any primitive sense, nevertheless does not include any sequence for deriving squares, as Chomsky's early model does for deriving sentences. Furthermore, Chomsky's "ordering" principles are clearly not (or at least not all) merely arbitrary by-products of the way he happens to have constructed his particular theoretical device; in some of his later work, at least, some ordering constraints or "cycles" often represent substantive hypotheses about "psychologically real" and even potentially universal cognitive principles of human language (e.g., *LangMind* 45, 88, 131). Thus, while I think the square analogy is still valid for what it illustrates, it does not tell the whole story of what generative means. Any complete account of what generative means must show how generative "works," and no such account can ignore the derivational sequences inherent in Chomsky's model—at least in the early model of *Syntactic Structures,* where he actually called his phrase-structure rules "instruction formulas" (*SS*, 29).

It is interesting to note that Chomsky encloses instruction formulas in quotation marks. While I do not know his reasons for doing so, I think there may be a telling implication here. In what sense do these formulas give instructions for actually producing sentences? As we will see below, it is obvious that they must be followed in ordered steps to produce a derivation, as Chomsky explicitly notes (*SS*, 32–33, 44–45, 69). Does this justify our treating the derivational sequences in Chomsky's model as some sort of literal description of the chronological events in the mind during actual sentence production? Again, the answer is no. This is a misconception of his theory that Chomsky not only cautions against in *Syntactic Structures* (*SS*, 48) but has repeatedly warned against throughout his work (e.g., *KnowLang,* 67; *LangMind,* 117, 157); it is apparently one of those misconceptions that has become more widespread as his theory has become more complex. On the other hand, it is easy to understand how this misconception might arise, since any student who wants to grasp how the model works will also want to experiment with it by applying Chomsky's rules in their strictly ordered sequence to derive sentences. When students do practice with Chomsky's "top-down" sequence of generative rules, in fact, I have noticed that they often experience a kind of cognitive "resonance," which makes it very tempting to believe that there is something about the rule-order itself that is psychologically real. Indeed (though Chomsky might not agree), I believe there is something psychologically real about it. But if (as Chomsky warns) the chronological sequence of rules is not itself a description of the actual chronological sequence of events in the mind when someone formulates and speaks a sentence, then

what is it about this rule-sequence itself that can be called psychologically real?

The answer, I believe, is that the "temporal" order of rules in the
grammar models a "cognitive" order of principles in the mind. That
is, the chronological priority of certain rules in the grammar is a reflection of the logical priority of their parallel principles in the language. This distinction between logical and chronological priority is
crucial to an understanding of the quasi-mathematical sense of the term
generative, so before we look at how Chomsky's rules work in actual
examples of English, indulge me one last nonlinguistic analogy. (I
promise this one will be the last, and it is at least quasi-linguistic!)
Consider the following syllogism:

> All linguists eat quiche;
> Noam Chomsky is a linguist;
> Therefore, Noam Chomsky eats quiche.

The syllogism, of course, is the classic model of deductive reasoning,
consisting of a major premise ("All linguists eat quiche"), a minor
premise ("Noam Chomsky is a linguist"), and a conclusion ("Noam
Chomsky eats quiche"). Although the three parts of the argument need
not be presented in this order (the minor premise may precede the
major premise, for instance), the normal order of presentation in logic
books is as shown above, and there is a reason for this. The chronological priority of the major premise (in the normal order) is a reflection
of its logical priority—namely, a reflection of the fact that it is indeed
the major premise, which is logically but not necessarily chronologically prior to the other statements.

Surely no one would suppose that an ordinary human being who
happens to engage in the actual process of deductive reasoning would
necessarily have to begin with a major premise, then go to a minor
premise, and then to a conclusion. We know from ordinary experience
that people seldom actually follow this temporal sequence when they
present an argument—including an argument that may be accurately
characterized as "deductive." As a matter of fact, people usually present
a deductive argument in the form of what is called an "enthymeme,"
leaving out one part of the underlying syllogism altogether and often
changing its order (e.g., "Noam Chomsky must eat quiche, because

he is a linguist.") In all likelihood, people seldom if ever think in complete syllogisms (Noam Chomsky perhaps being the obvious exception!)—not even when their thinking has a clear deductive logic to it. Can we therefore dispense with the syllogism altogether as an artificial model that has no psychological reality with respect to the way people actually reason? Of course not. At least it is very difficult for me to imagine how any researcher would carry out a rigorous and systematic study of the facts of human deductive reasoning without an abstract model of it that was at least something very much like the syllogism. The syllogism is not a "production model" in the chronological sense, but it most certainly is not, for all that, irrelevant to the study of human reasoning. Further, any true and broad production model of human argument and persuasion (call it a "rhetoric") would surely be incomplete without, as one of its crucial components, some abstract generative model of deductive reasoning such as is provided by the syllogism.

Now Chomsky's generative-transformational model of human language is not a model of deductive logic, any more than it is a model of arithmetic or geometry; the above analogy should therefore be interpreted only as having the following point: Chomsky's model is not a production model, either; but it need not be construed as a production model in order to reveal crucial aspects of the structure of human language—abstract structural principles that surely underlie not only the actual production of human language but its infinite productivity, as well. As such, Chomsky's grammar is directly and critically relevant to any broader theory of human linguistic production that might be proposed (*RuleRep,* 202–5). Thus my intention here is not at all to rule out the possibilities suggested by his model for such a broader theory; throughout his earliest work, Chomsky himself clearly anticipated such possibilities (*SS,* 103; *LSLT* 5, 20). As a matter of fact, these possibilities even in the early and primitive version of generative-transformational grammar that Chomsky presented in *Syntactic Structures* are largely responsible, I suspect, for the enormous appeal of the book to technically minded psychologists and researchers in communication theory during the cognitive revolution of the 1950s, which (as described in the previous chapter) was an era of unparalleled excitement about the possibility of "language machines" and the like. While Chomsky himself did not share this particular enthusiasm, he convincingly demonstrated the superiority of his quasi-mathematical generative-transformational model to other mathematical models for purposes that can be viewed, at least, as having very much to do with the actual production of sentences. In any case, no description of what generative grammar is could hope to be accurate without some exploration of how it works.

How Does Generative Grammar Work? After demonstrating the inadequacy of a finite-state grammar as a model of natural human language, Chomsky next considers a much more powerful kind of model called a "phrase structure" grammar (*SS*, 26–33). *Syntactic Structures* does not give a complete account of how this sort of grammar works in actual examples of English, but it does give a much more complete demonstration than I can give here (see also *LSLT*, 223–91, for an even more thorough and formal account). The basic principle of operation, however, is easy enough to understand by considering a few examples of Chomsky's phrase structure rules, rules of the following sort (*SS*, 26):

Sentence → NP + VP

where NP stands for Noun Phrase, VP stands for Verb Phrase, and the arrow (→) can be understood as meaning "rewrite." Thus this sort of rule device starts out with the notion of a whole Sentence and then rewrites it in terms of its parts, the NP (corresponding to the subject in traditional grammar) and the VP (the predicate in traditional grammar). The easiest way to see the effect of such a rule is with a phrase structure diagram:

Already you can see one very important difference between this approach and that of the finite-state grammar, which starts out with a single word and then generates a sentence word-by-word from left to right. In contrast, Chomsky's rule starts at the "top," with the holistic conception of Sentence, and generates "down" to smaller structures within the whole. In this way, it introduces the crucial concept of "levels," something that is missing in the single-level approach of the finite-state grammar (*SS*, 11, 25). Notice that Chomsky's rule introduces the "vertical" or "hierarchical" level, here, without compromising the "horizontal" or left-to-right order of English, either—the NP (subject) still occurs to the left of the VP (predicate), just as it would in a simple finite-state grammar of English. This is part of what we mean by saying that the phrase structure approach is more "powerful": In a much simpler way, it accounts for everything a finite-state grammar can account for (left-to-right order), but it also captures something more (the abstract vertical or hierarchical levels of syntax). Thus, instead of merely producing a sentence, the grammar is generating its formal structure, thereby accommodating certain linguistic intuitions from traditional grammar about syntactic categories and their logical connections—which intuitions, by the way, Chomsky believes are largely correct (*SS,* 81).

The same top-down approach is followed at all lower levels in the phrase structure grammar with Chomsky's very simple (purely illustrative) rules for rewriting the NP (*SS,* 26):

NP → T + N

T → *the*

N → *man, ball,* etc.

where T represents something like an Article and N of course represents a Noun. These rules can expand the diagram as shown below:

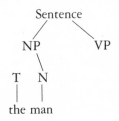

Chomsky also gives some rules for expanding or rewriting the VP (*SS,* 26):

VP → Verb + NP

Verb → *hit,* etc.

By applying these rules—and then reapplying the NP rules at a lower level—we can have a complete derivation:

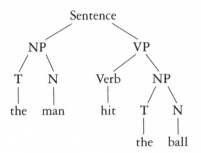

This is of course a very simplistic derivation of the sort given in *Syntactic Structures* for illustrative purposes only. It does, however, demonstrate the greater power of this approach when compared to the finite-state grammar. Not only does the phrase structure grammar preserve the grammatical left-to-right word order, but it introduces the important grammatical intuition of hierarchical structure, the intuition by which native speakers sense that sentences are made up of whole groups of words or "constituents" (instead of just left-to-right, word-by-word chains).

Notice that the phrase structure grammar achieves this greater power with greater simplicity: While a finite-state grammar could produce the left-to-right sequence of words in the example above, in order to do so it would have to provide a complete set of instructions for the word-options available after each word; thus, on reaching the Verb *hit*, the finite-state grammar would have to give a whole new set of instructions for what might come next. Conversely, the phrase structure grammar merely stipulates that an NP must come next. No new set of instructions is required to generate this NP (*the ball*), because precisely the same NP rules that work for the subject-NP (*the man*) will also work for the object-NP (*the ball*). That is, phrase structure grammar can use the same generative processes or rules recursively at different syntactic levels and positions within a sentence, thereby avoiding unnecessary duplication of rules and instructions. This theme of "simplicity" plays a crucial part in Chomsky's later work, as well, especially as it relates to the problem of language acquisition: How is it, for instance, that young children so quickly master the production of complex sentences? In part, it must be because complex sentences contain a finite number of constituent types, each of which is generated by a set of rules that will work for that type of constituent no matter where it occurs or how often it occurs or how long and complex the sentence in which it occurs. Thus, once children know the generative rules for making a Noun Phrase, for instance, they can use those same rules anywhere a Noun Phrase occurs in a complex sentence.

Of course the above sentence is hardly "complex," and the phrase structure rules that are used to derive it are grossly oversimplified for illustrative purposes. Chomsky goes on in *Syntactic Structures* to consider some far more interesting phrase structure rules. The most powerful and exciting insights of his monograph spring from a consideration of the following three rules (*SS*, 39):

(1) Verb → Aux + V

(2) V → *hit, take, walk, read,* etc.

(3) Aux → C(M) (have + en) (be + ing) (be + en)

Rule (1) merely says that a Verb contains an Aux—an "auxiliary" or "helping" verb—in addition to the main Verb (V). This Aux Chomsky further defines, in rule (3), as consisting of one required element— C—and four optional elements: (M), (have + en), (be + ing), and (be + en), where the parentheses mean "optional."

How well I remember the first time I read *Syntactic Structures* and came upon this Aux rule. Up until this point, I had understood everything in the book fairly well, but when I got to the Aux rule, I had not the foggiest idea what was going on. Kellogg Hunt, the professor in my first syntax class (required) in graduate school, was already prepared to move forward with Chomsky's *Aspects of the Theory of Syntax,* but I was still stuck on page thirty-nine of *Syntactic Structures.* I had to interrupt Hunt's agenda for the class, in order to ask for help. Much to my surprise, he said, "You have asked a very intelligent question. If you will only understand this one little formula and all it implies, you will have understood the $e = mc^2$ of modern linguistics." It was something of an exaggeration on Hunt's part, of course, prompted by the fact that he had sensed my embarrassment, but by the end of class that day, I did not think it was an exaggeration at all. In fact, I had decided to switch my major field of study from American Literature to Linguistics. And I felt much better about the whole affair when I learned (some years later) that what first got Noam Chomsky himself "quite excited"—during his earliest work on a generative grammar of English in 1952—were the discoveries he made on the system of auxiliary verbs in various types of sentences (*LSLT,* 30–31).

I cannot duplicate Hunt's explication or Chomsky's, but let us look at the Aux rule more closely. In his Appendix II (*SS,* 111), Chomsky repeats the rule in a simplified form, deleting only the "passive" auxiliary element (be + en) which, as we will see later, he decides to introduce by a different rule, a different sort of rule (namely, the passive transformation). Without the passive element, the Aux rule looks like this:

Aux → C(M) (have + en) (be + ing)

The C basically stands for verb tense (past or present). Why not also a future tense? That is handled under the (M), which stands for Modal—words like *will, can, may, shall,* and so forth. Among the reasons for this separation of C and (M) is the fact that Modals are optional, whereas some minimal verb tense—past or present (nonpast)—is required. Note also that Modals have these same two tense forms: The past-tense form of *will* is *would,* the past of *can* is *could,* the past of *shall* is *should,* and so forth. [11]

In addition to the optional Modal, there are two other optional elements of the Aux rule: (have + en) and (be + ing). These elements specify what is often called the "Aspect" of the Verb: If we choose to include the (have + en) option in the Verb sequence we are deriving, we get the "perfect" Aspect (of completed action in traditional grammar), as in *have taken,* and if we invoke the (be + ing) option, we get the "progressive" Aspect (of ongoing action), as in *is taking.* Of course we can invoke both options: *have been taking.* We can even include a Modal: *will have been taking* or (if the tense were past) *would have been taking.* Indeed, the first indication of power in the Aux rule is the elegant simplicity with which it provides for a whole range of independent options, clearly defining a precise and regular system underlying what might otherwise appear to be purely aperiodic chaos or idiosyncratic irregularity in the English auxiliary. Given the assumption that there are only two verb tenses, and taking just a single Modal for illustrative purposes, we can see how Chomsky's one short Aux rule stipulates every possible combination in modern "standard" English. Consider how the rule would lay out these possibilities for a Verb phrase whose main V is *take* and whose NP-subject is *Mary* (assuming the present tense, which may or may not be indicated by a morphological inflection):

C   (M)   (have + en)   (be + ing)   V

1. pres   -   -   -   take = *takes*

2. pres can   -   -   take = *can take*

3. pres   have + en   -   take = *has taken*

4. pres   be + ing   take = *is taking*

5. pres can have + en   -   take = *can have taken*

6. pres can   -   be + ing   take = *can be taking*

7. pres   -   have + en   be + ing   take = *has been taking*

8. pres can have + en   be + ing   take = *can have been taking*

If we change the tense to past, of course, the possible combinations will be the same but the ultimate morphological forms of the verb elements will be different. In example 1 above, for instance, the past tense would result in *took* instead of *take*s; in example 2, it would result in COULD *take* instead of *can take*; in example 3, *ha*D *taken* instead of *ha*s *taken*; in example 4, WAS *taking* instead of IS *taking*, and so forth. This answers a question about Chomsky's rule that often arises: Why does he put the tense element (C) first in the order of elements stipulated by the rule? The answer is simple: Because the tense (C) will ultimately need to be "inflected onto" whatever element is chosen next. If the tense is past and the option of a Modal is selected to come next, the Modal must receive the past-tense inflection (COULD); if no Modal is selected but a *have* comes next, the *have* gets the inflection (*ha*D); if neither a Modal nor a *have* is selected and a *be* comes next, the *be* gets the inflection (WAS); and if none of these options is chosen, so that the main V itself comes next, then the main V gets the inflection (TOOK).[12]

The same sort of phenomenon explains the configuration of the elements (have + en) and (be + ing) in Chomsky's rule: The -*en* suffix, even though it is generated from the group (have + en), is never actually added to the *have,* nor is the -*ing* suffix of the group (be + ing) ever actually added to the *be.* Rather, just as in the case of verb tense, the suffixes -*en* and -*ing* are ultimately added to whatever comes next. Thus, if both options—(have + en) and (be + ing)—are selected, the -*en* gets added to the *be* of (be + ing), and of course the -*ing* of (be + ing) gets added to the main V *take* (*have be*EN *tak*ING). But if only (have + en) is selected, then the suffix -*en* gets added to the main V (*have tak*EN). Below are some schematic illustrations of how this very interesting and highly systematic phenomenon operates in the case of all three verb inflections in English: tense, -*en,* and -*ing.*

To put it somewhat crudely, Chomsky's Aux rule—with no way to "anticipate" at any given instant of its operation which of its own options might (or might not) be selected to occur next—must nevertheless make some abstract provision for whatever element might occur next to receive the proper inflection. In this respect, the problem faced by a phrase structure grammar is the same as that faced by a finite-state grammar. No matter what else a phrase structure grammar may account for (e.g., hierarchical structure), it still must take into account the same linear left-to-right distribution of elements that a finite-state grammar tries to capture.

While the problem is the same in this respect, the solution is markedly different: The finite-state grammar tries to "list" all the actual word-forms that might come next, but Chomsky's phrase structure rule attempts a much simpler (yet necessarily more abstract) solution, a solution that says, "No matter what word comes next, it must be inflected (at some level) with such-and-such a suffix." Because the finite-state grammar is *strictly* linear or left-to-right, it can only try to anticipate all the possible properly inflected words, to the ends of which have already been attached all of the proper grammatical suffixes. But because Chomsky's phrase structure rule is also abstract and hierarchical, it can "front-load" the proper suffixes, thereby providing for them to be attached to whatever comes next, no matter what the next actual word-choice may be.

Notice that this front-loading phenomenon is emphatically not some sort of arbitrary or manufactured artifact of Chomsky's grammar. Rather, it captures precisely (for the first time in linguistics, by the way) certain important facts about the auxiliary system of the English verb phrase. For instance, as a general law at least, it just so happens to be true that the first element of the verb phrase will carry the tense inflection, no matter what that element is and no matter how the element may ultimately be "spelled" with the inflection attached. In some dialects of English, for example, the past-tense inflectional form of the V *walk* may be simply *walk* instead of *walk*ED (just as in standard English the past tense of *hit* is simply *hit,* instead of **hit*tED), so that the sentence "I walk home" can be equivalent in these dialects to the expression (in standard English), "I walkED home." (*indicates ungrammatical form.) However, in no dialect of English (to my knowledge) does any native speaker say, "*I CAN walkED home" (unless the speaker is too drunk to walk home). Rather, as Chomsky's rule would predict, the grammatical form will be either "I can [*pres*] walk home" or I COULD [*past*] walk home." Similarly, in some dialects we may have a perfective such as "I have walk[Ø] home," or a progressive such as "I [Ø] walking home," but (in no cases that I am aware of) do we find a perfective like "*I have walkING home," or a progressive like "*I be walkED home," or a perfect-progressive like "*I have beING walkED home." At its abstract level, the Aux rule captures very precisely a general law governing the distribution of auxiliary elements—precisely by abstractly front-loading the standard suffixes, thus providing for their ultimate attachment to whatever words may follow.

Providing for the proper "attachment" of these suffixes to the following words is one thing; actually attaching them, even at an abstract level, is quite another. How does Chomsky propose to do this? His formal explicit proposal is a rule of the following sort (*SS, 39*):

Af + v → v + Af#

where Af = affix (suffix, in this case), v = verb-phrase element, and # = word boundary. In other words, the rule says whenever you have an affix (Af) followed by a verb element (v)—which situation the rule describes as Af + v—you should rewrite (→) this sequence as the mirror-image v + Af, and you should consider this new *v + affix* sequence as a word (bounded by #). This rule will neatly change *past + can* into *can+past#* (could), or *past + have* into *have+past#* (had), and so forth.

What sort of a rule is it, however? It certainly is not like the other phrase structure rules. If you look back, you will see that each phrase structure rule up until now has merely specified how to rewrite (→) a single abstract element, which always occurs to the left of the arrow, as a string of new elements, always occurring to the right of the arrow. But Chomsky's new affix rule has two elements to the left of the arrow (Af + v), and the same two elements to the right of it (v + Af). Instead of taking one abstract element and rewriting or expanding it in terms of its parts (e.g., Verb → Aux + V), this new rule takes two elements (Af + v) and basically switches them around (v + Af). If it is a phrase structure rule, it is a phrase structure rule of a very new and liberal sort indeed.

Actually, as you probably have already guessed, it is not a phrase structure rule at all. What it is, is a "transformation"—perhaps the very first ever written in the description of English. As such, it was (and is) only the beginning.

The Natural Algebra of Transformations.   All right, then, someone might reply, it is a transformation if you say so, but it merely looks like another of these silly quasi-mathematical computational formulas to me. What is so special or interesting about this transformation? A fair question. Consider again the fundamental difference between a phrase structure rule and a transformational rule:

A   → b + c   phrase structure rule

b + c → c + b   transformational rule

In this way of looking at it, a phrase structure rule takes one simple or whole thing (A) and rewrites or expands it into a more detailed, complex thing (b + c). Conversely, a transformation takes a thing that already has a detailed or "complex" internal structure to begin with (b + c) and rewrites it as another thing having a different internal structure (c + b).

So what? After all, when the phrase structure rule sees A, it changes it into (b + c); when the transformation sees (b + c), it merely changes it into (c + b). Thus a phrase structure rule "reads" a simple thing and turns it into a more complex thing, while a transformation reads a complex thing and turns it into a different complex thing. If all we are trying to do is to generate complex sentences from a few simple rules, how does the transformation represent any step forward? After all, in the case of both rules above, complexity is the "output"; and the transformation's output (c + b) is hardly more complex than the phrase structure rule's output (b + c), so what is the big deal about the transformation?

Obviously, the difference has more to do with the "input" (the stuff to the left of the arrow) than with the output (the stuff to the right of the arrow). What makes a transformation so special, in comparison to a phrase structure rule, is not its ability to "write" complexity but its ability to read it. This difference is important only if our goal is to understand the structure of human linguistic knowledge.

With some effort, for instance, and with a big enough "machine," it might be possible to construct a phrase structure grammar that could write all the complex structures of a human language; in *Syntactic Structures,* Chomsky himself concedes that he does not know whether or not this is possible for English (*SS,* 34). Outside linguistics, some recent discoveries in the natural sciences and mathematics—particularly those discoveries that are seen as relevant to what is called "chaos theory"—have suggested that astonishing arrays of natural complexity might be derived from a relatively few compact recursive formulas. For instance, after describing the incredibly complex branching "tree" structure of the air pipes in the human lung, a structure that leads into literally millions of microscopic air sacs called alveoli, James Gleick writes, "DNA surely cannot specify the vast number of bronchi, bronchioles, and alveoli or the particular spatial structure of the resulting tree, but it can specify a repeating process of bifurcation and development" (Gleick, 110). All that complexity must somehow be there—in abstract coded form, as a set of recursive principles—

written on a few strands of DNA in every living cell of the human body.

What sort of code could possibly serve this amazing function? Surely it could not be any sort of single-level linear chain, which would presumably have to specify, in advance, every single possible pathway that might be followed by every single bronchiole to every single alveolus. Would the code rather be a set of expansion rules? In order to generate such incredible complexity from such elegant compactness—with what might well turn out to be only a relatively few recursive functions—surely nature's own biological code must be something of this same general sort, at least in part. When it comes to human language, Chomsky's phrase structure rules are in fact of this very sort. But in *Syntactic Structures,* Chomsky also uncovered principles of a rather different sort—principles that he formalized (for the first time in linguistics) with rules that can not only write complexity but can also read it—read it and then transform it into something new. And, although I do not know very much about such matters, I would be willing to bet that if and when the scientists ever manage to unravel the complex self-organizing systems of organic nature into the basic code of life itself, they will discover rules of two general types: (1) those whose function is to generate complexity out of compact simple wholes (much like phrase structure rules), and (2) those whose function is to read this new complexity—read it even as it develops—and then transform it into a pragmatically functional (and aesthetically rich) natural diversity.

In short, what Noam Chomsky wrote of in 1957 as a "natural algebra of transformations" (*SS,* 44) may yet prove to be something beyond an apt metaphor. After all, if he is correct as to the ultimate biological foundations of human language, then those principles of language that most uniquely distinguish it as a dynamic and complex system may well turn out to reveal, at least abstractly, something important about the genetic principles of life itself—much in the way that abstract fractals can reveal, in macrocosm, the otherwise unnoticed microscopic intricacies of design in the natural images on which they are based. Significantly, however, this sort of fractal revelation is not always just a matter of replication or reproduction on a larger scale; rather, the operative principle of the fractal revelation itself often seems to involve a fracturing, a permutation of the original image, or what Gleick sometimes calls a transformation—a process by which a thing can reveal its own essence, not just by replicating or expanding itself, but by actually changing itself. A queer and paradoxical notion, perhaps, but let me try to divest it of mysticism: If we understand what Chomsky means by a transformation, it is not strange at all to think that a dynamic system might actually reveal its "simple" inner secrets in the very act of transforming its own growing complexity; for in order to so transform itself, such a system would have to be equipped to read itself—read its own complexity.

Perhaps this is only a metaphor, after all, but in this respect I think we really are dealing with something much more like an "organism" than a "mechanism" in Chomsky's transformational theory. If what you want to do is just to build a machine to write complex structures, you may not in fact need transformations at all; you may be able to make do with recursive phrase structure rules alone. But if what you want to do is to build a device (in the sense of a model) that will actually help you to understand that remarkable complexity of human linguistic knowledge, then you would be well advised not to neglect the special power of transformations—the power not only to write complex structures but to read complex structures, and thus to select just those structures that are suitable for rewriting in specific ways. This "self-reading" function of language—which might be called (again echoing Gleick) the "sensitivity" of language, not only to the so-called initial conditions but to the evolving conditions of its own internal structure as it expands—is what Chomsky was trying to capture, in *Syntactic Structures,* on the left side of the transformational arrow. It is what Chomsky himself has called "context sensitivity" or "structural dependency"; it is indeed a dependency, a constraint, a limitation, but as such (perhaps like the human abductive faculty itself) it also defines a special ability—not just the ability to "see" the identity of a thing as a whole (A), but the ability to see "into" it, to see its internal configuration of parts (b + c). The transformation can see this internal configuration, of course, only because it is itself so configured as to "look" for it. This is a limitation, a constraint on the transformation; it is "blind" to anything other than the particular structure on the left side of its arrow; but because what it is thus constructed to look for is, after all, not just some syntactic element but the *internal structure* of an element, the transformation has a unique capability of projecting the ultimate possible form(s) of this element.

In *Syntactic Structures,* Chomsky describes this unique capability of the transformational rule as its ability to "look back" into the "history of derivation" of a sentence in order to determine the "next step" in the derivation (*SS*, 37–38). This can be illustrated with a brief examination of Chomsky's (optional) passive transformation (*SS*, 43), simplified below (a more formal version at *SS*, 112). Beneath the rule itself is an illustration of its effect:

$$\text{Np}_1 \text{ Aux } V \quad \text{NP}_2 \quad \rightarrow \quad \text{NP}_2 \quad \text{Aux be en } V \text{ by } \text{NP}_1$$

Mom past take the book → the book past be en take by Mom

The two NPs are marked with subscripts (NP_1, NP_2) in this rule because the transformation of course causes them to switch places, and the rule needs a way to keep track of which NP is which, and which moves where: The first NP (NP_1, or *Mom* in the example) moves to the end of the sequence, and the second NP (NP_2, *the book*) moves to the front. Whatever the Aux was in the original sequence (in the example, it happens to consist only of the tense element, *past*, the other Aux elements being optional), it stays the same and does not change its position. The V (*take* in the example) also does not change. The only other changes effected by the rule are to insert the passive verb marker (be + en) immediately after the original Aux and to insert the preposition *by* in front of the final NP. Chomsky's affix transformation (discussed earlier) can now apply to the output of the passive transformation to complete the derivation as shown below:

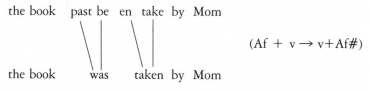

$$(\text{Af} + v \rightarrow v + \text{Af\#})$$

That is, when it sees the sequence *past be* and the sequence *en take*—both of which have resulted from the prior operation of the passive transformation, please note—the affix transformation in turn properly reads these sequences as instances of the particular string it is looking for (Af + v); having so identified them, it can then transform each of them into the properly concatenated elements of the structure (v+Af#). This may seem artificial, but notice that it could not have been done in advance: Since the passive transformation is optional, it need not have applied in this example at all; had it not been applied, then Chomsky's affix transformation (which is of course obligatory in all cases) could still have functioned properly, by applying instead to the original sequence, *Mom past take the book.* Specifically, it would have properly read the internal constituency of this string to find—in the sequence of *past take*—another instance of (Af + v), whereupon it would then have transformed the sequence into (v+Af#), or *take + past#* (*took*).

Here, then, we can see how two fundamentally different principles of generative complexity in the dynamic system of human language (as envisioned even by Chomsky's very early transformational model) mutually support one another in a remarkably powerful way. Namely, we see how Chomsky's phrase structure rule

$$Aux \rightarrow C(M) + (have + en) (be + ing)$$

works together with both his passive transformation and his affix transformation in the generation of different sentences that are nevertheless strongly and "genetically" related (by a common phrase-structure origin and yet through diverse transformational histories): *Mom took the book,* and *The book was taken by Mom.* While the Aux rule is only a phrase structure rule, it does expand a single element (Aux) into a complex string, thereby endowing it with an internal structure that is "readable" (and thus transformable) by the affix transformation under distinctly different eventual situations—situations that may vary drastically according to which other transformations (like passive) may or may not apply while the derivation is in progress. Hence, Chomsky's phrase structure rules generate, from simple (albeit abstract) unitary wholes, a detailed complexity of discrete elements or digits; these digits, being independent of one another, may then be computed with great flexibility in a variety of ways by Chomsky's transformational rules, which have that uniquely context-sensitive power to read and to rewrite digital complexity even as it emerges within the system.

The way in which the passive transformation reads and rewrites the internal complexity of the English "kernel" sentence [$_s$ NP$_1$ + Aux + V + NP$_2$ $_s$] and the even more narrowly focussed yet flexible way in which the affix transformation in turn reads and rewrites the appropriate elements [$_{AUX}$ . . . Af + v . . . $_{AUX}$] within any possible configuration of the Aux itself—well, of course these are only illustrative examples of the way transformations interact with phrase structure rules in Chomsky's early grammar. This account of it is intended only to give you a preliminary sense of how Chomsky's early version of generative-transformational grammar works, in the hope that you will go back to the original account—*Syntactic Structures* (or, if you are more ambitious, *The Logical Structure of Linguistic Theory*).

It is worth the effort. Although the formal devices of generative-transformational grammar have themselves been transformed drastically since *Syntactic Structures,* the book's central vision of English syntax is very nearly prescient about the next thirty-five years in theoretical development: From the alphabet of sound to all the complexity of meaning, human language is above all else a dynamic system predicated on the twin principles of digital expansion and novel recombination. Phrase structure rules are the formal devices for imagining the primitive digital complexity of sentences, and transformations are the formal devices for deciphering this complexity, even as it develops, and then reimagining it in terms of its possibilities for recombinant variety.

Whether or not this is anything more than a splendid early effort to formalize a few principles that are peculiar to human language remains to be seen. That would be enough for one short first book, but in view of how the transformation reads and rewrites the output of phrase structure expansion rules in *Syntactic Structures,* I cannot help thinking of something Chomsky told us in our first interview (Interview 1): "There are aspects of language that are continuous—like intonation and stress and gesture, and so on—but not language itself. It's a digital system, but an infinite digital system. Those things don't really exist in nature very much—maybe DNA is another case. . . ."

The Psychological Foundations

What is the ultimate goal of a grammar that can derive sentences in the fashion illustrated above? Obviously, it is not really to build a device that will replicate some old sentences or even invent some new ones; there are more than enough old and new sentences to go around without having a machine to make up some more. Looking only a little beyond *Syntactic Structures* in order to see it in the larger context of Chomsky's work, we soon realize what is really at stake: Chomsky will ultimately want his device to generate sentences so as to model (in certain well-defined and illuminating ways) the real cognitive system underlying the native speaker's actual production of sentences. (Again, the goal, so construed, is not to model production but one part of the system underlying it.) If the model is to provide any real insight to this cognitive system, the generative device constructed by the linguist must really be "like" the system itself, at least in principle, and not just "happen" to generate some of the same sentences by some other altogether different set of principles.

Herein lies the revolutionary rub: Is Chomsky's device of generative grammar really like whatever linguistic system actually exists in the mind of a native speaker? If so, in what way are they alike? A closely related question is the one raised and discussed in the previous chapter: Is Chomsky's basic theoretical approach to the construction of such generative devices really parallel, in any fundamental way, with the native speaker's own cognitive approach to the acquisition of language? If so, in what way are they parallel?

These interrelated issues about the psychological reality of Chomsky's generative grammar, while central to his later work, might seem to be somewhat difficult to address in the context of his earliest work, for the simple reason that he himself does not (explicitly) address them here. Understandably, this has made some readers of Chomsky believe that the school of linguistics to which at least the early generative model of *Syntactic Structures* belongs is essentially autonomous from any real concerns with cognitive psychology. John Lyons, for instance, seems to say exactly this, observing, correctly, that Chomsky did not make any explicit connections between generative grammar and cognitive psychology until his later work—notably, *Aspects* (Lyons, 91). Some readers who are less sympathetic to Chomsky than Lyons have seen in Chomsky's generative devices only a sort of "abstract speculation" that has "next to no foundation in linguistic facts."[13] It might even seem that Chomsky himself invited such assessments of *Syntactic Structures* when he said that the "ultimate outcome" of the kind of investigations he proposed should be a linguistic theory in which the "descriptive devices" of particular grammars are "studied abstractly, with no specific reference to particular languages" (*SS*, 11). To some who read no farther than the book's introduction, this may have meant that Chomsky was doing some sort of artificial, highly abstract mathematical linguistics that has no relation to anything outside the Platonic world of its own making, a conception of his work that he has pointedly denied (*KnowLang*, 33–36). Given the rigorous and formal (quasi-mathematical) elegance of Chomsky's devices in *Syntactic Structures*, all such general impressions are as understandable as they are totally incorrect.

It must be remembered that *Syntactic Structures* was essentially a set of class notes in which Chomsky's main concern was to present some of his generative devices in the context of automata theory, a topic that was of particular interest to the students in his class at that time. It is thus the abstract and seemingly autonomous design features of such formal systems in themselves with which Chomsky is occasionally concerned in this work, rather than whatever psychological reality his own devices may or may not possess. Nevertheless, such questions of psychological reality were clearly in the immediate background of Chomsky's thinking when he wrote *Syntactic Structures,* and even earlier in his much more formal work, *The Logical Structure of Linguistic Theory.* Thus it was Chomsky's student, Robert Lees, who first pointed out (in his review of *Syntactic Structures*) the relevance of Chomsky's model to language acquisition—with good reason, for Chomsky had already been talking about this and related psychological questions (specifically in relation to generative grammar) for some time. Chomsky also explicitly addressed the relevant issues in his immediate follow-up work (*LangResp,* 113). In his (unpublished) 1958–9 revision of *The Logical Structure of Linguistic Theory,* for instance, Chomsky presented this "psychological interpretation" as "the framework for the entire study"; the only reason he had left it out of his original version is that it had seemed (even to him) "too audacious" (*LSLT,* 35–36).

Perhaps any claim of psychological reality for the formal devices of *Syntactic Structures* would indeed have been too audacious, given the times. For instance, in the same year that *Syntactic Structures* was first published (1957), B. F. Skinner's *Verbal Behavior* also appeared.[14] Skinner's book was actually the published version of his William James Lectures, which he had delivered at Harvard in 1947. When Chomsky himself arrived at Harvard in 1951, Skinner's ideas were still being talked and written about with great enthusiasm. To say the least, Noam Chomsky's reception of these ideas was somewhat less enthusiastic. Skinner, of course, was the preeminent behaviorist of American psychology who attempted to account for the acquisition and use of language in terms of "stimulus-and-response"—that is, without taking into account any of the innate cognitive or so-called mentalistic properties of language that Chomsky was assuming from very early in his work. Chomsky wrote a scathing review of Skinner's book, a review that is now a classic.[15] It clearly indicates how deeply concerned he was at this time about psychological questions of language (both as to the cognitive devices by which it operates and the cognitive system by which it is acquired), even though he did not himself raise such questions explicitly in *Syntactic Structures.*

These psychological concerns are nevertheless implicit within the book's generative theory of language. After all, cognitive psychologists like George Miller (who, interestingly enough, was quite enthusiastic about Skinner's converse approach before encountering Chomsky's) were much more receptive to Chomsky's early work than the professional linguists were. Recall the importance of Chomsky's "Three Models" paper in the birth of the cognitive revolution; this paper's abstract and mathematical formalizations make the formal devices of *Syntactic Structures* look downright concrete, language-specific, and what some might call humanistic by comparison. To see the psychological implications in Chomsky's early work, one simply had to be receptive to a view of human psychology that was essentially "cognitivist"—the sort of view that sees nothing whatsoever antihumanistic in the abstract study of any and all human capacities, including the study of how one human capacity might reveal (whether by similarity or by contrast) something important about another.

The Intuition of Grammar. Nowhere are the ultimate psychological foundations of *Syntactic Structures* more apparent than in Chomsky's discussion of the concept "grammatical." This is a key concept, of course: Chomsky does not want his device to generate just any sort of sequence; he wants it designed so as to generate any grammatical sequence, without at the same time generating any ungrammatical sequences (*SS*, 13). This is part of the reason for calling the device a grammar—its output is to be strictly grammatical. Right away, though, there is room for controversy: Who gets the final say as to which sequences are grammatical? While he specifically disavows any intention of giving a complete answer to this question (*SS*, 14–15), Chomsky does have some specific proposals for helping to determine what is grammatical. He begins with one that would not have seemed, at least on its surface, particularly new to linguists of the time: Use the native speaker as a source of evidence for what is grammatical; thus, he says, grammatical means "acceptable to a native speaker, etc." (*SS*, 13). The question of grammaticality is thus not to be decided by some academic authority (as in traditional prescriptive grammar); rather, it is to be decided (at least in part) by reference to evidence gathered from ordinary native speakers, who were commonly used as "informants" in the descriptive linguistic "field work" of the day.

It quickly becomes apparent, however, that Chomsky has no intentions of going out to do field work on the linguistic "behavior" of native speakers of English; he rather proposes to do something that must have seemed quite radical and dangerous to the empiricist and behaviorist-minded linguists and psychologists of the day: At least for purposes of this discussion, he proposes, let us assume an "intuitive knowledge" (presumably our own) of which sequences are grammatical sentences of English and which are not (*SS*, 13). In other words, assuming we are ourselves native speakers of English, and since we are studying English at the moment, we do not have to do any field work or behavioral studies in order to determine what is grammatical English, for the simple reason that we already know it—intuitively!

No great point is made of it in this short book, but out of Chomsky's rather quiet little assumption of intuitive knowledge would arise one of the major and most controversial psychological themes of his work. In 1957, true scientists of language and human behavior were not supposed to make any assumptions at all about mentalistic phenomena like "intuition," let alone base any part of their investigations upon such assumptions. Perhaps they could not entirely rid their minds of all previous conceptions about language, but they were certainly not supposed to gather evidence through introspection of their own intuitive knowledge. These anticognitive attitudes were deeply rooted in the empiricist-behavioristic view of language that dominated the scene in American linguistics during the early 1950s. In fact, Howard Gardner has pinpointed "the refusal of behaviorism to countenance mental entities and introspective accounts" as one of three chief obstacles to the cognitive revolution of the 1950s; he also names Chomsky as one of the principal figures who assisted in the "exorcism" of these obstacles (in *Debate*, xxv–xxvi). The revolutionary status of Chomsky's appeal to intuition is surely one reason why perhaps no other single aspect of his approach has been so widely misunderstood.

In *Syntactic Structures* the assumption of intuitive knowledge might seem to be little more than a matter of pragmatic convenience, but Chomsky was later to say that "the first goal" of generative grammar is to explore the nature of "the intuitive, unconscious knowledge" that permits language use (*LangResp*, 109), and he had already said much the same thing in his work prior to *Syntactic Structures* (*LSLT*, 95). Perhaps the most controversial aspect of this goal is Chomsky's notion that linguists—in their effort to determine the nature of the linguistic intuition—need not limit themselves to observing the linguistic behavior of other native speakers but may, via introspection, explore their own grammatical intuitions as native speakers (*Managua*, 46). This notion is commonly misconstrued, however, as meaning that Chomsky thinks the actual structural properties of the language (the rules or principles a linguist needs to discover in order to construct a grammar) are themselves directly accessible to introspection. Nothing could be more incorrect. Indeed, Chomsky strongly criticizes the Cartesians— for whom he otherwise has great admiration[16]—on just this point: The Cartesians thought the properties of the mind were directly accessible to introspection, whereas Chomsky believes that the "deeper principles of mental organization" may be "as inaccessible to introspection" as are "the mechanisms of digestion" (*LangMind*, 25–26). In other words, linguists cannot simply "look inside" and discover the rules of the language directly; as Chomsky mentioned in our first interview, the principles and models and theories of modern science are in fact often directly counterintuitive (Interview 1).

What role, then, can linguists' introspection upon their own intuitions about language possibly play in their efforts to construct a grammatical model? The answer is simple: data. Introspection and intuition are only sources of linguistic data. Chomsky is quite clear and emphatic about this in both his earlier work (*LSLT*, 62–65, 86–87, 101–3) and his later work (*LangMind*, 104; 186–87). If they are themselves native speakers of the language they are studying, Chomsky believes, linguists should feel free to draw upon their own intuitive knowledge of which sentences are clearly grammatical and which are clearly ungrammatical (the same sort of judgment a structural linguist might attempt to elicit from an informant). But these observations about grammaticality merely produce some facts to be explained, not the explanation itself; the task of explanation (constructing, evaluating, and testing a formal theory to account for the facts of grammaticality) is a matter for linguistic science, not simple introspection. That is, having made some very preliminary observations about some intuitively obvious data (as to what is or what is not a sentence of the language), the linguist must then construct a formal, explicit hypothesis that would explain these data; if it is explicit enough, it will (in all likelihood) also hypothetically project the existence of still more data—and these hypothetical projections must then be evaluated and tested empirically against the actual facts of language. However intuitively attractive a given hypothesis may be to the linguist, it is only an empirical hypothesis that is subject to confirmation, revision, or disconfirmation through further careful evaluation and testing against a wide variety of additional data from many sources (*GenPrize*, 33; *KnowLang*, 247–48; *Sophia*, 39; *Managua*, 61).

It is strange indeed that Chomsky has had to defend himself on this matter so frequently throughout his later work, in view of the fact that the clear and precise research agenda he proposed in *Syntactic Structures* is as follows: observation → hypothesis → evaluation → prediction → testing through further observation → revision of hypothesis → further evaluation → further prediction → testing through further observation, and so on (*SS* 49–50; see also *LSLT,* 96). This is in fact a rather common research agenda in the physical sciences. Chomsky's innovation was merely two-fold: First, he proposed to make it the agenda of linguistic science, as well (which, during the 1950s, might otherwise have seemed to consist almost entirely of observation → observation → observation); and second, he proposed that the linguist's own intuitions about grammaticality can be one source of data for the observation step.

Simple and candid as Chomsky's appeal to intuition may have been from the very first, however, it was controversial for still another reason in 1957, and it remains so for this same reason today. Even among those linguists who are prepared to assume intuitive linguistic knowledge of grammaticality as a given, another question is sure to arise: What if your intuitions, Professor Chomsky, do not agree with mine? Are there not many cases on which even highly educated native speakers of English disagree as to what is and what is not grammatical English? But even in *Syntactic Structures,* Chomsky has already anticipated the question and is ready with a reply: Yes, he says, there are troublesome cases upon which many of us may disagree, but there are also many clear-cut cases upon which most of us are bound to agree. The existence of troublesome cases must not make us forget the clear-cut cases. If we design our device so that it can handle the clear-cut cases (by generating sequences that are clearly grammatical and not generating sequences that are clearly ungrammatical), then that will at least be something, will it not? Furthermore, if we can ever make our device so refined that it will include all the clearly grammatical sequences and none of the clearly ungrammatical ones, then we can allow the device itself to decide about the troublesome cases in between (*SS,* 13–14).

As surprising as this reply may seem in the context of grammar, it sounds a familiar theme in the philosophy of science: Construct your theory so as to handle the clear cases, and then see what your theory can tell you about the unclear cases. In order to construct a coherent theory in the first place, however, you will often have to ignore the unclear cases for the time being and rather concentrate on the facts that are clear. Chomsky's notions along this line come straight out of the natural sciences; they are connected, for instance, to what the theoretical physicist Stephen Weinberg has described as "the Galilean style" in physics.[17] In his most provocative exploration of how this scientific "style" of inquiry should apply to the cognitive psychological domain of human language, Chomsky points out that the Galilean style necessarily requires the "far-reaching idealization" and in fact the "radical idealization" of "abstract models," as well as a "readiness to tolerate unexplained phenomena or even as yet unexplained counterevidence to theoretical constructions"—much as Galileo went forward with the construction of his theory of astronomy despite the fact that he could not explain, in that context, why objects did not fly off the surface of the earth (*RuleRep*, 9–10; 218–19). "Time after time," Chomsky writes, "people have been able to construct remarkable explanatory theories on the basis of very limited evidence, often rejecting much of the available evidence on obscure intuitive grounds as they sought to construct theories that are deep and intelligible" (*RuleRep*, 250).

Chomsky's scientific idealism is clearly apparent here, but it is not without a strong common-sense appeal. To put the argument somewhat crudely, there will always be shades of gray in the natural world, but for the moment at least, there are also some fairly compelling cases of black and white, as well; if we can build a device (call it a camera) that responds to strong light/dark distinctions reasonably well, we may perhaps refine it to register subtle shades of gray. In any case, what is the alternative? To abandon—as a basic design principle of our camera—the admittedly ideal distinction between black and white is hardly to make the camera more sensitive to shades of gray; it is rather simply to abandon any hope whatever of building a camera. Similarly, as Chomsky has often argued more eloquently and at some length, the "idealization" of a "homogenous speech community" within which there is a strong intuitive accord as to clear-cut cases of grammatical and ungrammatical constructions is only a very reasonable place to begin. While he thinks we must always be alert to the potential danger of such idealization (namely, that it may cause us to "overlook" something "terribly important," as he says), Chomsky nevertheless insists that this danger inheres in all "rational inquiry"; and in no way does such an idealization gloss over the very interesting linguistic diversity to be found in the world (*LangResp*, 54–58; 73; see also *Reflections*,

137–227). Quite to the contrary, this idealization provides precisely the necessary theoretical foundation for studying such diversity (*Kyoto*, 72; *Sophia*, 30–31).

The Cognitive Method. Right from the first, then, in *Syntactic Structures,* Chomsky's vision of science foresees the whole agenda of the new linguistics. It is, in fact, a common style of scientific inquiry applied with remarkable simplicity and directness to some of the most ordinary and obvious facts of human cognition and common sense: On the basis of a "partial knowledge of sentences" (*SS,* 11), or a relatively few cases of grammaticality that are intuitively clear to any native speaker (the linguist included), Chomsky proposes to begin constructing hypotheses that might account for these cases. Notice again that the boldness with which Chomsky proposes to leave the field work of structuralist linguistics at its perpetually incomplete state (at least for the time being) and get on with the business of constructing a generative theory does not at all mean he is oblivious or insensitive to the need for evidence (see his succinct refutation of one such charge, *Debate,* 51–52). Rather, it merely implies what his understanding is about how any scientific enterprise should proceed. Basically, it is this: You begin by making some preliminary observations. You may go into the "field" and gather some data, if you like, but you already have at your disposal—in your own intuitive knowledge of what is and is not a sentence in your language—more than enough data to occupy (and confound) any linguist for a lifetime. So begin by considering some clear cases of what you already know.

Next, on the basis of these early observations, you hypothesize ("abduce," in the terminology of the previous chapter) a model or device that would explain or account for your data. If your hypothetical model is sufficiently explicit and precise (i.e., generative), it will most likely make certain projections. That is, it will predict or imply the existence of still more data—data that has perhaps not even been discovered yet! Now what do you do about this? Do you say, "No, no, this is only abstract theoretical speculation"? Of course not. In such a case as this, you will be quite eager to check your model's predictions against the actual facts of the language. So you go back (into the field, if you prefer) to see if you can observe any evidence of the projected phenomena.

Sometimes you will not find what your model has led you to expect. Sometimes you will find just the opposite of what it has led you to expect. Does this now mean it is "back to the drawing board"? Well, not just yet. If your model still explains some data that are crystal clear, surely it is not completely wrong. So you do not give up on it just yet. Maybe some extraneous factors are clouding the picture. Maybe, if you keep checking, these factors will themselves become crystal clear. So you keep checking and cross-checking and experimenting and searching. Sometimes, however, the results of all this work will be so overwhelmingly contrary to the projections of your hypothesis that you will be compelled to modify it substantially or even abandon it altogether in favor of some other hypothesis. Still, you are not discouraged; these "negative results" represent progress in the sense that they have allowed you to cross one possible hypothesis off the list and go on to the next most likely one. In any case, you keep looking and hypothesizing and projecting and then checking your projections because you know that someday something else may happen. . . .

That is, you know that you may occasionally find exactly what your model has led you to expect. Voilà! You have, at least tentatively, made a discovery! (This is actually no more a discovery than is a convincingly negative result, but most human beings simply cannot help feeling more excited about the positive sort of discovery.) You may have found something exquisitely exotic, perhaps from a part of the field where no one would ever have thought to look, or it may be something quite ordinary, something that has been right there under everybody's nose all along. In either case, though, it will be exciting and surprising to you, if only because the field workers (yourself included, at the outset) have somehow managed to miss it altogether up until now.

Very often in Chomsky's investigations of language—in which the instrument of discovery, in one sense, is also its object—the facts uncovered will be so compellingly obvious, once observed, that we may wonder: How did so many talented linguists miss these obvious and interesting facts about language for so long? The answer again, I believe, lies in the difference between induction and abduction—induction being the general method of discovery to which the American structuralist tradition confined itself, and abduction being the special theory of discovery that is implicitly assumed in the generative approach of Chomsky's *Syntactic Structures*. Thus, many empiricist-minded linguistic field workers in the past, eschewing mentalistic constructs and slavishly bent on collecting and classifying all data in general, failed to develop from that exercise a clear enough idea of which additional key pieces of data they needed to look for in particular. They were looking as hard as they could, but they had adopted an impoverished theory about where to look.

This is not at all to say, if you just "wander into the field" and start looking, that you will never discover any interesting and surprising phenomena. To the contrary, this is exactly how Chomsky began, I believe, and it is exactly how we must begin: Go with an open (though not blank) mind, receptive to any and all facts that may catch the eye. This is the beginning of science. But if you want to get beyond this beginning, then you must begin thinking about something in particular that has caught your eye. After all, it has caught your eye for some reason, has it not? Perhaps it is strikingly similar to something else you have observed in a previous but totally different context. Perhaps it is surprisingly contrary to something else you observe in the present context. You are curious about it: How can you explain it? "What if . . .?", you ask yourself. Now you are formulating an explanation. It may be dead wrong, but it is at least the beginning of an empirical hypothesis. If your formulation is precise enough to be considered a generative hypothesis, it should project the existence of other phenomena that ought to be true if the hypothesis is true. This is precisely the step toward depth discovery at which American structural linguistics balked, I believe. The natural sciences have never balked at it. Chomsky did not and does not balk at it. Generative grammar uncovers surprising and illuminating facts about language precisely because its projections give the researcher a very precise idea of which key facts would be needed for confirmation or disconfirmation of the theory.

People are of course entitled to decide for themselves whether or not the results really are surprising and illuminating, confirming or disconfirming. It is both unfair and unreasonable, however, to assume (without examining the results) that Chomsky's sort of model building or theory construction is a matter of his turning his back on the evidence; rather, it is a matter of his figuring out precisely where to look for evidence. It is in fact a means of hypothetically or abductively projecting evidence and thus—in the abstract, quasi-mathematical sense discussed earlier—of generating evidence. It is no surprise, then, to find Chomsky (throughout his work) making up sentences to consider as evidence. If these sentences are wrong, then they are wrong; if they are nonsentences, then they are nonsentences. But they cannot be labeled "wrong" or "nonsentences" simply because they are "made up."

No one who has the slightest interest in discovering what a sentence is, or how one is made, could seriously advance that objection. If Chomsky's critics believe that generating evidence in this sense means fabricating it, let them show that the evidence itself is false. It is not enough for them to point out that he has found such evidence only by first projecting it. Such a criticism portrays a rather deep misconception, not only about the nature of science, but about the creative character of human cognition in general.

To other linguists who have honest misgivings about Chomsky, the problem seems to be their feeling that he is premature in building his generative hypothesis before gathering a large enough corpus of data. Chomsky's answer to this possible objection, even in *Syntactic Structures*, is at first the most surprising and then the most disarming of all. One might have expected him to answer, "We already have enough data! The field workers and the scribes have been at it for centuries!" Actually, that is true, but it is not at all Chomsky's answer. In no way does he wish to minimize the extraordinary achievements of other linguists in gathering data on the thousands of languages in the world. Nor does he wish to discourage such pursuits. In fact, Chomsky believes we do not now and can never have enough data to account fully for even one language. The corpus will always be incomplete. The field workers know this better than anyone else. In the vast body of already-recorded sentences, there are very, very few "repeats"; almost every sentence ever recorded, in fact, is novel. (If you were to search through all the books in all the libraries of the world, for instance, how many times do you suppose you would find the particular sentence you are reading right now?) So the field workers know that if they stop recording sentences even for one minute, some ornery informant is bound to utter a brand new sentence that has never before been recorded in all the annals of linguistics and human literature. That one little sentence may punch a small hole in our theory of language; from that one small hole may come a crack; that crack may lead to a total collapse! To linguists who are less idealistic than Noam Chomsky, this realization might be cause for a certain private sense of weariness or discouragement: The field work can never be done; there will always be one more new sentence.

Gratefully acknowledging this, Chomsky is considerably more cheerful about it: Let there be new sentences. Let them punch holes in our theoretical walls. Let the walls crack and fall. We will rebuild. Why should we linguists fret about this, if children do not?

"In this respect," he writes, "a grammar mirrors the behavior of the speaker who, on the basis of a finite and accidental experience with language, can produce or understand an indefinite number of new sentences" (*SS*, 15). It is perhaps the closest he comes, in the conservative sparseness of *Syntactic Structures,* to an explicit statement of a goal that would soon emerge with bold freshness in his subsequent work—the goal of fashioning a formal linguistics whose principles and whose very methods in many ways resemble the abductive processes of language acquisition itself—"a successive maturation of specialized hardware." It is a goal that still compels attention today, even more so as we look back thirty-five years at *Syntactic Structures.* After all, a gifted college student today often requires years of diligent study and careful training in order to approach mastery of a computer language like those now available; yet the most elaborate and formidable of these languages is puerile, infantile, in comparison to the enormous complexity of natural human language—a system in which every normal child (without special training and without really trying) becomes fluent before reaching school age. Any theory that even alludes to the goal of understanding this remarkable phenomenon must be deeply grounded in the foundations of cognitive psychology. In view of this, it seems only a little disappointing, here, that Chomsky says the grammar mirrors the behavior of native speakers, instead of saying plainly that what it really mirrors is their knowledge.

"Behavior," however, was a choice of terms he was soon to improve upon. Perhaps it was his one last (farewell) nod to what in 1957 was the reigning establishment in the behavioral sciences.

Chapter Three

From Standard to Extended Standard Theory

After the publication of *Syntactic Structures* in 1957, Chomsky's career in linguistics began to accelerate. In 1958–59, he was appointed as a member of the Institute for Advanced Study in Princeton, where he undertook a full-scale revision of his big book, *The Logical Structure of Linguistic Theory*—with a view towards resubmitting it for publication, now that some interest was being shown in his approach. It was a revision he was never to complete, however, mainly because he became too deeply involved in his work on generative phonology,[1] applying to English the morphophonemic approach of his master's thesis on Hebrew. And of course there were other distractions. *Syntactic Structures* had begun to cause a stir in the professional community of American linguistics; in 1958 Chomsky was invited to present his new model of syntax at the Third Texas Conference on Problems of Linguistic Analysis in English, organized by Archibald Hill. Discussion of his paper, "A Transformational Approach to Syntax,"[2] was what Chomsky calls "animated and sharp," but what Mitsou Ronat perhaps more accurately characterizes as an "epic confrontation" (*LangResp,* 114, 133). Apparently, some structural linguists were attracted to the formal rigor of Chomsky's grammar, but what disturbed so many of them so deeply was his basic approach to linguistic science: They were not prepared to abandon their inductive "discovery procedures" in favor of Chomsky's more abstract, essentially abductive methods of theory construction and evaluation. And so, despite the excited stir *Syntactic Structures* was causing, "generative-transformational grammar" hardly rose to the level of a "standard theory" overnight.

Most of Chomsky's other publications during the late 1950s and very early 1960s, in fact, were in journals outside the field of linguistics proper (much of the work being on so-called pure mathematical linguistics; see Chapter Two). Nevertheless, in 1961, at age thirty-two, he was appointed full Professor of Modern Languages at MIT (the first of several titles),[3] and the real beginning of his meteoric assent to world preeminence in the field of linguistics may perhaps be put as early as 1962. This was the year when the Ninth International Congress of Linguists was held at MIT. It was then that Chomsky presented an important address, "The Logical Basis of Linguistic Theory," which was later published (in revised and expanded form) as his second monograph, *Current Issues in Linguistic Theory*.[4] In his presentation Chomsky explained—in the first fully comprehensive way—the difference between structural linguistics and generative grammar. The impact was apparently immediate and perhaps worldwide. In any case, things began to happen very rapidly around 1962. For instance, *Syntactic Structures*—which, at the time, had been only in its first printing for five years—went through a second printing in 1962, a third printing in 1963, a fourth printing in 1964, and so on, with another printing annually for years to come. Truly, 1962 seems to have been a watershed year, although the most dramatic torrent of activity was still to come.

Also in 1962, Chomsky was appointed Research Fellow at Harvard's Center for Cognitive Studies. His return to Harvard—some seven years after completing his first stint there as a Junior Fellow in the Society of Fellows—may not exactly have been a case of his "coming home in glory," but by 1967 (after a busy five years that had taken him all over the world), when he finally returned to MIT as the new Ferrari P. Ward Professor of Modern Languages and Linguistics, he was truly coming home, and coming into his own. Indeed, by 1967—prior to his thirty-ninth birthday—Chomsky had already been awarded the first two of at least nine honorary doctorate degrees, one from the University of Chicago and one from the University of London.[5] Additionally, his monograph *Topics in the Theory of Generative Grammar* was first published in 1966; it was the text of four lectures he had delivered in June of 1964 by invitation of the Linguistic Society of America at the Linguistic Institute held at Indiana University.[6] In 1965, at the invitation of Princeton University, he had given his series of Christian Gauss seminars, the material that formed the basis for his *Cartesian Linguistics* (also published in 1966), which put everything that was happening in a deeper historical perspective. In the summer of 1966, he had also served a term as Professor of the Linguistic Society of America at UCLA. During his prestigious appointment as Visiting Beckman Professor of English at the University of California Berkeley in the fall of 1966, Chomsky had written his important Beckman Lectures (delivered in January 1967), on which was based the book that may still be the clearest, most accessible, and yet one of the most profound statements of his philosophy of language—*Language and Mind* (first published in 1968).

A slightly busy five years indeed, 1962 to 1967, and this was not the half of it. If there has ever been a time in his life when Chomsky's ideas reached a sort of "critical mass," ready to expand the new theory with explosive force, it was this five-year span. The tenor for this whole period of the 1960s, in fact, was set by his *Aspects of the Theory of Syntax,* which Chomsky completed and sent to press while at the Harvard Center for Cognitive Studies in 1964. First published in 1965 (my 1988 copy is from the fifteenth printing), it was the technical centerpiece of the standard theory and was perhaps largely responsible for Chomsky's sudden fame.

Despite how it all might look from thirty years' hindsight, however, it is important to point out that this explosion of theory in the mid-1960s was not (at least not for Chomsky) an unmotivated, unforeseen, or isolated episode. For instance, Chomsky actually had been working on the long and crucial methodological discussion in the first chapter of *Aspects* ever since around 1958–59; this foundational treatise in the book may have seemed dazzling and sudden, but it was actually many years in the making, and, despite the many changes in the theory since *Aspects,* this foundation would prove to be equally enduring: Some twenty years later, Chomsky remarked during an interview, "I do not think that I would rewrite that discussion in almost any respect" (*GenPrize,* 62). Finally, the much greater conceptual breadth of *Aspects* (compared to *Syntactic Structures*) definitely did not occur as an isolated event in Chomsky's mental life; once again—just as in the case of *Syntactic Structures*—it had very much to do with what was happening between Chomsky and his students and colleagues. Clearly, his ideas represented the radical "core" of the new theory, but this is precisely what drew the minds of several brilliant students and teachers close around him at MIT, and their contributions are a vital part of what brought *Aspects* to its own special critical mass.

As we will see, the resulting "nuclear chain reaction" was in many ways as short-lived as it was dynamic. It spread rapidly into new territories, some of which have now been abandoned in dust and ashes. After all the smoke had cleared, however, and all the shock waves had dissipated, one principal thing was left intact: the original core itself, dense but simple—and Noam Chomsky holding on to it, virtually alone once again.

Competence vs Performance

One vital aspect of the original core of Chomsky's theory that was crystallized in the standard theory of *Aspects of the Theory of Syntax* is an idea that has endured and remains as controversial today as from the beginning. Early in his important methodological chapter (the first), Chomsky introduces the crucial contrast between linguistic *competence* and *performance*. Competence he defines as "the speaker-hearer's knowledge" of a language, and performance he defines as "the actual use of language in concrete situations" (*Aspects*, 4). Chomsky's primary goal in *Aspects* is to describe and explain elements of human linguistic competence—the structure of our internal linguistic knowledge that underlies our external linguistic behavior—and not the behavior itself (performance).

At first this might appear to represent a major shift in Chomsky's thinking, for in his earlier work, *Syntactic Structures*, he had used the term *behavior* (instead of *knowledge*) to designate what the linguist's grammar "mirrors" in one respect. But in precisely what respect did Chomsky say the grammar reflects behavior? The context of the passage in question makes it absolutely clear: The linguist's grammar must "project" the formal structure of sentences from an incomplete corpus of utterances; similarly, the native speaker—on the basis of "a finite and accidental experience with language"—must somehow acquire the capacity to "produce or understand an indefinite number of new sentences" (*SS*, 15). In other words, it is the linguist's method of discovery (hypothesizing from partial data) that mirrors the behavior of the native speaker; what the linguist does to construct a grammar is parallel in this respect to how the native speaker "behaves" in acquiring a language. This parallel between theory construction and language acquisition—one of the most provocative and persistent themes of his thought, from his very earliest work in transformational grammar—gets its first extended and forceful treatment in *Aspects* (e.g., *Aspects*, 24–37; 53–59, as well as "Language Acquisition and Explanatory Adequacy" below).

In context, then, Chomsky's earlier use of the term *behavior* is not really "behavioristic," as is sometimes thought; it is rather thoroughly compatible with his use of the new term *competence*. What the native speaker does to acquire language (like what the linguist does to construct a theory of language) is surely behavior of a sort, but the product of such discovery is obviously knowledge—and a very remarkable sort of knowledge, in view of the fact that it is (in both cases) acquired from fragmentary information. As I hope both preceding chapters have already made clear, Chomsky's primary interests (ever since his earliest work on Hebrew) have always been both what and how the native speaker "knows." His designation of such knowledge as competence in *Aspects*—instead of referring to the acquisition of this knowledge as behavior—is therefore a step forward only in the sense that it offers a forceful terminological clarification of the goal.

Chomsky's development of this new terminology provides a further clarification of the same parallel: While the linguist's discoveries obviously lead to conscious and explicit knowledge, the native speaker's knowledge of the language (competence) is largely and often entirely unconscious (*Aspects*, 8). To illustrate this fact, Chomsky offers numerous examples, one of which is the sentence "flying planes can be dangerous" (*Aspects*, 21). The sentence is of course (structurally) ambiguous because the phrase "flying planes" can mean either "the act of flying planes" or "planes that are flying," but many thoroughly competent speakers of English who hear the sentence in a specific context may assign it only one of these interpretations (as fits the context) and may be completely unaware of the other possible interpretation. Once it is pointed out to them, however, most native speakers of English will acknowledge the other possible interpretation; all along they have had the unconscious competence to see it, even though they did not invoke this aspect of their competence in their initial "performance." On the other hand, it is also interesting to observe that some speakers of English—having already committed themselves to only one interpretation of an ambiguous phrase—may actually refuse altogether to accept the possibility of a second interpretation, rejecting it as forced or unnatural after it has been pointed out to them. (I have seen people actually get angry about this kind of thing.) Thus, all sorts of psychological factors affect our linguistic performance: previous mental commitments, conscious beliefs, moods, biases, even personal pride. But the faculty of the human mind that Chomsky refers to as competence—being deeply intuitive and largely if not wholly unconscious—is itself unaffected (though often obscured) by such vagaries.

The notion that linguistic competence is somehow independent of these other natural (and perhaps valid) dimensions of the human experience, however, has led to a considerable controversy, one that is still raging today. Many reasonable and intelligent people—particularly in the humanities, where there is a devout and wholly justified concern for the actual use of language in social (including literary) contexts—have questioned whether it is desirable or even possible to study human language or any aspect of human language without taking into account all the variables that arise from such contexts. And so Chomsky's notion of competence as linguistic knowledge has often been attacked for failing to address our knowledge of the appropriate use of language in real-world situations, where all sorts of human psychological and sociological factors come into play. This controversy has motivated Chomsky, particularly in his later work, to attempt a further defense and clarification of the aim he set for himself in *Aspects*.

The specific target of Chomsky's approach to linguistic competence is what he calls "grammatical competence"; but he also acknowledges the reality (and the importance of studying) a different kind of competence with language—namely, "pragmatic competence" (*RuleRep*, 59), or what he elsewhere calls "communicative competence" (*Know-Lang*, 48, note 10).

It is important to understand that Chomsky does not view pragmatic competence as another term for performance. Performance, as we have seen, simply refers to the whole of our actual linguistic behavior— including mistakes, false starts, memory lapses, prejudices, and so forth—whereas competence (of ANY sort) refers to our knowledge, the knowledge that accounts for the regularities of our actual linguistic behavior. Thus pragmatic competence, in Chomsky's view, is not mere performance but is indeed a kind of competence, a quite valid kind of knowledge—a kind of competence that is largely concerned with matters of sociolinguistic context. This does not happen to be the kind of knowledge that Chomsky himself is interested in studying—his target is rather grammatical competence—but he does clearly acknowledge the reality of pragmatic competence, as well as the importance of studying it. In his further discussion of pragmatic competence, and in his choice of scholarly works to cite in this regard, it seems clear that Chomsky is thinking (at least in part) of what is sometimes called "speech act theory" or the "logic of conversation" (*RuleRep*, 224–25).[7] As the names of such theories suggest, their proponents (like Chomsky) are vitally concerned with understanding certain orderly rules and principles of linguistic knowledge, not the mere accidents or happenstance of performance. It just so happens that the speech-act theorists want to study a different aspect of this knowledge than the one Chomsky wants to study.

To get an initial sense of this difference, consider the following simple example:

Did you take the garbage out?

This ordinary question, in many contexts, would be understood as a simple request for information: The speaker wants to know if the hearer has in fact already removed said garbage from the premises. But what if we put the question in a special social context?

For instance, suppose you have invited me over to your apartment for dinner, and I have thoughtlessly arrived an hour earlier than I was supposed to arrive. You are right in the middle of preparing a complicated gourmet feast for me. I offer to help, so you suggest that, to start with, I might empty the kitchen garbage container in the backyard dumpster. But instead of doing as you have suggested, I pour myself a tall glass of your most expensive bourbon, sit down in your kitchen, prop my feet up on your kitchen table, and begin a long rambling discourse on generative theory, demanding to hear your opinion on certain highly technical points—all this while you are frantically trying to finish your complicated dinner preparations. After putting up with this for forty-five minutes or so, you suddenly turn to me and ask, "Did you take the garbage out?"

Even such a boorish dinner guest as I—assuming that I am at least a competent speaker of English—would surely understand that the bottom line of your question (given this context) is hardly a request for information. You already know (all too well) the answer your question pretends to ask for, and I know that you know this, so the question immediately breaks down into a considerably different (and somewhat less pleasant) "speech act."

Surely this sort of knowledge about how language can be used is a vital part of our human competence with language itself. As the speech-act theorists have shown, it is governed by orderly rules and codes and sociolinguistic principles and is certainly not just a matter of unpredictable variation in performance. That is precisely why Chomsky calls it pragmatic competence instead of performance (the broader term). Indeed, the study of this sort of pragmatic linguistic competence is rich and fascinating; it would furnish any linguist more than enough challenging material for a lifetime—many lifetimes—of rigorous study.

If this is true, however, what does it leave for Chomsky to study under the alternative heading of grammatical competence? What does he mean by grammatical competence, anyway? His answer: "I mean the cognitive state that encompasses all those aspects of form and meaning and their relation, including underlying structures that enter into that relation, which are properly assigned to the specific subsystem of the human mind that relates representations of form and meaning" (*RuleRep*, 59). Admittedly, a complicated answer, but notice that the end of the statement qualifies the first part of it: Grammatical competence does not (finally) include *all* aspects of meaning, but only "all those aspects of form and meaning" that belong to a "specific subsystem of the human mind." What sort of subsystem? What does he mean by form? What sort of meaning, and what sort of form-meaning relation? It is not an oversimplification to answer that he means the "computational" subsystem of the mind; it "computes" in the sense that it uses "the rules that form syntactic constructions or phonological or semantic patterns of varied sorts" (*RuleRep*, 54). Chomsky believes that these computational elements of form and meaning are fundamental to what might be called "implicational" meaning—in short, that grammatical competence is fundamental to pragmatic competence.

In order to understand one way in which this might be so, consider again the question, "Did you take the garbage out?" As already noted, in the special context of the dinner episode described above, the question is not (pragmatically) a request for information; its practical force is something much more like a request for action—tinged, perhaps, with the implication of a polite rebuke (or at least a reminder that I have not yet taken the garbage out). Pragmatically speaking, in that special context it might even mean something like, "Mike, you are beginning to annoy me," or (depending on your tone of voice when you speak the "question") maybe it means simply, "Shut UP!" But if this pragmatic meaning is the end of the matter—that is, if we look no deeper into it than this—then we will have missed a very important issue that is fundamental even to pragmatic competence itself. And that issue is this: If all you mean to do with your question in the kitchen is to make me shut up, then why do you not just come right out and say, "Shut up!"? Why do you rather formulate your command/rebuke as a question about the garbage? The answer seems obvious, once you think of it, but it is nonetheless interesting: If you say "Shut up!" or anything of the kind, you will appear to be even ruder than I have been, and I will be quite justified in feeling righteously indignant. Conversely, by phrasing your command/rebuke in the form of an innocent question, you gain a certain "rhetorical advantage." If I take offense at your question, you can always remind me that it was "only a question."

The first and most obvious point to be made from these observations is that in order for you to carry out your clever pragmatic strategy on me in the kitchen, you must of course first know how to "form" (or "compute") a question syntactically in English. That is where Chomsky's transformational syntax initially comes in, as a model of grammatical competence. The knowledge of how to form such questions in English (even though it is unconscious knowledge for most speakers of English) is no elementary matter, either; the process is in fact too sophisticated to go into with any detail at the moment. But Chomsky has shown (even in *Syntactic Structures*) how the "question transformation" in English involves the movement of a variable element in the auxiliary phrase to the front of the sentence; this transformation must be formulated to "read" the rather complicated internal structure of the English auxiliary—under a variety of possible configurations (as discussed in Chapter Two)—so as to reflect how the speaker of English invariably knows precisely which element to move, even under the several different structural and morphological options available in the English auxiliary phrase. Because this kind of computational knowledge is unconscious knowledge for most people, it may seem transparently simple, but it is actually a rich and intricately structured form of knowledge that is clearly fundamental to whatever practical use we find for questions in actual discourse. In this rather obvious respect, then, pragmatic competence presupposes the more fundamental grammatical competence.

There may be, however, a more important sense in which the "pragmatic strategy" of your question in the kitchen depends upon grammatical competence. In order for this strategy to work, not only must you first know how to form questions syntactically, but you also must first know—in fact, we both must first know—how such questions characteristically differ from statements and commands in their grammatical or formal meaning and significance. To many people, it seems strange to talk about the grammatical form of an utterance as having any "meaning" or "significance" in itself, but that is precisely one very important revelation of Chomsky's focus on grammatical competence. Utterances do indeed have a formal or grammatical meaning that is both distinct from and fundamental to their pragmatic significance in special contexts like that above; in fact, this very example of pragmatic meaning we have just been considering illustrates the point. In strictly grammatical terms, the question, "Did you take the garbage out?" is an example of what is called a "yes/no" question, and there is an obvious reason for this. By a regular grammatical principle of English, the syntactic form of such a question (specifically, the fronted auxiliary element) clearly signifies or signals—at some level—a query, as well as the anticipated form of the response: yes or no. There is surely no denying that such a "signal" is indeed a meaning of all yes/no questions in some well-defined sense. You may think at first that "Did you take the garbage out?" does not at all carry the meaning of a query in the special context described above, but if that is what you think, please think again: If the question does not signal—at the grammatical level, even in this special context—a request for information, then what rhetorical advantage could it possibly afford you in this context? Your rhetorical strategy of using the (antecedent and general) form of a yes/no question to evoke in my mind the (subsequent and special) inference of a command or rebuke is a clever strategy indeed, albeit a common one in the use of language. But if the strategy affords you any "defense" at all from a possible retort or from any recrimination on my part, it does so precisely by mixing or equivocating between two different signals of two different sorts—one grammatical (a simple question), the other pragmatic (a command/rebuke). That is, no matter which of these two signals I may react to in the kitchen, you will always have recourse to the other meaning of your utterance (and therein lies its rhetorical advantage).

This observation suggests only one minor reason why it is potentially important that we heed Chomsky's distinction between grammatical and pragmatic competence. That is, as long as we maintain a principled (and thus necessarily ideal) theoretical distinction between the two kinds of competence, we have the opportunity to examine the very interesting relations and interactions between them. On the other hand, if we abolish the distinction altogether—as some students of "pragmatics" have proposed (on the basis of examples rather like the one above, oddly enough)—then we forfeit any hope of studying the way grammatical knowledge interacts with other faculties of human language and cognition, for the simple reason that no interaction is conceivable, let alone analyzable, between phenomena that are somehow construed as one and the same. This particular argument begs the question of whether or not the phenomena at issue really are different, and I will return to that question under the heading "Deep Structure, Surface Structure" below, but it is important that we understand at the outset just what the consequences are of refusing even to countenance Chomsky's "divide-and-conquer" approach to the complexities of human linguistic competence.

Throughout his work, Chomsky has given other, more important theoretical justifications for this divide-and-conquer distinction between competence and performance (as well as for his distinction between different aspects of linguistic competence per se), maintaining that they arise from distinctly different though interrelated faculties of mind (e.g., *LangMind,* 111–17; 150). As we will see in the next chapter, this approach might be viewed as culminating in his current "modular" theory of mind, in which the language faculty is conceived as one distinct "module" of the overall cognitive system, a module that is thought to consist of a complex network of interacting linguistic subsystems (*KnowLang,* 204; *Managua,* 161). Once again, the notion of a "fractal" organization and development seems descriptive: In both the theory and its object of study, we have an increasingly intricate vision of subsystem within subsystem within system. While the direction seems clear enough from Chomsky's earlier work, in *Aspects* we have the first clear bifurcation of the global human linguistic experience into competence and performance; later, we have the finer subdivision of competence itself into grammatical versus pragmatic competence; and ultimately (perhaps inevitably), we find the further separation of the grammatical module per se into still finer subsystems. Thus, beginning at least with *Aspects,* the theory is moving inexorably away from the view of human language as some sort of uniform, undifferentiated colloid of general intelligence, culture, and pragmatic experience; it is rather moving more and more towards the view that language is a complex, dynamic (perhaps seemingly chaotic) cognitive system composed of many different but interacting subsystems at different levels.

Two facts are easily lost sight of in this direction of movement in Chomsky's theory, especially by those of us who may feel inclined to resist having sharp theoretical boundary lines drawn across any aspect of the human experience. The elementary competence/performance distinction in *Aspects* should remind us of both of these facts.

First, this development of abstract distinctions—while it might seem only to be complicating the already difficult task of studying so complex a phenomenon as human language—actually has the effect of simplifying the task: Chomsky isolates one palpably distinct aspect of

language for study at a time. Every single aspect of language is complicated enough for study in itself; by comparison, the task of trying
to study all of its different aspects at once, all lumped together in some
sort of seamless whole, appears hopelessly complicated. Chomsky's divide-and-conquer approach may prove to be dead wrong (it will, after
all, have to be confirmed or disconfirmed by its own explanatory results), but in no case can it be wrong because it complicates things.
To the contrary, if it does ultimately prove to be wrong, it will probably prove to be wrong precisely because of the way it simplifies
things.

This brings up the second fact we should remember in connection
with Chomsky's competence/performance distinction (as well as all the
future distinctions that seem to follow from it): The distinctions are
not only a matter of methodological necessity, for the sake of simplicity
or convenience; they rather constitute an empirical hypothesis about
the nature of human language and, more broadly, about the nature of
human mind—a hypothesis that boldly and explicitly claims these exceedingly complex phenomena of human language and mind actually
arise from the dynamic (perhaps ultimately unpredictable) interplay of
separate (and comparatively simpler) component subsystems. If this
hypothesis is discovered to be wrong, such discovery will represent
significant progress in the science of language, and our civilization will
be indebted to Noam Chomsky for having formulated the hypothesis
explicitly for the first time. It had to be proposed and it has to be
considered. Especially in view of recent findings in the natural sciences
(with which Noam Chomsky is attempting to keep the science of language abreast), we cannot afford to ignore this hypothesis on the a
priori grounds that it contradicts our traditional assumptions. Indeed,
at the very heart of the resistance to Chomsky's competence/perfor-
mance distinction (and the like) is the myth—a myth that has been
exploded by modern "chaos theory," in particular—that complex effects arise only from complex causes; that global systems can be
characterized only in terms of global properties; and, hence, that the
whole of the human experience with language can only be successfully
studied from the broad perspective of some "holistic" model that re-
jects any theoretical separation of levels or any isolation of component
subsystems.

On the other hand, to suggest that "global phenomena"—the
weather, for instance, or the overall complex of factors that Chomsky
calls linguistic performance—may at least be partly understood in

terms of the properties of their component subsystems is not at all to exclude purely "global properties" from the total picture. In fact, Chomsky himself brings up global properties in his discussion of performance. He shows that judgments of "acceptability" about various sentences, for instance, are often not at all explainable in terms of individual grammatical principles—not even when such judgments are entirely reasonable. Rather, such judgments often seem to depend on the way in which several different principles interrelate, and such interrelations Chomsky calls global properties (*Aspects,* 12). The study of competence, then, especially when it is construed as purely grammatical competence, cannot fully explain such performance phenomena as our judgments of sentence acceptability; formal grammaticality in fact is "only one of many factors that interact to determine acceptability" (*Aspects,* 11). Other factors might include memory limitations (causing us to reject a sentence that is too long and complicated, for instance, even though it may be grammatical, in the formal sense), appropriateness to the context, stylistic considerations, and so forth. All of these factors (along with our grammatical knowledge or competence, of course) interact to influence our overall performance with language.

For these and similar reasons, in his later work Chomsky has expressly rejected the definition of competence as "ability" (*RuleRep,* 59). If we understand performance properly, it does seem natural to think that competence must simply mean our ability to perform, but this is a frequent mistake in discussions of Chomsky. Many factors affect our ability to perform with language; grammatical competence (in Chomsky's sense) is only one factor involved in language ability (*LangMind,* 190–91). As a simple analogy, consider a bird's ability to fly. Obviously, many factors affect this: If the bird is too sick, too weak, too severely injured, or perhaps too "drunk" on berries to fly, or if it is paralyzed by fear of a predator or if the weather conditions do not allow it, the bird may not be able to fly; its ability to fly depends on its state of health and the environmental situation at any given time. Surely, though, there is one other (fundamental) factor involved in the bird's ability to fly—those anatomical and neurological structures of the bird that permit flight. Considered abstractly, the physical properties of these biological structures (when mature) precisely constitute the bird's competence for flight, in Chomsky's sense of the term, even though of course other factors are necessarily involved in determining the bird's ability to fly. Similarly, when it comes to human language, perhaps some external circumstance makes it absolutely impossible for you to speak or to write a single word; or there may be internal factors: You may be too tired, too weak, too drunk, or too upset even to "think" of a single word. If so, you may not have the ability to perform under these circumstances, but you have not lost your basic linguistic competence, in Chomsky's sense of the term, for the simple reason that your brain (presumably) still contains the "hardware" whose properties, considered abstractly, make up the basic underlying mental structures of grammatical competence (*KnowLang*, 224; *GenPrize*, 34–35). You may even suffer some illness or injury that utterly blocks your access to these brain structures; in this case, your loss of language ability may persist for as long as the inhibiting condition goes unremedied. But as long as the condition does not result in the destruction or deterioration of those neurological structures whose abstract properties constitute your grammatical competence, in Chomsky's sense, then you still have your competence.

A further and more important implication of this contrast with ability, however, is that grammatical competence (while obviously a human mental faculty) is not, in Chomsky's view, a generalized mental capacity like "intelligence"; it is rather a highly specialized and species-specific mental faculty—that is, a cognitive subsystem (*LangMind*, 102; *LangResp*, 140; *KnowLang*, 18; *Sophia*, 2). Intelligence (construed as general or global mental ability) may of course vary rather significantly from normal person to person, whereas the mental faculty Chomsky is talking about as grammatical competence varies only very slightly (if at all) from normal person to person (*LangMind*, 79); it is a species-specific and species-wide faculty—a faculty with which all normal human beings are as uniquely and specially gifted as in fact birds are gifted for flight (*Managua*, 38; *GenPrize*, 69). Of course intelligence is a gift, too, but it is not unique to human beings, as grammatical competence surely is. Human beings may indeed have a higher degree of intelligence than all other known species, but there is no more reason to suppose that our general intelligence is responsible for this highly specialized faculty of grammatical competence than there is to suppose that other species are somehow more intelligent than us by virtue of their own highly specialized cognitive faculties. Certain pigeons and fish and wasps, for instance, are equipped with incredibly specialized navigational faculties for finding their way home—a feat that human beings are not very well adapted for at all, and in fact cannot begin to match (without special instrumentation); but we do not for that reason say that these animals are more intelligent than us (*Managua*, 148–49). Such specialized and species-specific adaptations are simply not a matter of mere differences in "degree of ability"; in one of his most amusing spoofs of this notion, Chomsky writes:

Efforts to induce symbolic behavior in other species might illuminate the specific properties of human language, just as the study of how birds fly might be advanced, in principle, by an investigation of how people jump or fish swim. Some might argue that more is to be expected in the latter case: after all, flying and jumping are both forms of locomotion; both involve going up and coming down; with diligent effort and special training people can jump higher and farther. Perhaps some hopelessly confused observer might argue, on these grounds, that the distinction between jumping and flying is arbitrary, a matter of degree; people can really fly, just like birds, only less well. (*Reflections*, 41)

In *Aspects of the Theory of Syntax* and in his subsequent work, Chomsky is appropriately agnostic as to the specific neurophysiological foundations of grammatical competence (*Aspects*, 193; *LangMind*, 87), but it is clear that he is thinking of it as a faculty that is every bit as "highly specialized" in human beings as are the other special "cognitive capacities" of "every known species" (*Aspects*, 206)—specializations that are in no way predictable or explainable by considering the different species' general intelligence or other abilities. In his later work (while still acknowledging that not much is known about the specific mechanisms of language in the human brain), he often insists the human mind is constituted of "mental organs"—of which the language faculty is only one—that are as specialized and different in functions as any physical organ of the body, above or below the neck, from the visual system to the little finger (*LangResp*, 81–83; *KnowLang*, 2; *Sophia*, 2, 6, 18, 25–26). Chomsky further believes that mental organs that evolved for one or another apparent function may come to serve an entirely different function, in the same way that insect wings may originally have served the function of heat-transfer before being adapted to flight (*Managua*, 167). And most importantly, like other organs of the body, mental organs interact, as for example when the language organ interacts with the visual system: Speaking about what we are looking at may actually sharpen our visual perception of it (*LangResp*, 46). Chomsky conceives the goal of cognitive psychology, and perhaps of an even broader semiotics (or a pragmatic theory of signs), as being the study of the structural properties of these mental organs and their mode of integration in different but interrelated mental functions, from mathematics to language to systems of belief and even to our artistic sensibilities (*RuleRep*, 252–54).

Needless to say, Chomsky's generative-transformational grammar (his model of competence, and only of grammatical competence, at that) does not purport to constitute such a cognitive psychology, and certainly not such a broader semiotics. As already discussed in Chapter Two, Chomsky's theory is not even a global theory of linguistic ability, not a "production" theory—in short, not a performance theory, as he strongly reiterates in *Aspects* (139–40). Surely, though, any such global performance theory of language would have to incorporate a model of grammatical competence as one of its components, and because of the fundamental character of such competence, the broader theory of performance would depend crucially on having a model of competence to begin with (*Aspects,* 10). Finally, however, notice again that Chomsky's divide-and-conquer distinction between competence and performance—as well as his belief that grammatical competence is actually basic and preliminary both to pragmatic competence and to performance—in no way implies that he thinks competence studies of any sort can or should proceed in some sort of "autonomous isolation" from the facts of actual human linguistic behavior (see *LangResp,* 44). Quite to the contrary, just as performance theory depends crucially on competence theory, in Chomsky's view, so "evidence about the actual organization of behavior may prove crucial to advancing the theory of underlying competence. Study of performance and study of competence are mutually supportive" (*RuleRep,* 226).

To explore the possibilities of this mutually supportive relationship between competence and performance studies, consider how it might work in our bird analogy above. In general, let us say, you want to know how birds fly. Beyond that, you would also be interested to know how different species of birds fly differently. Beyond that, you would like to know how birds (including different species of birds) adapt their flight behavior to various environmental conditions—to changing weather conditions, for instance, or to a variety of dietary constraints or sources of food, or to different situations of danger and predation, and certainly to the ever-changing conditions of bird "society" such as flocking, mating, and the inevitable territorial imperatives.

Pretty curious about birds, aren't you? Even supposing that you limit your inquiry just to the "flight behavior" of birds under all these different circumstances, you are still asking for something like a global, comprehensive theory of "avian performance." It is, to say the least, an ambitious undertaking, and you had better develop some sort of research agenda. If what you honestly want to know is how birds fly in general and under all these various conditions, I believe Chomsky would say that the first thing you need is a basic model of "avian competence," a model of the fundamental principles of bird flight, principles that will have to be construed as abstract (albeit physical) properties—ultimately, of anatomy—that are rather common to all birds; these properties will have to be construed abstractly, of course, because of the variety of their particular anatomical realizations across the bird kingdom. Of course it will be impossible to develop such a model of avian competence without having first collected some preliminary data of some kind on the "flight performance" of at least one bird. Some sort of "performance data" must initially inform any model of competence, and this is the first respect in which competence and performance studies should be mutually supportive.

It is important to notice, however, that it would not at all be necessary for you to observe the flight performance of all or even many different species of birds—nor to observe their flight behavior under differing environmental or social conditions—before you could (with clear justification) "abduce" a basic model of flight competence for further exploration. (See Chomsky's argument to this effect with respect to linguistic competence and language variety at *Aspects,* 36, 209; *LangMind,* 189). In fact, an extremely powerful and useful model of avian competence could probably be formulated on the basis of some carefully recorded observations of, say, one single robin making one successful flight on one sunny spring day. Of course you need not limit yourself to this, but even if one solitary robin was all you had to work with, you could no doubt develop ample performance data from which to extrapolate some important abstract principles of bird flight that would probably apply equally well (albeit in different particular ways) to all birds, not just robins. The reason this is the case has nothing at all to do with any notion (probably false) that the basic principles of bird flight are a simple matter. For instance, if you were to record the flight of a robin from different angles and distances with a series of high-speed movie cameras, you would probably have enough data to keep you studying and analyzing principles of bird flight for a rather long time to come, and the result of your work might very well be a model of avian competence that could have massive implications for all such future studies—and beyond.

At the least, surely someone else whose special interest happened to be how birds fly under different wind and atmospheric conditions would be vitally interested in your findings. Another scientist—studying how birds, say, adapt their flight behavior during migration in dense flocks—would also be interested in your findings, as would still another who wanted to investigate something as seemingly far removed from your study as how the flight of the bald eagle differs from that of the golden eagle. Indeed, the abstract findings of basic competence studies like yours would in some sense be fundamental to these other studies. Even here, though, the mutual support system should be reciprocal. Comparing the flight of the golden eagle to that of the bald eagle of course may lead to new discoveries about avian competence in general, causing you to modify or even completely abandon your earlier theory of such; it might, for example, cause you to look at your old photographic studies of the robin in an entirely new way. It is even conceivable that some incidental discovery about, say, the wing rotation of sparrows during aggressive mating-flight behavior could radically change our whole theory of how birds in general fly.

Needless to say, the mutual support that all such studies can provide one another ought to have one further consequence: As studies of avian competence progress, informing—and being informed by—pragmatic and performance studies, they ought also to inform (and be informed by) new discoveries about the basic anatomy and neurophysiology of birds, which after all must be the ultimate biological foundations of avian competence. Similarly, Chomsky believes that studies of the highly specialized cognitive subsystem of grammatical competence should ultimately lead to new discoveries about the physical structures of the human brain that permit such competence (*Aspects*, 193; *Kyoto*, 2; 10; 47–48; *Sophia*, 2–3; 6; 36–37); even more accurately, he believes that brain science and the study of linguistic competence ought to mutually inform one another, with discoveries in the one guiding discoveries in the other (*Managua*, 7–8).

For obvious reasons, it is far easier to study how the anatomy and neurophysiology of birds is related to their basic competence for flight than it is to study how human brain structures are related to linguistic competence. As complicated as it may be, avian competence is a "motor capacity," whereas human linguistic competence is a "cognitive capacity"; much about the biological foundations of bird flight can be understood in terms of the gross external anatomy of birds, whereas the external anatomical mechanisms involved in human speech (or writing) are rather peripheral to human linguistic competence (the prime mechanisms, in this case, being internal neurological structures). Of course bird flight involves neurological systems, too, perhaps quite intricate ones, but biologists are permitted by our society (rightly or wrongly) to perform live experiments on animals, experiments of a sort that neurolinguists obviously cannot perform on human beings. And so, for the most part, inquiries about the relation of human linguistic competence to the neurological mechanisms of the human brain must await the development of experimental methods that are safe and morally appropriate; otherwise, we can only wait for "Nature's experiments"—cases of brain injury or other pathologies—to provide the (less than ideal) data for this side of the inquiry.

This does not mean, however, that there is nothing now to be done towards the development of a theory of linguistic competence whose ultimate foundations are in human biology. Indulge me one last extension (even if to the point of absurdity) of the bird analogy: Imagine, for instance, that you have never seen a bird and have no idea of a bird's anatomical structure; imagine that you now have no prospects, in fact, of ever being permitted to examine even the wings or feathers of a bird. Imagine that all you have to go on is some sort of nonexplanatory but descriptive record of the achievements of birds in flight: They leap, travel through the air for impressive distances, and then come down. Under these circumstances, how would you proceed to investigate the foundations of bird flight-competence? Surely you would suspect some sort of biological foundation—no creature could possibly perform such "tricks" who did not have the necessary physical traits to perform them—but what is the nature of these traits and how do birds acquire them? Are birds genetically endowed with these traits by their own innate anatomy? Or are these traits only secondarily acquired characteristics that birds have somehow developed through special training and exercise in the trick of flight (much in the same way that human high jumpers or pole vaulters or broad jumpers or even aerial acrobats and skydivers have learned to "fly")?

You might have your suspicions as to the most likely of these two possibilities, but with only a "descriptive record" of the achievements of birds in flight, you could never be confident as to which possibility must be the correct one . . . or could you? What if, for instance, your descriptive record of the birds' performance also included copious details about how much (or how little) actual "flight training" (and of what sort) they receive? What if your record provided all the chronological details as to the birds' actual progress in acquiring this trick of flight—a record that spanned their flight training and levels of achievement from the time when they are mere fledglings in the nest to the time when they reach full mastery of the trick?

Now from this sort of descriptive record, you might just have the makings for a serious theory about the innate biological foundations of the birds' competence for flight—a theory which, in Chomsky's terms, could achieve "explanatory adequacy" even with no direct evidence on anatomy and neurophysiology.

Language Acquisition and Explanatory Adequacy

In his first chapter of *Aspects*, Chomsky is also concerned with several questions bearing on what emerges as a central theme of the book and perhaps the most enduring and unifying theme of his whole approach to human language: the *explanatory adequacy* of linguistic theories (*Aspects*, 24–62). He leaves no doubt as to what he has in mind: The problem of explanatory adequacy in linguistic theory is "essentially the problem of constructing a theory of language acquisition . . ." (*Aspects*, 27). To those for whom the goal of linguistics is simply to assemble a descriptive record of human achievements in language, it might seem that the question of how children actually acquire a language is an altogether separate topic of inquiry, one that belongs not to linguistics proper, but to developmental psychology. Yet Chomsky believes (and has always believed) that explaining how native speakers acquire language is THE central task of linguistic explanation, which is the main reason he in fact now conceives of linguistics as a branch of psychology (*LangMind*, 88, 103; *LangResp*, 43–44; *RuleRep*, 4; *Managua*, 6)—or, more specifically, of cognitive psychology (*LSLT*, 39; *LangResp*, 46; *Sophia*, 6).

Chomsky specifies "cognitive" as the sort of psychology to which linguistics belongs for reasons that are clearly related to the competence/performance distinction discussed above. After all, the object for description and explanation in linguistics, as Chomsky views it, is human linguistic "cognition" or knowledge (competence)—how it is structured (the real descriptive task) and how it is acquired (the real explanatory task)—not behavior per se, in the sense of performance. Thus, even though he sees linguistics as a part of psychology, and even though psychology is often called a "behavioral science," Chomsky has been very leery of bringing linguistics itself under the more general rubric of behavioral science as commonly understood. This is not a self-contradiction on his part, but only a rather clear indication of what he conceives the essence of the human psyche to be: It is not a "habit" system (like the behaviorist's "reinforced response to stimuli") but a system of knowledge (*Aspects*, 204). Thus, human behavior per se is only evidence for the brand of psychology to which Chomsky assigns linguistics; to call this particular brand of psychology a behavioral science, he says, would be as misleading as calling the discipline of physics a "meter-reading science" on grounds that much of the data used in physics comes from reading meters (*Sophia*, 10; *LangMind*, 65).

As you might expect, many behavioral psychologists have resented Chomsky's attempt to redefine their own discipline for them in this way, not to mention his claim that the task of explaining the child's acquisition of language—a task the behavioral psychologists have long considered an important province of their own special domain—is instead a matter for linguistics proper; nor has it exactly meliorated any of their resentment to hear that Chomsky is willing to bring linguistics into psychology itself in order to pursue this important explanatory goal. They have no particular objection if Chomsky wants to spend his own time theorizing about the abstract structure of linguistic knowledge—after all, that is his own business as a linguist—but how can he presume to challenge established "learning theories" in psychology with his abstract theories about language structure?

Chomsky's provocative answer, whatever its merits, certainly indicates that behavioral psychologists are generally right to feel challenged: He has called their learning theories (at least those of a behavioristic bent) an "impoverished" theoretical framework (*LangMind*, 191). He has further said it is "absolutely suicidal" for a discipline to define itself the way psychology often does—namely, "as dealing only with processes but not with the structures that might enter into them" (*GenPrize*, 69). And as to the counterclaim that the study of such language structures is linguistics and not psychology, in that same passage Chomsky dismisses this notion as a "weird idea"— weird in that it would be like saying "the way a bird flies is biology but the structures that permit flight are not biology, that is some other field." The alternative he proposes to this "weird idea," he goes on to say, nevertheless "requires a leap of imagination," a willingness "to contemplate systems that are not overtly displayed," adding that this leap of imagination is simply "not a move that many psychologists are willing to make." Indeed, Chomsky believes that the role of these "systems that are not overtly displayed" is so profound in the process of language acquisition—and that the leap of imagination required for psychologists to contemplate these systems is so drastic—that nothing less than the total abolition of learning theory itself might very well be the ultimate consequence. At least "in certain fundamental respects," he writes, "we do not really learn language; rather, grammar grows in the mind" (*RuleRep*, 134). Citing recent findings in biology—such as those that reveal how the immunological system adapts through the "selection" of antecedent resources rather than by "learning" from stimuli, as was previously thought—Chomsky even goes so far as to speculate that it "is possible that the notion 'learning' may go the way of the rising and setting of the sun" (*RuleRep*, 139).

Learning theorists in psychology who are disturbed by such statements might at least be somewhat mollified to learn that Chomsky has been equally severe with the discipline of linguistics itself—and for the very same reason. For instance, the reigning school of structural linguistics as he found it when he entered the field in the late 1940s had in fact evolved, he says, as a "specific branch of the psychology of its time"—this, despite its "militant anti-psychologism," an attitude which Chomsky goes on to say is a reflection of the "anti-psychologism" to be found in "much of contemporary psychology itself, particularly of those branches that until a few years ago monopolized the study of the use and acquisition of language. We live, after all, in the age of 'behavioral science,' not of 'the science of mind'" (*LangMind*, 65). One very important symptom of this so-called anti-psychologism within linguistics was in fact those structuralist discovery procedures discussed in Chapter One, for these procedures generally eschewed any appeal to pre-existent "mentalistic" structures in favor of a strictly inductive method for constructing linguistic taxonomies from scratch, or from the bottom up—that is, with a heavy emphasis on gathering data about performance or behavior. Chomsky's longstanding antipathy to these procedures explains why, if he has called some of the learning theories in contemporary psychology impoverished, he has also applied that same term to the methodological doctrines of structural linguistics (*Sophia*, 15). Whether in psychology or in linguistics proper, all such empiricist dogmas are fatally flawed: "Had the physical sciences limited themselves by similar methodological strictures," Chomsky writes, "we would still be in the era of Babylonian astronomy" (*LangMind*, 112).

For these reasons, Chomsky's concern in *Aspects* with explanatory adequacy and language acquisition is really nothing new; again, just as in the case of the competence/performance distinction, what is new is the explicit emphasis on the explanatory goal. Even though he had not directly raised the problem of language acquisition in his earlier work (*LSLT* and *SS*), it was clearly a driving concern of his investigations of language from the very beginning, going all the way back to his thesis work on Hebrew, where generative grammar had its birth in Chomsky's epic intellectual struggle with the structuralist discovery procedures and the problems of explanation raised by these procedures. His words in *Aspects* reflect how he resolved that personal struggle when he finally rejected the structuralist discovery procedures as wrong in principle: "In fact, it would not be inaccurate to describe the taxonomic, data-processing approach of modern linguistics as an empiricist view that contrasts with the essentially rationalist alternative proposed in recent theories of transformational grammar. Taxonomic linguistics is empiricist in its assumption that general linguistic theory consists only of a body of procedures for determining the grammar of a language from a corpus of data, the form of language being unspecified . . ." (*Aspects*, 52).

In addition to making it more explicit, *Aspects* also provides a new philosophical depth and weight to this issue of "empiricism" versus "rationalism," which is really what is at stake in Chomsky's feud with behaviorist psychology and structural linguistics. The book provides this philosophical depth by setting the issue of empiricism versus rationalism in a rich historical perspective (*Aspects*, 47–52): It is not, we discover, really just Noam Chomsky versus the establishment in contemporary psychology and linguistics, but René Descartes, Lord Herbert of Cherbury, Ralph Cudworth, the Port-Royal Grammarians, Gottfried Wilhelm von Leibniz, Baron Wilhelm von Humboldt AND Noam Chomsky on the rationalist side, versus those philosophers on the "empiricist" side as represented by the likes of John Locke, David Hume, Ludwig Wittgenstein, W. V. O. Quine (with some forgiveness in footnotes 25 and 26 of *Aspects*, 203–4), and B. F. Skinner (also mentioned in footnotes 25 and 26, but without forgiveness). It is certainly beyond the scope of this book to investigate all the subtleties of this background in the history of ideas; for that, see Chomsky's *Cartesian Linguistics* (which was forthcoming at the time *Aspects* was published); and for a sympathetic philosopher's lucid and insightful introductory overview see Justin Leiber's book on Chomsky (especially his Chapter Three, "Psychology, Philosophy, Politics," 135–83).

For our purposes here, it perhaps suffices to confine this age-old debate to the opposing views of Descartes and Locke. With Locke, of course, is associated that notion of the human mind at birth as a tabula rasa—literally, an "erased tablet" or "blank sheet"—the unformed and featureless mind before it receives (through the senses) the impressions of experience. In this view, experience itself is the source of all our ideas (empiricism coming from the Greek word for experience). With Descartes, on the other hand, is associated the theory of "innate ideas"—cognitive forms and principles of various sorts that are already in the mind (at least as potentialities) prior to experience. According to this view, all our conceptions (even those of sense) are shaped by strong inborn propensities or predispositions to see the world in certain specific ways and thus to conceive ideas of a certain specialized kind.

Where this debate touches the problem of language acquisition, then, the issue might be posed (at least as a first approximation) in the following way: Are children born with a formless and featureless mind of soft "clay" that can be rather freely "molded" by their linguistic experience into just any sort of linguistic knowledge, or are children born with a mind that comes equipped with its own "mold"—an innate mold that forms linguistic knowledge of a rather restricted and specialized sort (perhaps as the mold itself is "filled in" with the clay of linguistic experience)? While posing the question in this way might work as a first approximation, it is a little unfair, I believe, to both sides of this classic debate. Chomsky is more careful in noting that the dividing line between rationalist and empiricist positions is not always quite so sharp as analogies like my clay/mold metaphor would make it seem (e.g., *Aspects,* 52).

In the first place, while the rationalists certainly accept the notion of innate ideas, it is not the case that the empiricists, on the other hand, accept nothing at all as innate to the mind; Chomsky notes exceptions to the "blank mind" view in the thought even of Locke (*Aspects,* 49), and more particularly of Hume (*Aspects,* 51). He points out that Hume, for instance, believed that a method of "experimental reasoning" is instinctive in humans; in this respect, at least, it seems to be on a par with animal instincts, which Hume says are derived not "from observation," but "from the original hand of nature." He refers to it as the kind of instinct that "teaches a bird, with such exactness, the art of incubation, and the whole economy and order of its nursery."[8]

On its surface, Hume's description of the bird's "instinct" seems hardly distinguishable from that of Peircean abduction, which is the epistemological model assumed in Chomsky's work (tacitly, until shortly after *Aspects*) from very early on (*KnowLang*, 54–55). Now notice that abduction is naturally much more compatible with rationalism than with empiricism in at least one respect: Unlike strict (empiricist) induction procedures—which are only a method for gradually synthesizing (or learning) ideas by generalization from experience, ostensibly with no preconditions at all as to what ideas might be so synthesized—abduction creatively "leaps" from limited experience to certain ideas or hypotheses for which the mind already has a distinct and highly specialized predilection. Hume's description of the bird's instinct therefore seems much more like a case of abduction than induction—this, despite the fact that Hume is otherwise decidedly on the empiricist side. So the dividing line between rationalism and empiricism is not always entirely clear, and the two intellectual currents may often cross.

In the final analysis, Chomsky may be right, as he told us in an interview, that Hume's instinct—at least in the case of the human instinct for experimental reasoning—is essentially "inductive" (albeit innate) rather than "abductive" (Interview 1). This interpretation would seem to be supported by Hume's designation of the human reasoning instinct as *experimental.* It is also supported by what Chomsky says about the matter in *Aspects* (51): Hume's experimental reasoning, he claims, is merely an empiricist procedure for the acquisition of knowledge, whereas the rationalist position is that the actual form of the acquired knowledge (not just the procedure) is part of what is "fixed in advance" or experience. This seems to be the crucial point upon which the sides of the debate rather consistently part company: While both sides believe that something is "innate" to the human mind, what is that something? For the empiricist, it is only a generalized learning method that can be used to acquire any sort of knowledge whatever; for the rationalist, it is rather a highly specialized faculty that predisposes the mind to certain forms of uniquely structured knowledge.

To illustrate this crucial concept about the antecedent form of linguistic knowledge, Chomsky borrows an interesting analogy from Leibniz.[9] It is better than my mold/clay analogy above, which oversimplifies not only the empiricist position but the rationalist position, as well. That is, while the notion of the mind as a mold seems reasonably accurate as a metaphor of the rationalists' antecedent form, it may be a little misleading to suggest that the Cartesian rationalists conceived of experience itself as providing the substance (clay) to be molded by the mind into ideas; rather, they apparently believed that the very substance of our ideas, too, is in some sense "given" by the mind in advance of experience. Consider instead, then, a paraphrase of Leibniz' famous analogy of "Hercules in the marble" (*Aspects,* 52): Imagine two blocks of marble, one of which has "veins" (seams or grains of differing texture) running through it, and the other of which is "wholly even" (uniform and undifferentiated in texture throughout). While a sculptor might set out to carve any number of statues from either block of marble, the wholly even block would be equally "receptive" to the sculpting of any figure whatever, whereas the veined block would be receptive only to a more restricted range of designs—that is, to sculpt this particular block successfully, the sculptor will have to "work with the grain." Depending on how definite and stubborn the sculptor discovers these grains and textures to be, it might even be the case that the marble's veins more or less dictate to the sculptor the emerging form of a single viable figure—say, Hercules. In such an (admittedly extreme) case as this, the shape of Hercules would in some sense be innate to the marble, and the role of the sculptor would be, in the words of Leibniz, "to discover these veins, to clear them by polishing, and by cutting away what prevents them from appearing. Thus it is that ideas and truths are for us innate, as inclinations, dispositions, habits, or natural potentialities, and not as actions. . . ."

Similarly, Chomsky believes (following what he calls "rationalist speculation") that the "general form" of linguistic knowledge is "fixed in advance as a disposition of the mind," and that the role of "experience" (like that of the sculptor) is merely to bring out this innate general form, causing it "to be realized and more fully differentiated" (*Aspects,* 51–52). Further, as his use of the Leibniz analogy implies, the antecedent properties of the human linguistic potential predetermine "in a highly restricted way" not only the general form but also "in part, even the substantive features" of the language that finally emerges (*Aspects,* 53). Chomsky's choice of the phrase *general form,* here, as well as his use of the phrase *in part* to describe the degree to which even the "substantive features" of a language may be predetermined, suggests a further extension of the Leibniz analogy (one that Leibniz did not make): Even with a block of marble that was so strongly veined that it predetermined Hercules as the only viable figure to be carved from it, the artistry of different sculptors—with their differing styles and techniques and tastes in cutting and polishing—could of course still lead to quite an interesting diversity of finished artistic conceptions; the rationalist presumption here is merely that all of these different conceptions (given the sort of highly veined marble we are assuming) would nevertheless still be different conceptions of Hercules—recognizably so—and not some other figure (certainly not, at least, a weasel or a whale). Similarly, Chomsky's notion that the general form and, in part, the substantive features of human language are innate in no way discounts the actual variety of languages to be found in the world. As he puts it, "The existence of deep-seated formal universals . . . implies that all languages are cut to the same pattern, but does not imply that there is any point by point correspondence between particular languages" (*Aspects,* 30).

Chomsky's emphasis in *Aspects* on language "universals"—which emphasis, as we will see in the next chapter, survives the *Aspects* model itself and comes to a rather dramatic culmination in his most recent and radically novel approach—does not imply (I must repeat) any hostility at all on his part to the study of language diversity. Rather, it merely implies his belief that there is, after all, some real form and substance to be attributed to the notion of "human language"—that there is something that is distinctly recognizable as human language, not just despite the natural diversity of particular languages, but especially in view of such diversity. It is not clear why the notion human language should be any more problematical than the notion of "human being," an idea that surely has some salience for us, some distinctive form and substance and weight in our minds, and all the more so even as we contemplate the rich natural diversity of human societies and cultures and races. While anthropological studies that concentrate on cultural diversity have the crucial pragmatic consequence of sensitizing our minds to the ways in which various civilizations differ (and differ importantly), what greater or more profound goal could there be in anthropology than the goal of those other studies that focus on the universals of human nature, helping us to understand what it really means to be distinctly human in ways that transcend race and culture? Similarly, Chomsky writes, "Real progress in linguistics consists in the discovery that certain features of given languages can be reduced to universal properties of language, and explained in terms of these deeper aspects of linguistic form" (*Aspects,* 35).

Perhaps the problematical element of this statement for many people would be the term *reduced*: They do not like the idea of "reducing" linguistic diversity to a set of universals. For some, it may come as a surprise to learn that Chomsky himself is in fact very aware of this as a distinct problem, especially as it concerns his explanatory goal of accounting for language acquisition in terms of innate mental structure. "The real problem," he says, "is that of developing a hypothesis about initial structure that is sufficiently rich to account for acquisition of language, yet not so rich as to be inconsistent with the known diversity of language" (*Aspects*, 58; see also *LangMind*, 170).

Here the term *rich*—a favorite term of Chomsky's in talking about all aspects of human language—is especially telling, and it ought to dispel any misconception that Chomsky's explanatory goal implies some sort of "reductionist" approach that ignores the various "flavors" of different languages. That is, Chomsky has no intentions of reducing the natural diversity of languages in the sense of simplifying them to a set of bland or insipid generalities; rather, he wants to reduce the features of given languages in the sense of "boiling them down to the very essence of language," in the sense of "rendering" language to a set of universals that are "rich" enough—concentrated and detailed and powerful enough—to explain how children can (and do) achieve mastery of any one or several of the world's thousands of natural languages in an astonishingly brief time.

Indeed, therein lies the central problem for anyone who will face it as honestly as Chomsky does: If we attribute to the minds of children enough innate richness and specificity of linguistic structure—as extrapolated, say, from a particular language like Spanish—in order to explain how children achieve fluency in Spanish as quickly as they do, then we face the problem of explaining how the same children can achieve the same sort of fluency in Russian or English—or even all three languages at the same time—just as quickly as they acquire mastery of Spanish. On the other hand, if we reduce this rich model of innate mental competence to a set of impoverished generalities about language or learning, then we will face the converse problem of explaining how children could possibly master the rich complexities of any natural language at all. This, in fact, is precisely the problem faced (though seldom acknowledged) by the empiricists, who—attempting to account for language acquisition with "general learning theory"—propose that the model of children's innate linguistic structure be "reduced to a conceptual minimum" (*Aspects*, 58). Thus it is the empiricist approach to human language that is truly reductionist, not Chomsky's. Chomsky squarely faces the problem of accounting for language acquisition across a diversity of languages and cultural conditions precisely because his proposal to investigate language universals is pointedly antireductionist. There is no solution to this problem for Chomsky, of course, in his merely stating it or facing it; in fact, the persistence of this and related problems is precisely what led to the virtual abandonment of the standard theory during the "second Chomskyan revolution," as we will see in Chapter Four; but of all the criticisms that have been leveled at Chomsky, perhaps the single most unfair is the notion that his focus on linguistic universals is insensitive to language diversity.

No doubt the criticism has been motivated, in part, by the fact that Chomsky (especially in his earliest work) often draws most of his evidence from a single language—English. Chomsky has sometimes responded to this by saying that the reason he does not work on other languages very much is simply that he does not know any others very well, adding that he has nevertheless consciously tried to extend the range of linguistic data he draws upon (*GenPrize*, 82). The response is perhaps overly modest, just as the criticism is somewhat facile: It completely ignores the fact, for instance, that generative grammar had its birth in Chomsky's work on Hebrew, not English, and the fact that in his latest work he has drawn upon evidence from Spanish, Italian, French, Arabic, Japanese, Korean, Chinese, and Miskito, to name a few languages (e.g., *Managua*, 12–17, 69, 126; *Sophia*, 6, 20; *LangResp*, 186). The criticism also ignores a substantial body of very detailed "generative-transformational" work carried out by others on various languages, work that is even now putting Chomsky's latest conceptions of language universals directly to the test with largely (and impressively) favorable results.[10] Chomsky has repeatedly acknowledged the importance of such cross-linguistic testing of any hypothesis on language universals (e.g., *Managua*, 55, 61; *Debate*, 48); he has pointed out that even the theory of a particular language is always subject to change (*KnowLang*, 38) or to complete disproof (*KnowLang*, 203, *LangMind*, 78) by evidence from other languages; and he has demonstrated his own interested receptiveness to such results (when demonstrated with rigor), even when they seem to contradict his own earlier proposals (e.g., see *LangResp*, 186, 193–94; *Debate*, 49). Therefore, while it is still true that Chomsky himself spends comparatively little time investigating other languages in detail, it is simply wrong to say that he is interested only in English.

The criticism is most seriously mistaken, however, in what appear to be its underlying assumptions. One of these seems to be the idea that if Chomsky really wants to discover language universals, he must necessarily devote himself to the investigation of cross-linguistic evidence. The idea seems to operate on the (faulty) assumption that a universal is necessarily a property or phenomenon to be found in all languages; thus, the reasoning goes, if Chomsky wants to know what all languages have in common, he will of course have to study all languages. But Chomsky is quite clear that this is not a necessary requirement for the sort of universals he has in mind. In his discussion of "substantive" universals, for instance, he cites the tradition of Roman Jakobson, who identified a set of some twenty distinctive phonological features that are proposed as universals of human language (*Aspects,* 28). These distinctive features are proposed as universals, however, not in the sense that every language will necessarily contain them all, but in the sense that they are all universally available—they belong to a "universal set" from which every language will choose its own subset.

Now the proposal of such a universal set is not at all vacuous, as it may seem. Notice that the proposed set is quite finite (consisting of only some twenty distinctive features). In part at least, this is an obvious function of human anatomy: Because of certain characteristic attributes of the human articulatory mechanism, human beings are innately predisposed to make certain kinds of sounds rather than others. The range of possible sound features available for use in language is also no doubt further constrained by limits on the human hearing capacity—certain sounds that we can in fact produce nevertheless are not usable in the phonological systems of human languages because they cannot be heard and discriminated by humans with any degree of reliability. Beyond that, there almost certainly are other purely neurological structures innate to the human brain that predispose us to the systematic use of only certain kinds of acoustical contrasts in language. Whatever the reasons, it seems clear enough that every human language must select its own particular subset of distinctive phonological features from the inventory of such features universally available to human beings. The features are universal in the sense that they are universally available for contrastive purposes in language, not in the sense that every language necessarily contains or uses them all.

A similar point can be made with regard to the "formal" universals that are of special interest to Chomsky. Unlike substantive universals of Jakobson's sort, which are features of a particular kind (phonetic features or particular syntactic categories like Noun or Verb), "formal" universals are abstract conditions on the kind of rules that may appear in languages (*Aspects*, 28–30). That is, formal universals are proposed as general principles that the rules of every language must adhere to, but this proposal does not require that any particular rule itself must appear in all languages, or even in any two languages (*Aspects*, 29). For instance, the phenomenon of "structure dependency" is a general principle talked about as a formal universal throughout Chomsky's work; it is crucially relevant to the general character of transformational rules (see *Aspects*, 55–56). Specifically, the structure-dependency hypothesis proposes that all transformations, in all languages of the world, will be structure dependent—that is, that they will manipulate only whole constituents belonging to certain well-defined syntactic structures. The hypothesis does not imply, however, that every language will have the same particular transformations. Some languages may not even have any transformational rules at all; the proposal is that all languages that do have transformations will have only structure-dependent ones.

As an illustration, consider how structure dependency relates to the yes/no-question syntax touched upon earlier. As a first approximation, we might suppose that forming such a question involves a simple inversion of the first and second words in a sentence:

> *You can* take the garbage out
>
> ╳
>
> *Can you* take the garbage out

Now admittedly, a simple inversion of this sort might not really involve any structure dependency, in Chomsky's sense; rather, it might involve only a linear, word-by-word transformation. That is, if the yes/no-question rule is construed as a simple inversion of the first and second words, it would not be necessary for the rule to read the underlying constituent structure of the input sequence (as discussed in the Chapter 2) before moving something—the rule could be as simple as, "Move the second word to the front." As a matter of fact, there is no logical reason why such an elementary linear rule could not work perfectly well for communicative purposes: We could all simply agree to form questions by inverting the normal word order of the first two words in any declarative sentence. With this rule, for instance, you could easily form a question for a slightly different sequence as follows:

> *The boy* can take the garbage out
>
> ╳
>
> *Boy the can take the garbage out

If I knew the "rule" you were using, I would know that "Boy the can take the garbage out" is the question form of the declarative, "The boy can take the garbage out," so you and I would be "communicating" just fine. Hence there is no "logical" reason why we could not use simple linear rules of this sort.

There is, however, a basic human reason why we do not in fact use such linear transformations, and that reason (in Chomsky's terms) involves an innate universal of the human linguistic mind—structure dependency. It is because human beings have a neurobiological predisposition toward structure-dependent grammars, in Chomsky's view, that speakers of English would transform the sequence above into a question by distinctly different operation, a transformation more like the following:

The boy *can* take the garbage out

Can the boy _____ take the garbage out

where it seems clear that the mind must be deciding what word to move by means of some deeper principle than any mere linear process like counting (in this case, to the third word). The real nature of this principle is even more apparent in more complex examples like the following:

$[_{NP}$ The boy from Anchorage] $[_{AUX}$ *can*] take . . .

Can $[_{NP}$ the boy from Anchorage] $[_{AUX}$ _____] take . . .

where the intent is to show that the question transformation must be formulated to read rather deeply into the structure of the underlying string to locate the proper structural element for movement. Indeed, the operative principle here is even more complex than the above diagram indicates; still further examples could be educed to show that the transformation must not only read the structure of the whole underlying sequence to locate the constituent AUX, but must actually "read within" the AUX itself, isolating the Tense-marker and the first optional element of the AUX—regardless of what it is (a Modal like *can*, or a *have*, or a *be*)—for movement to the front.

Now the point of this discussion is not to delineate the particular details of what might be called the yes/no-question transformation in

English; after all, what Chomsky claims is universal is not this or any other particular transformation, but the principle of structure dependency. Other languages may have different transformations for asking questions, but Chomsky predicts that all of these transformations will be structure dependent. Some languages may not use any transformational movement at all, but if they do—Chomsky predicts—these will necessarily be structure-dependent transformations. Chomsky's prediction of course might someday be refuted by evidence from other languages, but it is important to keep in mind just what sort of evidence this would have to be. It would not be sufficient to produce evidence of some language that has no transformations (and thus no structure-dependent transformations); rather, it would be necessary to produce evidence of some language that did indeed have transformations—but not structure-dependent ones.

On the other hand, this argument may sound like a complete misplacement of the burden of proof: Chomsky proposes structure dependency as a formal universal of all transformations, then sits back and waits for someone else to find a language with NON-structure-dependent transformations. It is certainly true that proposing or hypothesizing a universal is not the same thing as proving it, and Chomsky is careful to note that such proposals are only "highly tentative" if postulated on the basis of only a few languages (*LangMind,* 158). Still, he has never hesitated to propose a universal on the basis of even one single language (*Debate,* 48), and he insists that it is not necessary to wait for the achievement of descriptive adequacy in various languages before making such proposals (*Aspects,* 36). Furthermore, study of a wide range of languages is only one way to evaluate such proposals after they are made, in Chomsky's view; thus, consideration of a single language can not only "motivate" a theory of language universals but may also provide "significant support" for it (*Aspects,* note 2, 209).

How can this be? How on earth can the study of a single language provide significant support for a proposal about language universals? That question brings us right back to the basic problem of explanatory adequacy. The problem, again, is to explain how it is possible for children to acquire a language as quickly and naturally as they do, without any special instruction, and on the basis of very scattered, impoverished, and often contradictory evidence. Phrased in terms of the specifics we have just been considering in regard to English, for instance, the problem is to explain why children who hear such questions as "*Can you* take the garbage out?" do not make the mistake of assuming that

questions are formed in English by simply inverting the first two
words. It is indeed eminently clear that children never make this faulty
assumption; in fact, they apparently never even try it out as a possibility. Children do of course make mistakes in forming questions, like

> *Can you *can* take the garbage out?

> *Can the boy *can* take the garbage out?

in which the AUX element is "copied" at the front of the string, instead of being "moved" to the front, but children never try to ask a
question in the ungrammatical form

> *Boy *the* can take the garbage out?

in which the first two words are merely inverted.

Notice that this principle of "linear inversion"—which would seem
to be a thoroughly logical choice for children to try out, at least, in
that it could account (superficially) for a huge number of examples
children actually hear—is far more elementary than the principle of
structure dependency. It would be relatively easy, for instance, to program a computer to invert the first two of any string of words, but
extremely difficult (if not impossible) to program a computer so that
it could transform any declarative statement into a grammatical
question in English. The reason, as we have already seen, is that the
operative principle of such grammatical transformations is structure
dependency. This is an extremely complex phenomenon, from a computational point of view, a phenomenon to which it is thus (understandably) very difficult to adapt linear machines. Yet human children
unerringly prefer this far more complicated principle of structure dependency—to the extent that even their mistakes are structure dependent! How can these strange facts be explained? In terms of Chomsky's
theory of formal universals, it must be because human children are not
linear machines; their minds are innately predisposed to certain highly
specialized, species-specific, and species-wide proclivities—not the
least of which is an irresistible tendency towards structurally dependent
mental computations in language.

It is for reasons of this sort that Chomsky believes depth insights
about formal universals can arise from the intensive study of a single
language (*LangMind,* 113, 188). When a particular language is found

to exhibit (throughout its rule systems) abstract formal principles of this sort—principles that are far too sophisticated and highly specialized to be explained as mere instances of "inductive generalization" or rote learning on the part of children—then Chomsky's proposal that these principles may in fact be human linguistic universals seems rather natural and well motivated, at the very least as an empirical hypothesis. While it is always subject to disconfirmation (as any empirical hypothesis is), the theory of formal universals is not groundless speculation. It offers a sensible and coherent explanatory account of certain striking facts about language acquisition—even of a single language—that must otherwise remain inscrutable mysteries, and it has now in fact guided several decades of productive cross-linguistic research, including research into the problem of multiple-language acquisition.

It is no surprise, then, that the whole evolution of Chomsky's work before, during, and since the *Aspects* period can be described as a movement of greater and greater abstraction towards more and more universal principles of language. As we will see in Chapter 4, this very movement ultimately led to the overthrow of many formal provisions in the *Aspects* model. Such an outcome does not necessarily abnegate the earlier models (*Aspects* included) for purely descriptive applications, but it is more than justified by the achievement of deeper and deeper explanatory adequacy. Further, nowhere in his work (before or since) has Noam Chomsky given a more eloquent and compelling statement of the importance of explanatory adequacy as a goal of linguistic science than in the long first chapter of *Aspects*. It was not really new, but it was more explicit and forceful than ever before. It was an extraordinary moment of confluence and culmination of several old themes in Chomsky's thought, and it set the course of research in linguistic theory for at least the next three decades (and counting).

Deep Structure, Surface Structure

Two concepts that are (at least partly) new in *Aspects,* however, are those of *deep structure* and *surface structure.* The concept of deep structure, in particular, is not really definable within the framework of *The Logical Structure of Linguistic Theory* and *Syntactic Structures,* even though there are some loosely connected analogues to it in that earlier work (see *LSLT,* 16–17). This perhaps explains, in part, why deep structure is one of the most frequently discussed (and misunderstood) topics in generative-transformational grammar. The questions around which most of the confusion seems to arise share a common theme: Is deep structure the same thing as "universal grammar" in Chomsky's theory? Is Chomsky proposing that deep structures are the same for all languages? Does he believe that deep structures are innate—that they are built into the human mind?

Chomsky's answer to these questions is an unequivocal, no (*LangMind,* viii; *LangResp,* 171, 183, 193). The "deep" of deep structure does not mean universal or invariant or innate, although the confusion of these terms is perhaps natural, arising from a variety of philosophical questions about language that have been debated since long before Chomsky (*LangMind,* 16–17, 157–58; *LangResp,* 169; *Aspects,* 198–99, note 11). Some of Chomsky's own comments in *Aspects* (which probably is most remembered for its introduction of the deep-structure/surface-structure distinction) may have contributed to the confusion, as for example when he speculates in a footnote that "only those descriptions concerned with deep structure will have serious import for proposals concerning linguistic universals" (*Aspects,* 210, note 2). This footnote certainly does not draw any equation between deep structure and universal grammar, however, and it seems clear enough from the note's context that Chomsky is thinking only of certain key elements of deep structure as being potentially universal—certain fundamental grammatical categories (like NP, VP), for instance, which he assumes are "selected from a fixed, universal vocabulary" (*Aspects,* 66).

In any event, this confusion (and related confusions) about the "deep" of deep structure has led Chomsky, in his work after *Aspects,* to substitute some alternative terminology. In *Reflections on Language,* for instance, he argues at some length for the expression "initial phrase marker" instead of deep structure, not only to avoid the "deep = universal" misconception, but also to avoid any implication that deep structure is somehow more profound or more interesting than other aspects of language—including surface structure, where "surface" no more means superficial than "deep" means profound (*Reflections,* 80–84; see also *LangResp,* 172). Now, in Chomsky's most recent work, the usual terminology is "d-structure," which has been adopted instead of deep structure for some of the same reasons already mentioned (*KnowLang,* 205, note 8; see also *RuleRep,* 145–58).

Chomsky's current use of the term d-structure suggests that the fundamental conception he was attempting to capture in deep structure has not changed substantially since the *Aspects* model. This inference is largely correct (although, as we will see, d-structure plays quite a different role in current theory than deep structure played in the standard theory of *Aspects*). His interim use of the phrase initial phrase marker is also essentially an emphatic reiteration of the way he originally (and clearly) defined deep structures—as "structures generated by the base component" (*Aspects*, 136). The "base component" of *Aspects* consists of two subcomponents: (1) the "base rules" (rules such as S → NP Aux VP, much like the old phrase structure rules of *SS*) and (2) the "Lexicon," which contains the words to be inserted into the "tree" structures generated by the base rules. Chomsky calls these base-generated structures "base Phrase-markers" and says that they are the "elementary units of which deep structures are constituted" (*Aspects*, 17). They are thus "initial" ("base") structures—sometimes even called "underlying" structures—that exist "before" the application of transformational rules (a separate component of the grammar). In short, the base component "first" generates deep structures, and "then" the transformational component applies to these, converting them into surface structures (as shown in the schematic of Figure 3.1).

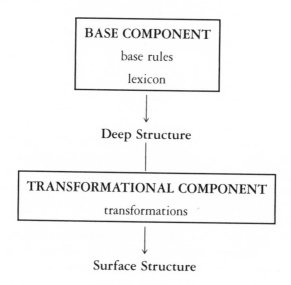

Figure 3.1

Caution should be used in how the "sequence" of this model is interpreted (and the same applies to words like *before* or *first* and *then* in the above description). As has been emphasized in Chapter Two, the derivational sequence of this and other models Chomsky has put forward makes no claim whatsoever as to the actual sequence of events in the mind of a speaker constructing or interpreting a sentence; Chomsky is quite clear and emphatic about this, calling any such misconception of his model an "absurdity" (*Aspects*, 139–40). The model's depiction of deep structure as "prior" to surface structure is an attempt to model its logical—not its chronological—priority (in the same way, perhaps, that the major premise of a syllogism is logically but not necessarily chronologically prior to its minor premise and conclusion).

In other words, it does not matter (so far as this model is concerned) what really happens first in the mind of a speaker/hearer of a sentence. The model's spatial-temporal separation of deep and surface levels is simply a way of diagramming the fact that certain necessary "logical" relations in the sentence (like Subject-of, Object-of) may not be readily apparent from the order in which its "grammatical" slots are actually filled in the surface form of the sentence. To understand this distinction between logical roles and grammatical slots is to understand the essential difference between deep and surface structure (*Aspects*, 70). Chomsky gives examples of it like the following:

John was persuaded by Bill to leave

where *John* is the grammatical Subject of the main sentence, but not the logical Subject—in the sense that we understand John is not the one who did the persuading. Rather, Bill is the one who did the persuading, so *Bill* is the logical Subject of the main sentence, even though at the same time *Bill* is the Object of the Preposition *by*, in terms of grammatical position. Further, even though *Bill* appears in surface structure immediately in front of *to leave*, every speaker of English knows that Bill is not the one who is supposed to do the leaving; that role is really played by John, so *John*—while being the grammatical Subject of *was persuaded*—is also the logical Subject of *to leave*. Finally, while *John* is the logical Subject of *to leave*, *John* is simultaneously the logical Object of the Verb *persuaded* (Whom did Bill persuade? John, of course.) In short, *John* is a grammatical Subject (of *was persuaded*), a logical Subject (of *to leave*), and a logical Object (of *per-*

suaded)—all at the same time—just as *Bill* is simultaneously a logical Subject (of *persuaded*) and a grammatical Object (of *by*)!

As you can readily see, keeping track of the difference between logical and grammatical relations can be a complicated affair. The *Aspects* model at least makes it far easier to examine these different roles and their interrelations, by proposing a deep-structure-to-surface-structure derivation (simplified as follows):

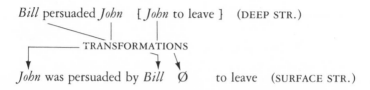

The transformations involved in this derivation would of course be a "passive" transformation (much like that discussed in Chapter Two) and a "deletion" transformation that eliminates the second occurrence of *John* (which would be a redundancy at surface structure, though it is not at all a redundancy at deep structure, where the purpose is to spell out all the underlying logical relations completely and explicitly). Details of the particular mechanisms of these transformations need not concern us here, especially since these have been abandoned in subsequent theoretical developments (see Chapter Four). What has not been abandoned, however, is the fundamental concept of an underlying logical configuration of roles and relations that are not always immediately apparent from the grammatical configurations of surface word order. It was perhaps the principal distinctive achievement of the *Aspects* model to have made this important conceptual difference clear and explicit for the first time with a theoretical separation of deep and surface structure.

While the distinction is powerful in the analysis of single examples like the one above, it is even more insightful for what it reveals about examples like the following:

I persuaded a specialist to examine John

I expected a specialist to examine John

where (from all appearances at the surface level) the two sentences have exactly the same syntactic configuration, differing only in what Verb happens to be filling the main Verb slot (*persuaded* vs *expected*). Chomsky convincingly demonstrates, however, that these sentences have very different deep structures, thereby showing the necessity of a separation of levels (*Aspects*, 22–24). He brings out the difference by presenting further evidence that puts the apparent surface parallelism of structure to the test. For instance, consider the second sentence above in relation to a rough paraphrase of it:

I expected a specialist to examine John

I expected John to be examined by a specialist

Here, in at least one way of reading them, the two versions are "cognitively synonymous," as Chomsky puts it: One sentence is true if and only if the other is true. This is not quite the same as saying the two sentences necessarily have exactly the same meaning in every sense (because there is at least a subtle difference of emphasis), but there is at least one sense in which the two versions could be read as having the same basic "truth conditions": If I expected that a specialist would examine John, then I must (logically) also have expected that John would be examined by a specialist.

Now if *I* PERSUADED *a specialist to examine John* really has the same structure as *I expected a specialist to examine John,* then performing the same test on the former as we have just performed on the latter ought to produce similar results; that is, any difference in meaning ought to be only a rather subtle difference in emphasis, not a logical difference in the basic truth conditions. This, however, does not turn out to be the case. Compare:

I persuaded a specialist to examine John

I persuaded John to be examined by a specialist

where the difference in meaning is clearly drastic. In the first instance, the specialist is the one on whom I used my powers of persuasion, but in the second instance, it is John. Thus, the truth conditions have changed dramatically, and the two versions are not at all cognitively synonymous: My having persuaded a specialist to examine John does NOT logically entail that John has also been persuaded to be examined. Under no reasonable interpretation of these two sentences, then, can they be construed as meaning even roughly the same thing.

Chomsky accounts for these interesting differences by using the provisions of deep structure, where the logical relations are fully spelled out and thus differentiated, despite whatever may be the surface similarities in grammatical order. Specifically, for the two sentences "I persuaded a specialist to examine John" and "I persuaded John to be examined by a specialist," Chomsky posits two different respective deep structures like the following (again simplifying certain irrelevant details):

I persuaded a specialist [a specialist examine John]

I persuaded   John   [a specialist examine John]

The difference in these deep structures, of course, lies in what is specified as the underlying logical Object of *persuade*: In the first instance, it is *a specialist,* and in the second instance it is *John*; otherwise, the two structures are identical. This very precisely isolates the origin of the fundamental difference in meaning, while at the same time accounting for elements of logical and grammatical parallelism: In both instances, it is I who does the persuading, a specialist who is to do the examining, and John who is to be examined; but in the first instance, it is the specialist who is persuaded that this examination should take place, and in the second instance it is John.

This approach also makes possible an analysis of how the two versions above differ in their "transformational histories." In the first case, we have

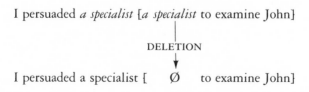

I persuaded *a specialist* [*a specialist* to examine John]

|

DELETION

↓

I persuaded a specialist [Ø   to examine John]

which involves only a deletion of the second (consecutive) occurrence of an "equi-NP" (an equal or repeated Noun Phrase, in this case *a specialist*), but in the second version, we have an additional step—a passive transformation—the result of which is another situation of con-

secutive equi-NPs (now, *John*) triggering the deletion transformation
in turn:

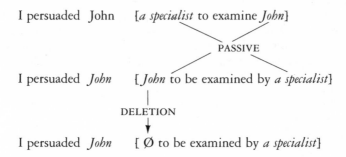

I persuaded John   [*a specialist* to examine *John*]

PASSIVE

I persuaded *John*   [*John* to be examined by *a specialist*]

DELETION

I persuaded *John*   [Ø to be examined by *a specialist*]

Now compare the derivations of the so-called parallel examples, "I
expected a specialist to examine John" and "I expected John to be examined by a specialist." In the first instance, we have a deep-structure
configuration that is basically unchanged in the grammatical order at
surface structure:

I expected   [a specialist to examine John]   (DEEP STR.)

I expected   a specialist to examine John   (SURFACE STR.)

In other words, no deletion or major movement transformations like
passive apply, so the structure surfaces in what is (essentially) its underlying form. Nevertheless, it is very important to notice how the
"role structure" of this particular underlying form differs from that of
the earlier sentences with *persuade*; consider them again, now side-by-
side with the above deep structure:

I expected   [a specialist to examine John]

I persuaded a specialist [a specialist to examine John]

I persuaded   John   [a specialist to examine John]

In all three cases, the internal deep-structure configuration of the
"embedded" clause (*a specialist to examine John*) is the same, thus cap-
turing the intuition that the specialist is to be the agent (logical Subject) of the examination, and John the patient (logical Object) of the

examination, in all three cases. Where the *persuade* deep structures obviously differ from that of *expect,* however, is with regard to what occupies the (logical) Object role of the two Main Verbs: The Object of persuasion is either John or the specialist, but the Object of expectation is neither John nor the specialist (at least not individually); rather, it is the entire construct [*a specialist to examine John*] that is "expected." In other words, it is neither John nor a specialist but a complete event considered as a whole that is expected—a specialist's examination of John. Once again, notice that this important difference between these (otherwise parallel) sentences with *persuade* and *expect* is in no way apparent in the surface form of the sentences. If we are to capture this difference at all, it is clearly necessary to capture it at some other level, and deep structure is simply Chomsky's provision for that other level.

It only remains now to ask how the fourth sentence ("I expected John to be examined by a specialist") is derived, and how its derivation differs from that of the other sentence with *expect* ("I expected a specialist to examine John"). The derivation of the latter is repeated (first) below, for comparison purposes:

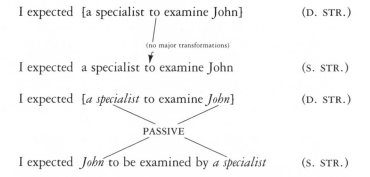

I expected [a specialist to examine John]   (D. STR.)

(no major transformations)

I expected a specialist to examine John   (S. STR.)

I expected [*a specialist* to examine *John*]   (D. STR.)

PASSIVE

I expected *John* to be examined by *a specialist*   (S. STR.)

In other words, the two derivations have essentially the same deep structure; they differ only in their transformational histories, with the passive having applied only in the latter case (and only within the embedded clause). [11] Thus, even though these two sentences have two different surface structures, it is appropriate that they should have essentially the same deep structure—appropriate, for the simple reason that they have basically the same (if not exactly the same) meaning. That is, whatever subtle difference in semantic emphasis may exist between "I expected John to be examined by a specialist" and "I expected a specialist to examine John," these differences are not germane

to what might be called the "propositional content" of the two sentences, which is fundamentally the same in both instances.

In sum, not only can deep structure show how radically different
underlying logical structures may be embodied in seemingly identical grammatical surface forms (e.g., "I expected John to be examined . . ." vs "I persuaded John to be examined . . ."), but it can also
show how the same basic underlying structure may be embodied in
rather different surface forms ("I expected a specialist to examine John"
vs "I expected John to be examined by a specialist").

This observation brings us to the single most important fact about
deep structure as it was first introduced to modern linguistics in *Aspects
of the Theory of Syntax.* It is a fact that has probably become more and
more obvious to the reader as this discussion has moved along, but
because it constitutes the most novel and controversial provision of the
Aspects model, it deserves explicit emphasis: Deep structure is the level
at which all essential (logical) elements of propositional meaning are
fully represented in the standard theory. It is thus the level at which
all formal semantic interpretation takes place. The greatest single technical innovation of *Aspects* was in fact its provision for a formal semantic
component that reads the propositional meaning of sentences straight
from their deep structures. It was a truly bold experiment, one which
is now generally regarded (even by Chomsky himself) as a failed experiment. But I believe it was an experiment that simply had to be tried
before generative grammar could move beyond the standard theory to
the new horizons of the so-called extended standard theory and Chomsky's current work in universal grammar. For these reasons, certain
issues relating to the Syntax-Semantics relation—as these were brought
to a culmination in *Aspects*—require at least a brief examination.

Syntax vs Semantics

One of the major criticisms leveled at Chomsky's early model of
generative-transformational grammar (as represented in *Syntactic Structures* and *The Logical Structure of Linguistic Theory*) is the charge that it
totally "excluded meaning" from the study of human language. This
is a misconception. In *Syntactic Structures,* for instance, Chomsky maintains that syntactic arguments per se should be "autonomous and independent of meaning," but at the same time he acknowledges the
"undeniable interest and importance of semantic . . . studies of language" (*SS,* 17). In fact, this short monograph includes a whole chapter
on the relation of syntax and semantics (*SS,* 92–105), in which Chom-

sky shows that meaning cannot be used to determine grammatical structure with any reliability (*SS*, 92–101), but that grammatical structure (once determined on independent grounds) has a very important relevance to studies of meaning (*SS*, 101–5). This important relevance of syntax to semantics is even given the last word in the book (*SS*, 108).

Similarly, in *LSLT* Chomsky does say that the unclarity of meaning is good reason "for refusing to admit meaning into linguistic theory," but it is clear from the immediate context that he means (more precisely) "for refusing to base the theory of linguistic form on semantic notions" (*LSLT*, 87). He goes on to distinguish carefully between the "*appeal* to meaning and the *study* of meaning" (emphasis Chomsky's), the latter (i.e., semantics) being "an essential task for linguistics" (*LSLT*, 97). In other words, Chomsky's intention was never to "exclude semantics" from linguistics, but only to avoid basing his descriptions of syntax on vague appeals to meaning. So many other factors (pragmatic knowledge, beliefs about the world, etc.) influence our conceptions of meaning that Chomsky has always been leery of allowing these conceptions to enter into what he thinks should be the formal and precise description of grammatical structure. This stance is therefore merely another instance of Chomsky's divide-and-conquer approach to the study of different aspects of the complex human experience with language. Contrary to the charge often leveled, it is not that Chomsky wants to study only one aspect of language (syntax); he simply wants to study one at a time. In fact, a major goal of the *SS-LSLT* theory was ultimately to advance the study of semantics by showing how "sufficiently rich" descriptions of formal structure can "provide the basis for the fruitful investigation of semantic questions" (*LSLT*, 21). Semantics has always been one of the greatest "promises" of Chomsky's syntax; *Aspects* presents his first systematic effort to make good on that promise.

Thus Chomsky's *Aspects* does not abandon his earlier hypothesis about the "autonomy of syntax," which simply means that semantics cannot be used as the basis for syntax. Rather, *Aspects* is thoroughly compatible with this hypothesis, for it makes syntax the basis for semantics. Specifically, *Aspects* provides a syntactic model of deep structure as the basis for semantic interpretation. The base generates the deep structure, that is, and a separate semantic component operates directly upon this deep structure to fully "interpret" its meaning.[12] This is possible because the base component contains two parts that are directly relevant to meaning: (1) the base (phrase structure) rules generate syntactic structures that embody all the structurally meaningful grammatical functions (like Subject-of, Object-of, etc.), and (2) the base Lexicon of course contains the words (along with their meanings) that are inserted into the base phrase structures. Furthermore, the base contains other information of a syntactic/semantic sort that is idiosyncratic to individual words. For instance, some Nouns (like *sincerity*) will have features like + ABSTRACT, which is (redundantly) − HUMAN. This imposes an important grammatical limitation on which deep structures are possible, because some Verbs (like *admires*) require a + HUMAN Subject. Thus we could have *John (+ HUMAN) admires sincerity,* but not *Sincerity (+ ABSTRACT) admires John.*

One of the consequences of this latter provision of Chomsky's base component, however, is that it often makes dividing questions of "form and structure" from questions of "meaning" extremely difficult. No sooner does Chomsky introduce the provision for "lexical subcategories" of this sort (like + ABSTRACT, + HUMAN) than he begins to grapple with his own syntax/semantics dividing line (*Aspects,* 75). Since his earliest work in transformational grammar, in fact, he has readily acknowledged related difficulties and has often grappled with what might be called "borderline cases" that put his own twin idealizations of formal grammaticality and the distinction between syntax and semantics to the test (e.g., *LSLT,* 68, 132, 148–49, 567). What needs to be remembered here, though, is the status of borderline cases in Chomsky's basic approach to scientific inquiry: One constructs one's theory, not on the basis of borderline or difficult cases, but on the basis of clear-cut cases; then (and only then), one attempts to determine what the theory itself can reveal about the difficult or borderline cases. Testing a model in this way may lead to further refinements in the model, but it does not necessarily call for abandoning the model's theoretical distinctions. Quite to the contrary, a consistent continuum or graded array of borderline cases is exactly what we should expect to find in the vicinity of any "border" that happens to be real.

To see how this principle might work with regard to Chomsky's syntax/semantics distinction, consider first some of the examples he grapples with in his earlier work (*LSLT,* 132):

(1) Look at the cross-eyed elephant

(2) Look at the cross-eyed kindness

(3) Look at the cross-eyed from

In the *LSLT*-model, Chomsky made an elaborate attempt to account for arrayed examples of this type by proposing ways to distinguish their differing "degrees of grammaticalness": Sentence (1)—with the pragmatically odd "cross-eyed elephant"—is proposed as the most clearly grammatical of the three, while sentence (3)—with its "cross-eyed from"—is clearly the least grammatical (and for reasons that are rather clearly syntactic). But sentence (2)—with the phrase "cross-eyed kindness"—is somewhere in-between; it is a borderline case, strange but not totally ungrammatical, and it is difficult to say whether the strangeness arises from formal syntactic or semantic considerations. Since Chomsky has subsequently rejected his early concept of "semi-grammaticalness" (e.g., *Sophia,* 33), we need not go into the *LSLT*-model's provisions for dealing with it. For our purposes, the relevance of examples of this kind is what they might show about Chomsky's ideal distinction between syntax and semantics. They also perhaps illustrate a further distinction Chomsky makes between "semantic systems" proper (lexical content and structurally meaningful relations like Subject, Object, etc.) and other "systems of knowledge and belief" that are often referred to as pragmatic knowledge (see *Aspects,* 159–60).

Starting with the most clear-cut case, most speakers of English would probably acknowledge that sentence (3), with *the cross-eyed from,* represents a definite violation of formal syntactic rules. An Article like *the* and a Modifier like *cross-eyed* are unambiguous markers of a Noun Phrase; but no matter how a Noun Phrase may begin, at some point in the generation or expansion of every grammatical Noun Phrase there must be a Noun. A Noun is the lexical "Head" of a Noun Phrase, the essential defining core of the phrase. In this particular phrase, however, the final word is *from*—a Preposition, rather than a Noun. Even very young speakers of English would surely know instantly that the rules of the language are not being followed, here. Now it is not a question of whether there might be some special context in which this rule violation could be deemed appropriate or even interpretable; it might be part of a language game with children, for instance—a game of "breaking the rules for fun"—or it might even be a potentially meaningful statement in a poem by a poet such as e. e. cummings. In either instance, though, notice that the statement achieves whatever special effects it might have (fun or poetic surprise) precisely by deviating from an ordinary rule of English syntax. Whatever meaning it may be assigned in context, it is ungrammatical from a strictly syntactic point of view. ("Ungrammatical," as we will see, is not intended as a pejorative term.)

Conversely, it seems almost as clear that sentence (1)—again from a strictly syntactic point of view—is entirely well formed. When you think of it carefully, the notion of a cross-eyed elephant is strange for reasons that are essentially pragmatic and/or semantic, having to do with meaning in the broad sense of real-world knowledge. We know—from our knowledge of the way elephants are put together, rather than from our knowledge of the way sentences are put together—that (real) elephants cannot be cross-eyed; the sentence expresses an odd belief (or perhaps a fairy-tale or cartoon conception), but it displays perfectly good English form and structure. If you doubt this, ask yourself how you would go about explaining the oddity of the sentence to a speaker of English who did not at first see anything odd about it at all. Would you give the person a brief grammar lesson, explaining some technical point about Nouns and Modifiers (as I did above with the case of *the cross-eyed from*), or would you merely remind the person that an elephant's eyes are normally on opposite sides of its head (and thus cannot literally be "crossed")? To explain the oddity of the sentence, we must draw mainly upon our extralinguistic (pragmatic) knowledge of real-world elephants—and of course on our linguistic knowledge of semantics, having to do with the idiomatic word-meaning of *cross-eyed,* and so forth—but our linguistic knowledge of English syntax proper gives no apparent clue as to what is odd about the sentence.

In the case of sentences (1) and (3), then, Chomsky's syntax/semantics distinction seems reasonably well supported: With *the cross-eyed from,* there is an instantaneous shock to our structural intuitions, no matter how sanely or imaginatively this sequence of words might ultimately be interpreted in context; with *the cross-eyed elephant,* on the other hand, there is no such structural anomaly, and we must think (for a moment, at least) about the meaning of *cross-eyed* (semantic knowledge) in relation to our knowledge of real-world elephants (pragmatic knowledge) before we can pinpoint the origin of the strangeness. In short, *the cross-eyed elephant* represents a semantic and/or pragmatic counter-factual; *the cross-eyed from* represents a syntactic deviation.

This still leaves us with the problem of what to say about sentence (2)—*Look at the cross-eyed kindness.* Surely most speakers of English would recognize something anomalous about this sentence—again, even if it is fully interpretable in some special imaginative or poetic context. Indeed, the very fact that any possible interpretation would have to be imaginative or poetic or at least figurative can be taken as evidence that the sentence has some property "marking" it as "unusual" (in comparison to ordinary literal discourse), a property that singles the utterance out for special interpretive treatment. But what is the nature of this marking property? Is it pragmatic/semantic as in the case of *the cross-eyed elephant*), or is it syntactic (as in the case of *the cross-eyed from*)? If it is a pragmatic/semantic anomaly, it seems a little more drastic than that of *the cross-eyed elephant* (an elephant, unlike kindness, at least literally has eyes that might be crossed in some possible way or in some possible world). If, on the other hand, *the cross-eyed kindness* represents a syntactic deviation, it seems somewhat less drastic than that of *the cross-eyed from* (*kindness*, unlike *from*, is at least a Noun, though not the right kind of Noun). In short, *the cross-eyed kindness* seems to be a borderline case, given Chomsky's ideal borderline between syntax and semantics.

In *Aspects*, Chomsky grapples more seriously than ever before with such borderline cases and the problems they raise about his hypothetical boundaries between syntax and semantics (e.g., *Aspects*, 75–79; 148–63). In effect, he is here demonstrating his readiness to attempt exactly what is tacitly promised in his basic scientific methodology, even as proposed in *Syntactic Structures*: Having designed a device that can deal fairly well with the "unequivocal cases," that is, he now is ready to look at some borderline cases (*Aspects*, 77), to attempt "an account of how an ideal listener might assign an interpretation" even to such borderline cases, in many instances (*Aspects*, 78). After all, one of the primary goals of *Aspects* was to present a model of syntax that permits full semantic interpretation. Thus, while these borderline cases "deviate in some manner . . . from the rules of English" (*Aspects*, 76), Chomsky feels the need to give an account of how such "deviant" sentences can sometimes be interpreted.

Given the nature of the problem, Chomsky envisions two possible versions of such an account. One would seem to be a purely semantic approach to the problem, in that it would allow the syntax itself to freely (over)generate sentences, thus producing many deviant sentences that would have to be interpreted, if at all, by special rules within the semantic component. The other approach—the one Chomsky decides to follow for the time being—puts more of a burden on the syntactic component, in that it would allow a deviant or borderline case to be generated or assigned an interpretable phrase structure "only by relaxation of certain syntactic conditions" (*Aspects*, 79). In other words, under this approach no deviant or borderline cases would be directly generated by the syntax to begin with, as long as its conditions were being strictly followed; only by bending the rules of the syntactic component could a deviant deep structure be derived, and it would thus be marked as such—labeled as a "violator" of specific syntactic conditions—before being turned over to the semantic component, which would have to assign an interpretation (if any is possible) by "analogy to nondeviant cases" (*Aspects*, 78). In short, a model constructed to handle the clear-cut (nondeviant) cases would be imposed on the borderline (deviant) cases in an effort to make some sense of them. The approach is vintage Chomsky.

As already mentioned, this sort of "imposition" (my term, not Chomsky's) of a clear-case model on all sorts of cases results in the less-than-clear cases being labeled as deviant. Specifically, cases like *the cross-eyed kindness* would be marked as "violations of selectional restrictions." For instance, we might suppose that the modifier *cross-eyed* has a selectional restriction on its use, a restriction of the following sort stipulating the environment in which it can be selected to occur:

$$ \underline{\qquad} \ N_{+\,\text{ANIMATE}} $$

This simply means that when *cross-eyed* appears in the "modifier slot" (_____) in front of a Noun, it must be a Noun with the feature +ANIMATE. The Noun *kindness,* on the other hand, would have the feature +ABSTRACT, which is redundantly − ANIMATE, so the expression *cross-eyed kindness* would involve a "violation" of a rather specific condition on grammatical "co-occurrence," resulting in a "clash" between − ANIMATE (in *kindness*) and +ANIMATE (in the selectional restriction for *cross-eyed*).

One can debate forever whether such features as ± ANIMATE are syntactic or ultimately semantic in nature; such cases always concern this very borderline, and Chomsky does not assume that syntactic and semantic considerations can always be "sharply distinguished" (*Aspects,* 77). In fact, the precise boundary between syntax and semantics is far from settled, in Chomsky's view, and his decision to incorporate selectional restrictions into the syntactic component is a "conservative compromise" (*Aspects,* 159). Whether their status is ultimately judged to be syntactic or semantic, however, it is difficult to deny that "selectional restrictions" of this sort can pinpoint rather precisely what is anomalous about expressions like *the cross-eyed kindness.*

On the other hand, if selectional restrictions marked as deviant only such expressions as *the cross-eyed kindness,* it is unlikely that very many people would have paid much attention to this provision of Chomsky's model. After all, how often do you hear anyone talking about cross-eyed kindness? When you reflect that you might very well read such an expression in a poem, though, you begin to realize that almost all kinds of figurative language—most notably, metaphor—involve what Chomsky would call "violations of selectional restriction" (*Aspects*, 149). Needless to say, many literary scholars have not at all appreciated Chomsky's designation of metaphor and other kinds of figurative language as deviant or ungrammatical or even borderline. Furthermore, there are many professional linguists who are vitally interested in the very prominent role of metaphor in ordinary conversation, as well as others who are centrally concerned with metaphor as an important perhaps universal process of semantic change in the history of words. These linguists and literary scholars have often wondered how Chomsky can relegate metaphor—one of the most fascinating and creative phenomena of human language—to the deviant or ungrammatical or even semi-grammatical fringe of language.

As one who has a special interest in metaphor, I must admit to having found some cause for regret in Chomsky's choice of terminology like deviant or ungrammatical to describe figurative language.[13] While metaphor is not an exclusively linguistic phenomenon, I believe, it is as natural to the human mind as language itself, and language makes prominent use of it; it is in fact one of the most profoundly creative aspects of human cognition and should not therefore be described in terms that are almost certain to be construed as pejorative. On the other hand, I am convinced that the only issue here is indeed a question of terminology; Chomsky is quite clear that he uses the term *grammaticalness* in a well-defined "technical" sense "with no implication that deviant sentences are being 'legislated against' as 'without a function' or 'illegitimate'" (*Aspects*, n.2, 227). Nor is this an empty or trivial disclaimer; from his very earliest work in transformational grammar, it is clear that Chomsky is trying to find a way to deal with idioms and metaphors in the grammar at a higher level of grammaticality than that of mere mistakes (e.g., *LSLT*, 148–49).

Ultimately, it is a question of whether a rigorously formal grammatical model should "generate" sentences of this sort (which are almost always at least potentially metaphorical in appropriate context) with or without marking them as exceptional in some precise way. Identifying a violation (or, if you prefer, a relaxation) of selectional constraints does turn out to be a remarkably precise way of pinpointing the linguistic condition that characteristically "triggers" figurative interpretation in metaphorical language.[14] Viewed in this way, Chomsky's formal provisions for codifying selectional criteria are not at all inimical to the study of figurative language. On the contrary, these provisions can actually provide a rather useful descriptive tool for discussing at least the linguistic manifestations (and further semiotic implications) of the "semantic shock" or "surprise" that is such a noticeable (and I believe crucial) characteristic of novel metaphors, particularly in creative literature. The naturalness and even prevalence of metaphor and other tropes—from conversation to poetry—should not obscure the fact that figurative language is nevertheless a palpably different, uniquely interesting, and truly exceptional mode of discourse. It is exceptional not for its rarity (it is, after all, rather ubiquitous), but for its imaginative and semantically fertile deviation from strictly literal discourse (taken as a generative and conceptual norm).

The so-called deviance debate that grew up around this aspect of Chomsky's efforts to fashion his model of syntax so as to address semantic considerations was largely a "theory external" controversy. That is, while it was a matter of concern to some literary scholars and non-transformational linguists, it was hardly of any significance within the evolving theory of transformational grammar per se. Among Chomsky's own students and colleagues, however, another debate arose around the standard theory of *Aspects* that was to lead to both a major division and a major revision of the theory itself. The division resulted in the emergence of a new model called "generative semantics"; the simultaneous revision of the old model led to the so-called extended standard theory. The extended standard theory, in turn, furnishes much of the technical framework for Chomsky's latest theories (see chapter four).

The Extended Standard Theory

As noted earlier, it was two young colleagues of Chomsky's at MIT—Jerry Fodor and Jerrold Katz—who suggested introducing the semantic component into the overall model of transformational theory. In *Aspects,* Chomsky attempted to accommodate this innovation by revising his model of syntax so that a semantic component of the type proposed by Katz and Fodor could read the deep structure and thus interpret the meaning of a sentence. Katz also collaborated with Paul Postal (also at MIT) in formulating what came to be known as the

"Meaning Preserving Hypothesis" (or the "Katz-Postal Hypothesis").[15] It is called meaning preserving because it postulates that transformations do not change meaning. Chomsky's use of this in the *Aspects* model meant that deep structure fully determines meaning "in some important sense of this notion" (*LSLT,* 22), though the "slight role" of surface structure in semantic interpretation was also noted in *Aspects* (221, 224–25). In short, the standard theory was built around the idea that the base rules and lexicon generate deep structures that fully represent the underlying propositional content of a sentence. Transformations operate on these deep structures, transforming them into different surface structures, but the basic meanings (as represented in the deep structures) do not change during the transformational process.

For instance, suppose we begin with a (very simplified) deep structure like the following, to which the passive transformation applies:

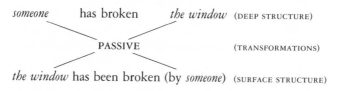

someone has broken *the window* (DEEP STRUCTURE)

PASSIVE (TRANSFORMATIONS)

the window has been broken (by *someone*) (SURFACE STRUCTURE)

Whatever fundamental meaning is represented in the deep structure above as the underlying proposition of this sentence, that meaning is not changed by the transformation. That is, if it is true that someone has broken the window, it is also undeniably true that the window has been broken by someone: The basic truth conditions of the proposition have not been changed by the passive transformation. As discussed in the section "Deep Structure, Surface Structure" earlier, the deep structure fully specifies all the logical roles (like Subject-of, Object-of) that are relevant to this sort of formal semantic interpretation; transformations may change the grammatical word-order slots occupied by these elements at surface structure, but transformations do not (at least in simple examples of this kind) change the underlying logical truth conditions. To put it the other way around, *Aspects* could afford to adopt the Katz-Postal Meaning Preserving Hypothesis because examples of this sort seem to prove that transformations (like passive) do not change the fundamental meaning of the logical proposition as represented in deep structure.

It is important to note, here, that we are talking about fundamental or propositional meaning, not pragmatic meaning. It is obvious, for instance, that the passive transformation in the above example does indeed change what might be called the practical "emphasis" of the underlying deep structure (simplified above as *someone has broken the window*), by shifting—more precisely, by "raising"—*the window* into the main Subject position, where it receives "topical" emphasis; that is, the window now becomes the topic of discourse, what the sentence "is about." Simultaneously, the passive transformation also "back-shifts" (or "lowers") the original deep-structure Subject *(someone)* into an ancillary Prepositional Phrase *(by someone)* at the end of the surface structure—a position of "deemphasis" in this case. This is such a de-emphasized syntactic position, in fact, that it can even be deleted without doing any violence to the grammatical integrity of the clause:

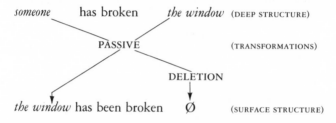

Now the implications of this sort of changed emphasis can be quite important to the pragmatic meaning of statements in context. For in-stance, I well remember my nephew (as a nine-year-old) playing "pass and catch" with himself by bouncing his new football off an outside wall of the house. Since his parents had left me temporarily in charge, I duly warned him that he might break a window, but he of course ignored me. He went right on throwing the football against the wall, and I went on about my business in another part of the house. Shortly afterwards, I heard the crash and the unmistakable shattering of glass. When I walked into his parents' bedroom, I found the offending foot-ball on the floor amid the scattered shards of the window. Curious as to how my nephew would handle this serious predicament he was now in, I peeped outside through the curtains: He was walking around aimlessly in the backyard, apparently rehearsing his explanation. Not wanting to rush his formulation of "rhetorical strategy," I returned to my business and waited patiently. It was worth the wait; about thirty minutes later, he appeared at the back door and announced, "Uncle Mike, Mom and Dad's bedroom window has been broken."

Whatever actual (and agonizing) mental steps he may have gone through to derive this sentence, his choice of the passive structure was an apparent compromise between conflicting necessities in his mind— the need to be evasive in pragmatic effect without neglecting the requirement to be truthful in a strictly formal sense. Borrowing (stealing, really) a Chomskyan model of sentence derivation as a model of actual language production, we might speculate that my nephew's mental "strategy" went something like the following:

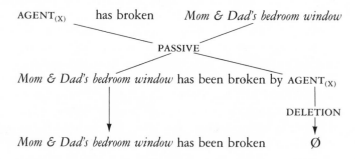

AGENT$_{(X)}$ has broken   *Mom & Dad's bedroom window*

PASSIVE

Mom & Dad's bedroom window has been broken by AGENT$_{(X)}$

DELETION

Mom & Dad's bedroom window has been broken   Ø

This would be to suppose that the basic proposition (deep structure) he felt the need to put before me in some form is that a certain AGENT—whom he chose to leave unspecified (X) for the time being— has broken the window. Of course, he might have formulated the final statement in this very form; he might have said, "*Someone* has broken the window," and in terms of its "propositional content" in the technical sense, this statement also would have been perfectly true as far as it goes: Someone indeed has broken the window. The pragmatic implication of this statement, however, would have been very dishonest: The speaker's overt (surface structure) choice of *someone* would strongly imply "someone unknown" or "someone else besides the speaker" or (even worse, for pragmatic purposes) "someone whom the speaker conspicuously chooses not to identify just now." Especially in the main Subject position, *someone* would have called far too much attention to the (deliberately) unspecified identity of the AGENT. In short, the whole question of the agent's identity would have become the topic of discourse—which is precisely the pragmatic effect my nephew wished to avoid (for as long as he could). Conversely, by using the passive construction with a total deletion of the unspecified AGENT (*the window has been broken* [Ø by AGENT-XØ]), he was perhaps attempting to minimize or to suppress the whole question of agency, and rather to put *the window* forward as a topic for conversation, a topic about which he could afford to tell the truth. In the formal technical sense, his statement was not a lie; pragmatically, however, it was still not entirely honest, and was furthermore quite evasive.

The point of all this is just to show one way in which transformations might be construed, under the Meaning Preserving Hypothesis, as affecting only such pragmatic factors as topic and focus without changing the formal truth conditions of the underlying proposition. (If my nephew's surface structure is not the whole truth under the above analysis, neither is his deep structure, for it also neglects to "specify" the agent's identity; his surface structure, by deleting any overt reference to AGENT$_{(X)}$, simply calls less pragmatic attention to this lack of specificity.) Even assuming arguments of this sort are accepted, however, the Meaning Preserving Hypothesis has more serious difficulties, as was soon discovered in the 1960s (*LangResp,* 151). Another of Chomsky's outstanding associates, Ray Jackendoff, showed that transformations *do* in fact change meaning, even to the extent of changing certain logical truth conditions, as formal propositional meaning was construed under the standard theory.[16]

The sort of arguments Jackendoff offered can be briefly illustrated with examples like the following:

The target has not been hit by many arrows

Under the standard theory, this surface structure would have been derived from deep structure in something like the following way (again, simplifying certain details):

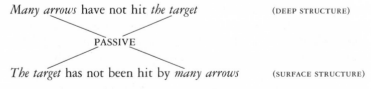

Many arrows have not hit *the target*   (DEEP STRUCTURE)

PASSIVE

The target has not been hit by *many arrows*   (SURFACE STRUCTURE)

Now it is very difficult to argue that the passive transformation does not change truth conditions in cases like this. It seems to be a clear logical presupposition or entailment of the deep structure above that many arrows exist and that these many arrows have not hit the target. But no such logical presupposition or entailment necessarily follows from the derived surface structure at all. That is, the statement, "The target has not been hit by many arrows" would still be perfectly true if only a few arrows existed in the whole world, and even if every one of these few arrows have struck the target dead center.

It is a tricky argument, but test your own interpretation against mine: The deep structure version, *Many arrows have not hit the target,* immediately gives me a mental picture of an archery target with perhaps a few arrows sticking in it but with many arrows sticking in the ground around it. In all likelihood, these many arrows have been shot at the target, but they have missed it. By thinking of it a little while, I can also picture other scenarios under which the deep structure version would still be true, but all of these necessarily involve many arrows that have not, in fact, hit the target. For instance, I can picture many arrows that have not hit the target AND many that have, but I must at least picture many that have not. That is, however many arrows may also be sticking in the target, the deep structure version also forces me to put many arrows somewhere else in the picture besides on the target. Many that have not hit is a logical necessity, if the deep structure version is true.

Contrast the surface structure version, *The target has not been hit by many arrows,* for which the mental picture of many arrows that have not hit is only an allowed possibility, not a logical necessity. Indeed, at least for me, this surface structure first merely evokes a mental picture of an archery target with only a few arrows sticking in it. The idea of "a few," of course, arises from the surface structure's word-order of "not . . . many"—something that is drastically different than "many . . . not" (which is exactly what we have in the deep structure version). The argument is that *many* is OUTSIDE the "scope of *not* in the deep structure version, thus logically presupposing at least the existence of many arrows, but the passive surface structure version has *many* falling INSIDE the scope of *not*. The inference of a few from this particular word-order (not . . . many) may only be an inference, but in no case is an inference of many a necessary presupposition of the sentence (as indeed it was in the deep structure version). The surface structure version, *The target has not been hit by many arrows,* of course allows the possibility that many arrows exist, but (unlike the deep structure version) it does not require that many exist. All it requires is that the target has not been hit by many. Perhaps many arrows were shot at the target, and only a few have hit it. But it is also equally possible (in full accordance with the surface structure) that only a few arrows were even shot. In fact, with the surface structure given as true, it is even possible that only a few arrows exist. If this possibility is in any way allowed by the deep structure version (*Many arrows have not hit the target*), it is extremely unclear and dubious, to say the least. Apparently, then, the truth conditions of the deep structure and surface structure versions of this sentence are rather drastically different.

One consequence of the many arguments of this sort that were pursued in the years following *Aspects*[17] was Chomsky's abandonment of the Meaning Preserving Hypothesis—and, along with it, the standard theory's provision that meaning is fully determined at the level of deep structure. What became increasingly clear was how important the role of surface structure (word order) really was in semantic interpretation, not just for such pragmatic considerations as topic and focus, but for such logical questions as scope and presupposition and entailment. Thus was born the "extended standard theory"—the version of generative-transformational grammar that has *all* semantic interpretation taking place at a level that is "in-between" surface structure and deep structure. This in-between level is that of "s-structure."

While it is in-between deep structure and surface structure, s-structure is "closer" to surface structure. It is not, however, a jargon abbreviation for surface structure, as is sometimes thought. What it is, in fact, is a highly enriched version of surface structure. For this enrichment, s-structure still depends as crucially upon the underlying logical relations of deep structure as it does upon the scope and word-order considerations we have just been discussing as phenomena of surface structure.

More will be said about this in the next chapter, but for now, here is a brief sketch of it (*RuleRep*, 145ff). Deep structure is now called "d-structure," for reasons discussed earlier, in part, but also because deep structure was the level at which all semantic interpretation took place (in the standard theory of *Aspects*), and this is no longer true in the extended standard theory. What, then, of all those structurally meaningful underlying relations in the old deep structure? Have these been abandoned, too, along with the theory of deep-structure interpretation? No, these underlying structures are still posited, and they are still preserved throughout the transformational cycle, ultimately to be represented in s-structure by the device of "traces." Traces might be thought of as the structurally significant remnants or place-markers of d-structure positions and relations at the level of s-structure. They are structurally place-marked "empty categories" that have been "vacated" by transformational movement. That is, when elements move from structurally significant d-structure positions, they leave behind traces of their original positions, and these traces are preserved and duly registered at the level of s-structure. Semantic interpretation is possible at the level of s-structure, in fact, only because s-structure is a trace-enriched version of surface structure. Thus s-structure incorporates all that is truly necessary to formal logical semantic interpretation, in Chomsky's sense: surface word-order (affecting phenomena like scope and presupposition, which, as we have just seen, can be changed by transformational movement) and traces of logical, structurally significant d-structure relations (like Subject-of or Object-of, which are not changed by transformational movement precisely because they are still trace-marked at s-structure).

Thus Chomsky has retained the standard theory's concept of semantically rich underlying structures, but he has retained it under the rubric of d-structure instead of deep structure. There are some interesting differences in the way d-structures are formed, in the extended standard theory, as opposed to the way deep structures were derived in *Aspects*. Recall that the *Aspects* model generates deep structures through the interaction of two components: (1) the base phrase-structure rules and (2) the Lexicon. The base rules generate the phrase structures (usually depicted as structural "trees"), and the words from the Lexicon are then "inserted into" these tree structures. In the development of the extended standard theory, however, the Lexicon plays an increasingly important role. It is perhaps not too much of an oversimplification to say that the words or "Lexical entries" now "come first"; that is, the words come from the Lexicon equipped with their own inherent structural "projections"—grammatical "slots" projected or anticipated by the word itself (as for example), *hit* projects or anticipates an NP Direct Object). These projected slots of course need to be "filled" by other syntactic constituents in order to complete or complement the "structural meaning" intrinsic to the word itself, and d-structures are now assembled largely in accordance with this phenomenon of Lexical complementation. The role of the "base phrase-structure rules" from *Aspects* has thus become increasingly redundant in the development of the extended standard theory, and in fact these elaborate, structure-specific rewrite rules have now been largely replaced by "X-bar theory." Unlike the old (and numerous) phrase-structure rules, the remarkably few general principles of X-bar Theory only assist or guide the derivation of d-structures. That is, d-structures "grow," largely from the intrinsic requirements of words for Lexical complementation; it is just that these d-structures also grow in accordance with the general structural principles of X-bar theory (more on this in chapter four).

Again, however, the biggest difference between the old deep structure and the new d-structure is the role of each in semantic interpretation. Deep structure was the level at which virtually all semantic interpretation happened, in the standard theory; in the extended standard theory, all semantic interpretation happens rather at s-structure. This does not mean that d-structure is now irrelevant; Chomsky still believes that the distinction between "underlying logical" and "surface grammatical" relations needs to be retained and accounted for in semantic interpretation. It is just that these underlying logical structures—for which d-structure is still needed to provide a full and explicit account—are not, by themselves, sufficient to permit complete semantic interpretation. For that, the theory also had to take account of the important role of surface structure. S-structure was the answer: It shifted semantic interpretation closer to surface structure, and still managed to "keep track" of the semantically important underlying logical functions and relations of d-structure through the device of traces.

Others in the generative school of linguistics took a very different approach to these problems of semantic interpretation. Rather than shift the burden of semantic interpretation closer to surface structure, they drew the connection between semantic representation and deep structure even more closely. Where Chomsky sought to incorporate the traces of all semantically relevant d-structure grammatical functions into s-structure, some of his students and colleagues sought to do just the opposite: They tried to incorporate, into deep structure, all the semantically relevant functions of surface structure. And they even went further: In the name of establishing a deep structure that could serve as the exclusive level for semantic interpretation of all sorts, they tried to build into their new deep structures the sort of "knowledge" and "beliefs about the world" that Chomsky has always called "pragmatic" and even "nonlinguistic" (*LangResp,* 152). This new school of generative linguistics thus came to be known as "generative semantics."[18]

For a while, generative semantics flourished and created a great deal of excitement in its efforts to formulate pragmatically determined deep (or deeper than deep) semantic structures. But it seems to have had a rather short life span, at least as a unified and coherent movement. Part of the reason for its early demise, according to Chomsky, is that the basic hypothesis generative semantics shared with his own standard theory (that deep structure can fully determine meaning in human language) was simply wrong (*LangResp*, 151); in fact, he thinks his own fundamental misstep in this regard was exactly what started generative semantics on the wrong path, adding that it was nevertheless a path that had to be explored because it just might have turned out to be right. [19] When it proved to be wrong, Chomsky merely backed up and changed his direction, revising his theory to get rid of the faulty hypothesis; generative semantics, however, continued on its own path, which seems ultimately to have led nowhere in particular; the generative semanticists perhaps lost their way in a "wilderness" of their own making.

Indeed, the failure of generative semantics as a coherent movement suggests that no discussion of it (in a book of this sort) is really justified—perhaps not even for purely historical reasons. The only real value in mentioning generative semantics at all (even briefly, as here) is that the ultimate causes of its disintegration as a theory reveal (by contrast) what is perhaps the most fundamental principle of Chomsky's alternative approach to theory construction. One of the most important reasons Chomsky has given for the fate of generative semantics is that it entangled itself with too many complexities of language all at once; the task it set for itself was thus too hopelessly "chaotic" (*GenPrize*, 44). It tried, for instance, to incorporate too many kinds of knowledge at the level of deep structure, including semantic considerations that are clearly of a pragmatic, perhaps even extralinguistic character. In short, it tried to account for the global complexities of human language with a seamless, monolithic global model that ignores the difference between syntax and formal semantics, as well as the difference between formal semantics and pragmatics.

By contrast, Chomsky's twin idealizations about language have always been the formal autonomy of syntax and the separation of computational elements of meaning from pragmatic elements of meaning in semantic studies (*LangResp*, 152–53). The extended standard theory was an effort to maintain these twin idealizations, but generative semantics abandoned them. As a direct result, the theory of generative semantics suffered a rather premature demise, apparently overwhelmed by its own chaotic complexities. It cannot be denied that language itself is just such a "chaos" (as understood in the modern sense of nonlinear and unpredictable complexity, as opposed to mere randomness), and Chomsky might at times sound hostile to the important study of such chaos (e.g., *LangResp*, 153). On the other hand, one of the principal insights of modern chaos theory in the natural sciences is that unpredictable complexity in the physical world may often be understood exactly as Chomsky proposes to understand it in human language: Simple systems give rise to complex behavior (Gleick, 304).

Generative semantics was an effort to make the system of linguistic description as complex as the circumstances of language use. In this it failed to understand that complexity often derives from simple systems. Conversely, Chomsky's method is to understand language complexity via divide-and-conquer idealizations—positing separate and relatively simple component subsystems that interact (albeit in nonlinear, often unpredictable ways) to produce larger and more complex global patterns. This is an approach to language that brings linguistics much closer to contemporary developments in the natural sciences, and it may very well someday be judged as Noam Chomsky's single most distinctive achievement.

Chapter Four
The Second Revolution

The so-called standard theory of "generative-transformational grammar" as represented by the *Aspects* model was in some ways perhaps the victim of its own success. Throughout the 1960s and 1970s, the generative-transformational revolution continued to gain momentum worldwide, with an impressive development in the number and complexity of structural conditions and transformational operations investigated and formalized in a rapidly growing body of technical literature. With this manifest success in formalizing the "rules" underlying human linguistic creativity, however, a kind of tension arose between the elaborateness of the theory's descriptive mechanisms and what Chomsky himself has always seen as the ultimate explanatory goal of linguistics. As discussed in the previous chapter, this explanatory goal is to account for the amazing facts of language acquisition by children. Without providing a feasible theoretical basis for explaining how children acquire language as rapidly and naturally as they in fact do, linguistics simply could not achieve explanatory adequacy. But if all these complex algorithmic rule systems that were being developed in the technical literature of transformational grammar were really a correct account of what a language is, then how in this context could there even be a feasible account of how children acquire such a language?

For this reason, the sophisticated descriptive superstructure of rule systems that grew out of the first "Chomskyan revolution" of the 1950s and 1960s actually turned out to present something of an obstacle in the way toward the theory's own ultimate explanatory goal. That is why the standard theory—despite the descriptive power and usefulness of its technical devices—had to be virtually torn down and swept aside to make way for the second Chomskyan revolution of the 1980s and 1990s. This is not at all to diminish the achievements of the first revolution. Aside from the significant (and, I believe, permanent) value of the earlier theory for purely descriptive purposes, there is a very real sense in which the first revolution was a theoretical step that had to be taken before the direction for the second (and more purely

explanatory) movement could become entirely clear. In short, the
structural and transformational apparatus of language had to be formalized in precise descriptive terms before linguists could understand
the true magnitude and complexity of the essential matter to be
explained.

Thus, while the formal edifice of rule systems that grew out of the
first revolution did indeed (in one sense) present an obstacle to the
second movement, in so doing it also presented something of a target,
helping to define the basic problem for the second revolution more
precisely. In our first interview with him, Chomsky offered a revealing
account of how the first revolution defined the problem for the second
"conceptual shift" (a phrase he prefers to *revolution*). The interview segment is rather long, but I think it is worth considering in its entirety
for the sense it provides of the historical background and chronological
sequence of events that led to both of the major movements associated
with Chomsky's work. It also provides an interesting personal glimpse,
I feel, of Noam Chomsky's characteristic attitude and demeanor whenever he is asked to assess his own work.

The following section, then, is the final segment of our first interview, conducted at MIT on 1 December 1989, with Ronald Lunsford
posing the questions (Interview 1).

Chomsky on the Chomskyan Revolutions

LUNSFORD: Maybe I can jump in and sort of pull back to a question
              of your place in modern linguistics as you perceive it.
              I'm aware that you reject—I believe it's in "On the Psy-
              chology of Language and Thought"—the idea that your
              linguistics constitutes a paradigmatic shift.[1]

CHOMSKY: It's just that I think all of that talk is very inflated. I
              think there are paradigmatic shifts in the history of
              thought, maybe about two of them, you know, three of
              them, something like that. There was certainly one in
              the seventeenth century; you can't trace it to a person,
              but throughout that period, roughly, there was a very
              substantial shift in the way lots of questions were looked
              at. This was true of the sciences in particular, but it had
              a big impact on lots of other things—often through mis-
              understanding. You could think of others: quantum the-
              ory, doubtless a paradigmatic shift. But to talk about it
              in fields like psychology or linguistics seems to me really

inflated. We're just much too primitive to have things like paradigmatic shifts. There are little changes here and there. So it's more a matter of scale than anything else.

LUNSFORD: As you look back on your contributions—

CHOMSKY: Well look, there was something in the 1950s that was waiting to happen. You go back, say, to the period we've been talking about, the seventeenth and eighteenth centuries, in my view culminating, really, in Humboldt. They were sort of groping for something, and what they were groping for was what Humboldt put in a nice phrase—a system that makes infinite use of finite means. He recognized, in one way or another, that that's what language is like. The means have to be finite, because they're in a finite mind and a finite brain, so we can't have an infinite number of sentences stored in our head, because our head is finite. So the means are finite, but they're unlimited. It was a big Cartesian insight that language is unbounded. And not only is it unbounded, but the use of language is unconstrained by stimuli. Language is appropriate to situations, but it's not caused by situations. So there's some property—this is in fact what he called the criteria of mind; that's why he thought mind wasn't a mechanism, because mechanisms aren't like this. But mind is revealed by the capacity to produce novel, innovative behavior, which is appropriate to situations though not caused by them. And that's a good characterization of normal language use. As far as we know, that's entirely accurate. And the mechanisms for it are some sort of mechanisms that allow for what today you would call recursive enumeration and digital infinity, and so on. So there was this kind of insight— you've got free, infinite, creative use of finite means. But there was nothing you could do with that insight, because nobody understood what that meant. It's sort of like a phenomenal description of what happens, but where do you go from there? And in fact it kind of terminated.

By the early twentieth century, it was beginning to be understood what that meant. In mathematics and in logic, and so on, there were the developments of a very clear understanding of what digital infinity meant— that's what we call the theory of computation and the theory of algorithms, Turing's theory and Gödel's theory, and so on.[2] All this stuff began to be understood in the abstract sciences; in the formal sciences this began to be quite well understood, in fact very well understood. It was no longer mysterious.

Here we have to be cautious—one thing remained and still remains mysterious, and that's the creative use of these mechanisms. So nothing is known about that; we're back just where Descartes was. We don't know anything about the appropriate use of language. Virtually nothing. But what we do know, what was already available, say by the 1940 or the 1950s, are the technical concepts required to put some meat on the notion of infinite use of finite means. And there had also been important developments in the study of language over this period. A lot of the sort of traditional mythology had broken down, through anthropological linguistics and so on. And languages were understood as being, in the Saussurian sense, a system where everything hangs together, and is not dictated by higher authority, and so forth. And there was a lot of descriptive material around; there had been a lot of interesting field work. So the time was right to put all this stuff together, and when you put it together you get generative grammar, period.

LUNSFORD: Moving from that kind of beginning way ahead to a long-range view of what's happened since then, I'd like to pick a quote out from *Lectures on Government and Binding* where you say, "For the first time there are several theories of Universal Grammar that seem to have the right general properties over an interesting domain of fairly complex linguistic phenomena."[3] I wonder if you could discuss what theories, properties, and phenomena you have in mind, and what new insights you might envision.

CHOMSKY: Have you seen a couple of little monographs that came out of Japan a year or two ago?[4] Remind me to give them to you when you leave, because I gave public lectures which dealt with these topics in detail.

What happened around 1980—*Lectures on Government and Binding* was lectures about it—what was going on through the seventies, from—look, let's go back to the fifties. When the framework of generative grammar was established, we say, OK now we understand the infinite use of finite means. I must say, incidentally, that this is very ahistorical—at that time nobody had ever heard of the relevant material in the work of Humboldt or Descartes; the understanding that there had been something before came much later, as is often the case; so this was not a reconstruction. What's called the "cognitive revolution," which is what was going on in the fifties, is really the second cognitive revolution,[5] which is sort of picking up and reconstructing a lot of stuff that was already done that nobody knew about. In fact, to this day, very few people know about it. So the sense of innovation is sort of right, but kind of wrong, too, because it was just our ignorance that made it innovative. But in this so-called cognitive revolution, in the linguistic part of it—which is probably the main part, or at least a main part—you have the notion of generative grammar, which means that we have a task now. The task is to present, say, for English or for any language, the mechanisms, the actual mechanisms, that are used to allow you and me to produce and understand arbitrarily many new expressions. So we try to find the means that we can—that we do—know, that are in our heads somewhere, that enable us to express new thoughts, and to interpret and understand new thoughts. That's the task.

Now as soon as that task was undertaken, there were a lot of quick results, which have the properties of what Kuhn calls a paradigm shift. One thing that happened is that all of a sudden vast amounts of new evidence became available. I mean things that people had never even noticed before, although they are perfectly obvious, immediately became problems. In this respect, it's a little bit like the apocryphal stories about Newton and the apple. As long as you're not puzzled by the phenomena of ordinary life, you haven't started on inquiry. If it's just obvious that an apple falls to the ground because that's its natural place—it's supposed to fall—then you don't have any physics. If you ask yourself why the apple is falling, then you've seen that it's a problem, and now you're into the area of inquiry. One of the hardest things to do, incidentally, is to recognize that things are problematic. Everything that happens in ordinary life looks like—you know, "Why shouldn't it?" But it's only when you begin to realize how puzzling these things are that are going on in ordinary life that you begin to start in-

tellectual inquiry. Now in the case of language, nobody
had ever even noticed some of the most trivial things—
for example, when I say, "John saw him," why is "him"
interpreted as somebody other than John, whereas when
I say, "John saw his mother," it's not, or when I say,
"John expected Mary to see him," it's not.[6] You can't
imagine a more trivial observation; but I don't think anybody had ever noticed it. This went on and on. As soon
as you begin to ask the question, how do the mechanisms
work, all of a sudden you realize you don't understand
anything about language. The most trivial facts are not
understood. And so this vast amount of evidence was
suddenly pouring on you, which was kind of there, but
nobody had ever seen it. And you had to try to work your
way through it and develop mechanisms that would account for it.

In the course of developing these mechanisms, you immediately found kind of a—if not a contradiction, at least
a tension. And the tension is between descriptive and
explanatory adequacy. That is, as you try to make it to
reach descriptive adequacy, that is to construct mechanisms that will at least be adequate to describing the
structures and their interpretations, you find that you
have to enrich the mechanisms you are allowing yourself
[in order] to gain descriptive adequacy. As you enrich the
mechanisms, the problem of explanation moves farther
and farther into the horizon, because explanation is basically the question of how a child ever knows it. Now
the richer the mechanism, the harder it is to explain how
anybody knows it, because if we have very rich mechanisms, how on earth did we figure them out, since we
have very scattered, marginal data. So there's a kind of
tension—to explain things, you want to show the mechanisms are really sort of simple and basically inherited to
begin with; to gain descriptive adequacy, you have to
keep enriching them. And that tension was obvious at
once.

So you take something like, say, forming questions.
There's an obvious mechanism—let's say WH-questions:
You have a Noun Phrase in "I saw John," you replace it
by a WH-phrase like "who," you stick it in the front of
the sentence, with other minor things, and you get
"Who did I see?" That's the basic mechanism. And you
can formalize that as a transformation. Trouble is, as soon

as you start applying it, you see it just wildly doesn't work. You start getting island effects and all sorts of other crazy things.[7] And so you have to increase the descriptive mechanism to account for these, and you start putting 50 different cases into the rule. Then comes the explanatory problem—how on earth did the kid ever figure out these 50 different cases? Why doesn't a child just assume that you can say, "Who did you read the book that wrote," let's say, for which the answer would be, "You read the book that John wrote." Why can't you say, "Who did you read the book that wrote?" Well, you can't.[8]

That's the kind of problem that comes up at once. Now it can't be that the child was taught that. Nobody's ever been taught that in history, and no grammar teacher ever even noticed that it was a fact. No grammar book describes it, yet everybody knows it. So you've got to put that into the rule. Well, you put that into the rule, and that's one case, then there's a thousand other cases; pretty soon you've got a rule which has a whole pile of mysteries in it. How does anybody know these particular features? That can't be.

Now in order to resolve that tension, it was very quickly recognized, by about 1960, that what you had to do was to show that there aren't any rules, really; there's no specific rule for forming questions, just a general principle. The intuitive idea is right: you take a WH-phrase and you put it in the front. But then there are conditions, universal conditions, which prevent certain things from happening. So there's the A-over-A condition,[9] and others of a similar sort. The reason the child knows these strange things is that the universal conditions are just there; they're a biological endowment.

So that sets another task. I'd say through the sixties and the seventies that was the major theoretical research task. Meanwhile, tons of other material is coming in, empirical material, as people begin applying these descriptive devices and facing descriptive problems that were never looked at before.

Now all this kind of work began to converge by about 1980. That's where *Lectures on Government and Binding* comes in. It summarized, and tried to organize, what had happened. What was beginning to become clear by then is that there was a fundamental error all along. The error was drawn from traditional grammar. Traditional grammar assumes that there are rules, and that there are constructions. Read a traditional grammar book, and there's a chapter on how to form the passive and another chapter on how to form questions, and so on. Now what you find in a traditional grammar is not really rules; you find examples and some loose hints and appeals to the intelligence of the reader to fill it out. The early task of generative grammar was to fill in what the intelligent reader was supposed to be doing. But by about 1980, it began to be recognized that the whole conception is wrong. There aren't any constructions and there aren't any rules. That picture of language, which goes back a couple thousand years, just happens to be wrong. So there's no passive construction. And there's no rule, or principle, of question formation or anything like that. There are just *very general* principles which are not particular to specific constructions; so the same principle will apply to passives and questions. And that's it.

How do languages differ? Well, they differ because these principles allow a very limited amount of variation—what are called parameters. So, for example, there are no rules for forming phrase structure; those are just fixed principles in the mind, and every language adheres to them. But you have minor differences. You can have the head of a phrase be at the beginning like English, or at the end like Japanese, so you get kind of a mirror image. What the child has to do in learning language is just to pick the values of these parameters, to figure out how to set the switches in some kind of finite switch box. But the whole network is sitting there. And the network apparently doesn't involve any grammatical construction of the traditional kind with particular rules.

Now that picture was beginning to emerge around 1980, and that set things off in a new direction. If there is a fundamental paradigm shift, that's it, not the first one. I mean the first one was just sort of doing what was natural; the second one is really different. It's presenting a picture of language and, correspondingly, of other mental systems, which is pretty radically different from anything in the tradition way back to Panini and the classical Greek grammarians. What it's saying is, Look, there are no rules, there are no constructions—these are just epiphenomena.

LUNSFORD: Do you credit yourself with that insight, and did it evolve over a period of several years?

CHOMSKY: By then, there were a lot of people working, and it was sort of falling together. In fact, a lot of this stuff came out of lectures that—

LUNSFORD: The Pisa Lectures?[10]

CHOMSKY: It was a seminar that I was giving in Pisa, where there happened to be some very fine linguists around. And it was kind of working out. And it sort of fell together in those lectures. There was just a lot of interesting work coming out at the time. The organization GLOW[11] had a meeting in Pisa, and it was very lively and exciting and a lot of stuff fell together in some workshops. By that time, it was kind of in the air, sort of waiting for somebody to write it down. That sets things off in another direction, which has been extremely productive. Again, there's been a huge expansion of data, and by now you're really flooded, and the theories have become much deeper.

Just to tell you, at the anecdotal level: In this department of seven or eight faculty members, fifteen years ago any one of us could be on anybody's thesis committee. Now it's just hopeless—I mean every one of us can be on some fraction of the thesis committees, because it's just much too deep; you can't keep up with the literature on the Empty Category Principle,[12] let along on linguistics. Now, for the first time, it's really becoming like the natural sciences. There's a lot of *general* understanding, which we can sort of share, but as soon as you begin to pursue things, the conceptual apparatus becomes rather intricate, the arguments become long and hard to follow, and you have to have a command of a lot of relevant material, and so on.

LUNSFORD: So that's what you mean when you say that we may have a system that has the right properties that may be wrong in concept?

CHOMSKY: Well, I think it's right in concept, but probably wrong in detail. For example, sure we have the wrong principles. It can't be that the binding principles are the way they're described in the Pisa lectures—in fact, by now, we know that they aren't. But it's the right idea. I think it's the right idea that there are invariant principles and a small number of parametric variations, which means, incidentally, that there's only a finite number of possible languages—which is a new conception, totally. It also carries with it a different conception of acquisition, a different conception of parsing. Surely the principles cannot be right in detail, but the picture could be right—maybe for the first time—in conception. Actually, I've got a lot of this stuff written up in these Japan lectures.

The Modular Principles and Parameters Approach

Indeed, the Japan lectures Chomsky refers to in the last sentence above (*Kyoto* and *Sophia*) offer a very lucid and careful summary of the developments from early generative grammar through the standard and extended standard theories and into the new "principles and parameters" approach of Chomsky's current work, which is often called "Government and Binding Theory" (although, as noted earlier, this is something of a synecdoche). As a matter of fact, these 1987 lectures in Japan may well have been a factor leading up to what is perhaps the single most important (official) recognition Chomsky has ever received for his work: On 24 June 1988, the Inamori Foundation awarded him the Kyoto Prize in Basic Sciences. This was indeed a substantial award (45,000,000 yen, or about $350,000); it is essentially Japan's version of the Nobel Prize.

The Kyoto lectures were thus a rather appropriate occasion for Chomsky to offer some of his most concise and insightful assessments of the past achievements, as well as the continuing problems and challenges, of the tradition in linguistics he has fathered. Speaking of the first major movement that culminated in the standard theory, for instance, he describes its "fundamental problem" as a certain "tension between descriptive and explanatory adequacy," further explaining: "To achieve descriptive adequacy, it seemed necessary to enrich the format of permissible systems, but in doing so, we lose the property of feasibility, and thus lose the possibility of explaining how it is that the child knows that such-and-such is the case, in the language in question. We thus continue to face Plato's problem" (*Kyoto,* 60–61). Where language is concerned, Plato's problem is of course the problem of explaining how the child comes to such a rich and complex knowledge of language at such an early age, despite the paucity and confusing mixture of evidence about language in the child's early learning environment. Hence the stronger and stronger emphasis in Chomsky's writings on the child's innate genetic endowment for language acquisition: Children do not learn "rule systems" at all; rather, the general underlying principles of what appears to be a rule system develop naturally from the genetic code of the human brain. It is important to understand the very abstract and general character of these "principles" whose origin Chomsky attributes to the human genetic endowment. He does not believe that children are born with a detailed knowledge about the rules of a particular language, but only with certain abstract properties of mind to which the rules (as epiphenomena) of all natural languages must generally conform. These general, innate principles of language make up the "Universal Grammar" in Chomsky's theory. In fact, the whole evolution of Chomsky's work can be seen as a movement towards greater and greater emphasis on the abstract universals of human language. Not surprisingly, then, his latest theories are often talked about under the rubric of Universal Grammar; while linguistic universals have always been a crucial part of Chomsky's ideas about language, Universal Grammar (UG) is an especially accurate label for his latest work, given its emphasis; it is a more accurate label, in fact, than Government and Binding (GB), which describes only the core set of universals now being talked about.

In his Japan lectures, Chomsky nicely reiterates how this emphasis on Universal Grammar has now led to the second conceptual shift, one that nevertheless grew out of the first revolution he led in the 1950s and 1960s: "The first [movement], within the framework of the 'cognitive revolution' . . ., changed the perspective from empiricist-behaviorist approaches to cognitive approaches, and from structural-descriptive linguistics to generative grammar. The second conceptual shift involves a change from rule systems to a modular, rule-free principles-and-parameters conception of UG [Universal Grammar]" (*Kyoto,* 68). Earlier in the same series of lectures, he also describes how this new "modular" and "rule-free" model of principles and parameters in Universal Grammar is conceived to function in language acquisition, as well as how it is related to the phenomenon of linguistic diversity:

In the past several years, a new and very different conception of language has emerged, which yields new answers to our . . . questions. The initial state of the language faculty consists of a collection of subsystems, or *modules* as they are called, each of which is based on certain very general principles. Each of these principles admits of a certain very limited possibility of variation. We may think of the system as a complex network, associated with a switch box that contains a finite number of switches. The network is invariant, but each switch can be in one of two positions, on or off. Unless the switches are set, nothing happens. But when the switches are set in one of the permissible ways, the system functions, yielding the entire infinite array of interpretations for linguistic expressions. A slight change in switch settings can yield complex and varied phenomenal consequences as its effects filter through the network. There are no rules at all, hence no necessity to learn rules. For example, the possible phrase structures of a language are fixed by general principles and are invariant among languages, but there are some switches to be set. One has to do with order of elements. In English, for example, nouns, verbs, adjectives and prepositions precede their objects; in Japanese, the comparable elements follow their objects. (*Kyoto,* 25)

And so the elaborate algorithms and rules of early Chomskyan grammar have now been all but replaced by the much more abstract principles-and-parameters approach of Chomsky's current work. The principles are the invariant universals of human language as reflected in the innate structure of the "network"; the "parameters" are the individual "switches" in the network that have to be set for each particular language, thus allowing for the fact that languages will of course differ, but at the same time predicting that they will differ only in highly systematic ways—and in a finite number of ways—instead of differing randomly or infinitely. The view is thus that all (normal) human beings have essentially the same language modules built into the mind; these modules are founded upon invariant genetic principles of human biology, but the modules themselves are linked together in a complex network, with switches that have to be set in accordance with a particular linguistic culture. This explains why the new theory is also sometimes called (in addition to UG or GB or principles and parameters) the modular theory of language, or even the "switch-box" or "network-and-switches" model, in reference to Chomsky's favorite metaphorical description of it.

The switch-box or network-and-switches metaphor may sound simplistic or "mechanistic" to some, but actually it implies a rather sophisticated conception of language that brings linguistics much more in line with some of the more recent and far-reaching conceptions of natural science, particularly those having to do with the study of chaos and nonlinear complexity in the physical world. Chomsky's assimilation of modern linguistics to these trends of contemporary scientific thought may prove to be his most profound contribution to the science of language and to the whole philosophy of science.

One key idea in the scientific theories having to do with chaos and nonlinear complexity is the "butterfly effect." In our first interview, Chomsky explained:

> For example, there are some insights developing now into what are called chaotic properties of systems. A lot of things in nature are what's called nonlinear. A system is linear, intuitively speaking, if a small change somewhere leads to a small effect somewhere else; a system is nonlinear if a small change somewhere is going to lead to wild effects somewhere else. And much of nature is nonlinear. That's why nobody can ever predict the weather. In fact, if I, say, drop my cup here—

HALEY: The butterfly effect?

CHOMSKY: Yeah, the butterfly effect. You know, if a butterfly flaps its wings, you get a tornado in Japan. That kind of thing is very common in nature, and that's a typical nonlinear thing. As soon as systems become the least bit complicated, with a couple of factors interfering, then you start getting chaotic effects. There's nothing immaterial about it; it just means that you don't get the kind of predictability you can have from linear systems. (Interview 1)

Viewed in light of such conceptions as these, Chomsky's network-and-switches metaphor is hardly "simplistic"; it may in fact be "deterministic" in one sense, but it is not really mechanistic in any simplistic or "linear" sort of way, precisely because it rests upon a conception of language as "nonlinear." Chomsky's analogy indeed suggests that there may be something like a "hard-wired" network in the mind—the principles of which are invariant among human beings and human languages—but note that he also explicitly maintains that small changes in the "switch-settings" of this network (as occasioned by different linguistic cultures) can produce seemingly vast phenomenal consequences (as seen in the development of different languages). This is a conception of language that is every bit as imaginative and open to complexity and phenomenal diversity as some of the most provocative notions of modern physics and molecular biology.

The parallel to biology, in fact, is one that Chomsky repeatedly draws in his most recent work in order to illustrate the same point about the nonlinear complexity of language. "Again," he comments, "there's a close parallel to embryology, where a slight shift in the gene mechanisms regulating growth may be all that separates a fertilized

egg from developing into a lion rather than a whale" (*LangPol*, 412).
He applies this notion to the evolution of human linguistic diversity
in an even more elaborate development of the parallel:

The logic of the situation is something like what underlies the determination
of biological species. The biology of life is rather similar in all species, from
yeasts to humans. But small differences in such factors as the timing of cell
mechanisms can produce large differences in the organism that results, the
difference between a whale and a butterfly, for example. Similarly, the languages of the world appear to be radically different from one another in all
sorts of respects, but we know that they must be cast from the same mold,
that their essential properties must be determined by the fixed principles of
universal grammar. If that were not so, it would not be possible for the child
to learn any one of them. (*Managua*, 65)

Indeed, his further application of the parallel to the specific problem
of language acquisition suggests that much more than a mere exposi-
tory analogy may be involved in this parallel: "As for the theory of
learning, I suspect that we'll find that at the level of cellular biology
there will be general principles applying to the various systems, and
then if we want to know what particular systems develop in the mind
or the rest of the physical body, we'll have to look at the specific instructions that our biological endowment determines. The theory of
learning would consist of the principles that govern the interactions
that take place between complexly constructed systems and the environment in which they can grow, develop and mature" (*LangPol*, 462–
63). In another interview in the same book, Chomsky's discussion of
this language-biology parallel leads him to express the hope that someday we may discover a real "relationship between molecular biology
and neural structure" of the sort that underlies language—relatively
simple structures, perhaps, that interact in nonlinear ways to produce
a very complex, essentially self-organizing system (*LangPol*, 757).

Be that as it may, Chomsky's development of the notion of nonlinear
complexity is a crucial point for those who would understand his latest
modular theory of Universal Grammar (*Sophia*, 45; *LangPol*, 274). The
principal idea, again, is that complex linguistic effects with apparently
drastic consequences can result from seemingly minor changes in the
switch-settings of the various language modules specified within the
theory—modules that in themselves may not be very complex at all.
Rather, it is the network of interactions between the language modules
that yields language complexity, and the nonlinear effects of small
switch-changes within the modules themselves that produce linguistic

diversity (see *Managua,* 63–64, for instance, where Chomsky gives examples of how simple alterations in the settings of a few switches could explain the development of diverse languages). Thus, while the discussions of this approach in the current literature are rather complicated and difficult for nonlinguists (and even many linguists) to follow, the theory itself is actually much simpler than the old model—simpler in terms of what it attributes to the innate language faculty. The new model thus brings linguistics closer than ever before to a solution for Plato's problem, that age-old epistemological problem of explaining how human beings can develop such richly specific and complex bodies of knowledge (best exemplified, of course, by knowledge of language) from such rudimentary and scattered bits and pieces of information as may be obtained from the environment through the senses.

Simpler though it is in this sense, however, the new theory involves too many interacting modules—and a mode of argumentation that is far too intricate and technical—to discuss with any rigor here. Readers who are looking for a secondary source that provides a fairly thorough introduction to the new theory—and one that is accessible to nonlinguists—will benefit from V. J. Cook's lucid and helpful book, *Chomsky's Universal Grammar.* Chomsky's own *Lectures on Government and Binding (GovBind)* and his *Barriers* are rather concentrated treatments that require the reader to have some previous acquaintance with the technical literature; his subsequent work, *Some Concepts and Consequences of the Theory of Government and Binding (Concepts),* is somewhat more accessible to nonspecialists; and perhaps eighty to ninety per cent of his much longer work, *Knowledge of Language (KnowLang),* requires little technical expertise, despite the fact that it may ultimately be considered his masterwork. The Japan lectures (*Kyoto* and *Sophia*) provide an excellent overview of recent developments in historical perspective, though these do not provide a great deal of detail on the new theory per se, and they may not be as readily available as many of Chomsky's books. Of his available book-length treatments, by far the most accessible (and one of the most provocative, in my opinion) is his *Language and Problems of Knowledge (Managua),* outstanding for its abundant and clear illustration (especially with parallel examples from English and Spanish) of how certain key concepts of the new theory apply, as well as what they imply about human language and about human knowledge in general.

Since accessible primary and secondary sources are available, I will not attempt any more here than a brief outline of the new theoretical framework. As already suggested, the new theory actually involves a whole group of interrelating sub-theories, which address the various modules, principles, and parameters of language as the overall theory now conceives it to be. What follows is a brief description of some of these; the description is necessarily oversimplified, but perhaps it will give something of the flavor of the new theory.

X-bar Theory. One of these subtheories, for instance, is "X-bar theory." In essence, it is what replaces the "phrase structure" component of the old theory. Like the old phrase structure grammar, "X-bar" (X′) syntax describes the structure of phrases, but it does so at a much more general and abstract level—a development that typifies the direction of movement in the new theory as a whole. In the old theory, as you will recall, we had phrase-structure trees starting with Sentence (S) that branched into a Noun Phrase (NP) and Verb Phrase (VP), with the NP then branching into Determiner (D) and Noun (N) and the VP branching into Auxiliary (Aux) and Verb (V) and NP or Prepositional Phrase (PP), among other possibilities, and so on. In the new model of X-bar syntax, universal structural principles that are to be found in all these different syntactic flora and fauna—S, NP, VP, PP, and so forth—are captured as mere particular instances of "X-double-bar" (XP, or X″). That is, all these different constituents (S, NP, VP, PP, etc.) are really just tokens of the same basic type of phrasal design— XP—the same basic structure replicated in different ways. Each XP consists of a Specifier (e.g., an "Article" or Determiner) and an X′, which in turn consists (optionally) of another X′ modified by an "Adjunct" (an option that may be repeated, thereby recursively "stacking" X's and Adjuncts). The final X′ consists of an X (the lexical "Head" of the phrase) and its "Complement(s)";[13] see Figure 4.1:

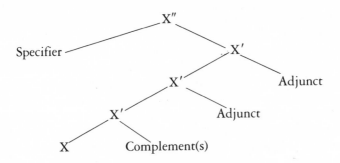

Figure 4.1

In this theory, the Specifier, the Adjuncts, and the Complement(s) are themselves XPs (X″s) which follow the same structural principles and options as their dominating XPs. In fact, even the uppermost S(entence) itself is ultimately nothing but an XP! This means that you can have extremely long and complex or extremely short and simple constituents—constituents that are, from all superficial appearances, as different from one another as an elephant is different from a yeast. But just as the elephant and the yeast have the same basic biochemical constitution, so all phrases and clauses—from the smallest to the largest—have the same basic syntactic constitution in the new theory: a lexical Head (X) with its Complements, together forming a minimal phrase (X′ or X-bar), which in turn (together with its Adjuncts) constitutes a maximal phrase (X″ or X-double-bar).

Here, then, is a good example of how the new theory achieves a kind of simplicity through greater abstraction. Children do not have to learn a whole series of particular phrase structure rules showing how to form a whole host of different constituent types (Noun Phrases, Verb Phrases, Prepositional Phrases, Adjective Phrases, Clauses, Sentences, etc.); rather, according to X-bar theory, they have one basic type, one basic design involving only a small handful of structural principles (Headship, Complementation, Adjunction, and Specification), which principles can be realized in a variety of different forms depending on what particular category of word (N(oun), V(erb), P(reposition), A(djective), etc.) happens to be the lexical Head (the X). Notice, too, that the new theory achieves this simplicity without failing to provide for complexity: What we really have, here, is essentially a conception of syntactic structure within structure within structure, a (potentially) infinite fractal-like replication of the same basic structural design at ever increasing or decreasing scales and levels of formal complexity.

The new theory also captures the uniformity of this basic structural design without sacrificing provisions for linguistic diversity, either. This is true because X-bar theory contains certain parameters to be set—switches that have to be thrown one way or the other, in accordance with the linguistic culture in which the child is acquiring language. As pointed out earlier, for instance, English is a "head-first" language, while Japanese is a "head-last" language. Thus, if the XP happens to be a Verb Phrase—of which the Verb itself is always the lexical Head—then we have Verb-last word order in Japanese ("I Japanese am") but Verb-first order in English ("I am Japanese"); if the XP happens to be a Prepositional Phrase, of which the Preposition is Head, then we have Preposition-last word order in Japanese ("Japan in") but Preposition-first order in English ("in Japan"). The claim is that all languages have phrases that contain lexical Heads and Complements, but they differ in the order of these: In some, the Head parameter is set as Head-last, in others as Head-first. Languages may not always be entirely consistent—that is, they may have "marked" constructions that do not follow the general Head-parameter setting for normal phrases—but major generalizations about previously hidden regularities in the phrase structure "core" of various languages have been made possible by this basic approach. This is but one example of a significant achievement in the new theory, a generalization that brings the theory one step closer to a solution for Plato's problem.

Movement Theory.   Questions of word order, of course, raise other questions that have long been a staple of Chomskyan grammar—issues having to do with the movement of whole constituents from one position to another in a syntactic construction. What has become of the "transformation" in the new model? You may have been shocked to notice that Chomsky (in the longer interview segment and in other quotations above) now says there are NO transformational rules like the "passive" or "question" transformation, which (along with a host of other transformations we have not discussed) occupied a prominent place in the old theory. If there are no longer any transformational rules like the old passive or question transformations, is Chomskyan grammar no longer even "transformational grammar" at all?

Well, the change is not quite that drastic. As in the case of other components of the theory, the old construction-specific transformations have simply been replaced by a single general principle of movement—"Move-α" or "Move-alpha," which basically means, "Move anything anywhere," or even "Affect-α," which gives the still more startling set of instructions, "Do anything to anything" (see *Kyoto,* 65). Students of Chomsky's political philosophy may think, at this point, that they have at last discovered the long-sought link between his theories of language and society: Sheer anarchism is now to be unleashed upon the world, in linguistics as well as in politics!

People's excitement about the anarchistic sound of Move-α usually subsides, however, as soon as they learn that "Move anything anywhere" does not really mean just anything or anywhere. Chomsky's current conception of Universal Grammar is so structured by constraining abstract principles and general conditions affecting movement that only certain "anythings" wind up having the practical freedom to move. Movement occurs only from certain well-specified d-structure positions, only under certain peculiar "triggering" conditions, only within certain clear constraints on the "distance" of movement, and only to certain well-defined final destinations. In short, Move-α does not turn out to be as much fun as it may have sounded like it was going to be; moving "anything" to "anywhere" with Move-α is somewhat like turning a homing pigeon loose with instructions to fly wherever it pleases; you do not give the bird any specific rules about where to fly for the simple reason that it does not need any.

In other words, the initial "input" conditions assumed by Move-α— the lexical and syntactic circumstances of a particular "deep structure" (or "d-structure,"[14] as it is now called) prior to movement, along with more general constraining, blocking, or filtering conditions that affect movement—merely obviate the need to specify any special instructions for a particular kind of movement, or to specify any particular "output" surface structures that are supposed to result from such movement. The allowed points of origin, available destinations, possible channels, and structural boundaries for movement are so well defined in advance that the simple instruction "Move" will suffice to ensure that any candidate for movement (α) responds appropriately, with everything ultimately being positioned in a grammatical slot.

Before we look at how this works, let us review how the English passive sentence was handled in Chomsky's theory at its earlier stages of development. To derive the sentence "The man was beaten" under the model of *Syntactic Structures,* Chomsky's Phrase Structure Rules would first have had to generate an active "kernel" string like the following (where [SME] = an unspecified agent, "Someone" or "Something"):

> [SME] past beat the man

to which the "optional" and output-specific passive transformation (NP_1 Aux V $NP_2 \rightarrow NP_2$ Aux be en V by NP_1) could then be applied to produce

> The man past be -en beat [by SME]

To this string, the (obligatory) "Affix" transformation would then apply (attaching *past* to *be* and *-en* to *beat*), as well as a special deletion transformation to get rid of the unspecified agent [SME], thereby producing the appropriate terminal string.

Under the provisions of the *Aspects* model, the "phrase structure rules" and "Lexicon" in the base component of the grammar would be used to generate a deep structure like the following:

[SME] past beat the man—*by passive*.

where the (abstract) "Manner Adverbial" *by passive* is a way of specifying—at the level of deep structure—that the passive transformation must subsequently be applied (also with an extra deletion step to eliminate the unspecified agent [SME]). In other words, a specific passive transformation very much like that of *SS* still exists in the *Aspects* model, but it is no longer optional, as it was in *SS*; it is now rendered obligatory and automatic by the triggering presence of the "dummy element" *by passive* at the level of deep structure. This provision for a mechanism that automatically "triggers" movement can be seen as a step in the direction of contemporary movement theory, even though what the *by passive* marker triggers in this case is obviously a very specific kind of movement (namely, passive), instead of the generalized movement transformation now favored: Move-α.

The *Aspects* proposal in this regard solves many of the problems presented by the optional passive transformation of the *SS* model (see *Aspects*, 103–6, for discussion), but notice that there is still an arbitrary (and now a rather artificial or ad hoc) quality to it: It depends entirely on the ad hoc provision of the artificial dummy element *by passive*, whose sole reason for existence at the level of deep structure is to trigger the subsequent application of an output-specific transformation, so that a specialized kind of surface-structure can be described—the English passive construction. If the goal of the grammar is merely to provide a catalogue of descriptively specific instructions for how and when all the possible surface-structure configurations in a given language can be generated, and of how these are related to one another transformationally, then the *Aspects* model is very powerful and useful indeed. But if the goal is to capture universal principles of mind that explain how children can master, not just the passive, but a host of other such constructions involving movement in English—not to mention how they can master (equally well) the constructions of other languages that do not even use overt movement for passive constructions, and perhaps no overt movement at all—then the *Aspects* proposal quickly loses its feasibility.

Now consider how this problem has been addressed in the current theory, which would propose a d-structure something like the following for our example (with inflectional details simplified for present purposes):

[$_{NP}$ *e*] was beaten the man

where [$_{NP}$ *e*] represents an "empty NP category" in the d-structure subject position. Given a d-structure of this sort, notice that no dummy element like *by passive* is needed to trigger the appropriate movement of *the man* to the front of the sentence; the real and actual morphological elements of the passive voice in English (*be* and *-en*) are already present in the d-structure, and these can take the place of the artificial marker *by passive* as a triggering mechanism for the movement of *the man* to the appropriate position (although there is, as we will see later, an even better explanation for what triggers the movement). In fact, the old output-specific passive transformation itself is no longer needed: Since there is only one available empty category (*e*, at the front of string) to serve as a destination, and since *the man* is the only NP-element available for movement to this empty NP-slot, the generalized transformation Move-α can suffice:

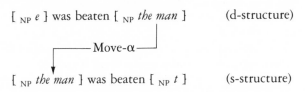

[$_{NP}$ *e*] was beaten [$_{NP}$ *the man*] (d-structure)

—— Move-α ——

[$_{NP}$ *the man*] was beaten [$_{NP}$ *t*] (s-structure)

where *t* represents a "trace" marking the original d-structure position (the underlying logical position) of *the man* at the new level of s-structure.[15] In short, with a d-structure that contains "empty categories" and an s-structure that contains "traces," complicated output-specific transformations like passive can now be abolished in favor of a single generalized transformation—Move-α. This alternative thus puts the new theory a step closer to a solution for Plato's problem: Children do not have to learn a whole catalogue of specific transformations like passive, yes/no-question, wh-question, cleft, pseudo-cleft, extraposition, and so forth; rather, for languages that employ movement, Move-α is all they need.

Very simple examples like the one above avoid the most interesting questions about movement in the new theory; we will take up some of these later, but there is one obvious question that cannot be avoided even here: Why posit an empty category in the subject position of a passive sentence in the first place? That is, why put *the man* AFTER the Verb *(was beaten)* in the d-structure above, and then go through the motions of shifting it to its final position in FRONT of the Verb at s-structure? If simplicity is what we really want, why not simply collapse d-structure with s-structure, generate everything in its proper surface-structure position to begin with, and dispense with transformations altogether by abolishing even Move-α? If reduction of the number of transformations from scores down to one has been desirable, why not reduce the number even further—from one down to zero?

This has in fact been proposed by some linguists, and Chomsky has specifically addressed the question (e.g., *GenPrize,* 72–74). One of the most important reasons he gives in his answer is that abolishing the transformation altogether does not actually simplify matters at all; it really leads to massive complications in other components of a generative grammar. Specifically, it requires abandoning the powerful abstract generalizations made possible by X-bar theory and going back to a word-order-specific phrase structure model, which would have to be elaborated enormously with hundreds of intricately indexed recursive rewrite rules in order to account for every possible syntactic configuration, even for a single language. (This is in fact the very sort of thing Chomsky tried—and soon gave up—in his own pretransformational grammar of Hebrew.)

The necessity of developing a theory of universal principles to explain how children can acquire any one or several of the world's thousands of different languages rather leads in the very direction implied by Chomsky's current theory of d-structure, empty categories, and general principles that govern and guide alpha-movement. In this connection, it is perhaps worth noting briefly how the above proposal of d-structure and Move-α to account for passive constructions in English happens to adapt the grammar rather nicely to the facts of other languages as well. As Chomsky points out (*Managua,* 119–20), the movement of the logical object *(the man,* in our example) is obligatory in languages like English and French; that is, Move-α is automatically triggered. But in languages like Spanish or Italian, this movement is optional; that is, the empty subject-position in the d-structure above ("*e* was beaten the man") could be left empty at s-structure in languages like Spanish or Italian. The examples Chomsky gives are from Spanish, where it is permissible to say

Ha sido devorda *la oveja* por el lobo

"It-has been devoured *the sheep* by the wolf"

where the surface position of *la oveja* in Spanish is also the proposed D-STRUCTURE position of *the sheep* in English. Of course this d-structure does not reflect the final grammatical word order in English, which would require Move-α to shift the logical object *(the sheep)* into the empty subject position (producing, "The sheep has been devoured by the wolf").

Does Spanish have a Move-α transformation? Yes, because it is also permissible to say

La oveja ha sido devorda por el lobo

"The sheep has been devoured by the wolf"

which of course is the exact word order for English. The difference is simply that the movement here is optional for Spanish, because languages like Spanish allow the subject position to be left empty. The question of whether or not a given language permits the subject position to be left empty is merely another parameter or switch to be set for particular languages; the switch is called the "null subject parameter" in the current literature: If the switch is set to "on," the language will allow null subjects at s-structure, but if the switch is set to "off," the language will not allow null subjects at s-structure.

For this reason, Chomsky's proposal that the D-STRUCTURE of a passive has an empty subject (which must be filled by Move-α in languages like English, but which may be left empty in languages like Spanish) happens to make the theory more universal, at the same time it facilitates the study of how languages differ. The d-structure Chomsky would propose for the English examples above, for instance, might seem strange and artificial to you:

[$_{NP}$ e] has been devoured the sheep by the wolf

but one of its many advantages is that it just happens to work equally well for languages like English and Spanish, at the same time it permits a very precise specification of how English and Spanish differ: The child acquiring Spanish need only learn that the null-subject parameter is set to on—allowing the [$_{NP}$ e] above to be filled by Move-α or not—while the child acquiring English need only learn to set this parameter to off—requiring Move-α to fill the empty slot.

Now an important qualification must be appended to my discussion of this point: It is emphatically not the case that Chomsky is proposing exactly the same d-structures for various sentence constructions in all languages (see *LangResp,* 193); thus, d-structure is not the same thing as Universal Grammar (*LangResp,* 171). What is universal in this regard is the principle of d-structure—the principle of an underlying level of grammatical representation that captures the same basic logical relations (like subject, object, goal, etc.), and which may assume different "surface" syntactic forms within each language, as well as across languages. It is also emphatically not the case that Chomsky is proposing Move-α as a universal for all languages; in fact, some languages may not exhibit any (overt) lexical movement at all (see Cook, 18). What is universal in this regard is the set of principles that govern Move-α, constraining and guiding lexical movement wherever it does occur. Thus, while some languages may not employ overt movement at all, any language that does (it is proposed) will obey the same basic principles of movement: All movement will be structure-dependent (moving only whole constituents), will originate only from certain characteristic (properly governed) syntactic locations, will be blocked from crossing certain syntactic barriers that are rather typical of all human languages, will always leave behind empty traces of what is moved, and will always terminate in certain identifiable and predictable empty categories.

Finally, though I have (so far) discussed only some of the above factors in connection with movement, it is important to note that they are not just "movement factors"; they are proposed as universal principles of language that always affect the phenomenon of movement whenever it occurs, but they also have many other effects as well. Thus, in languages where no overt movement occurs, these same factors are exhibited in a variety of other ways. Indeed, one of the strongest indications that Chomsky is on the right track in his new conception of language (as a system whose nonlinear complexity is the function of interacting subsystems or modules that are governed by the same relatively small set of simple and ubiquitous principles) is his repeated demonstration of how the factors affecting movement will manifest themselves in other aspects of human language as well.

Government, Binding, Bounding, and Case Theory. There is no better illustration of the above claim than Chomsky's work on the structural principles of "Government"—perhaps the core concept of the new theory—especially as these principles manifest themselves, not only by their "Bounding" effects on the phenomenon of movement, but also by their effects on the phenomena of "Binding" and "Case," two other important modules in the current theory. More accurately, all these modules interact with one another in some rather surprising and very interesting ways, helping to illuminate certain patterns and regularities that had previously seemed to be unexplainable instances of mere random or chaotic complexity in language.

First, some preliminary definitions: Government, as you might have guessed, is a special kind of syntactic or structural relationship that obtains between a "governor" and the constituents it lawfully governs. That probably sounds rather vacuous, but what may not be quite so obvious is the fact that only certain words or syntactic elements can act as governors, and these can govern only within certain surprisingly well-defined and consistently predictable "domains." Governors of course exercise certain forms of "authority" over the constituents within their domains; for one thing, governors have the power to "bind" their constituents—or, consequently, to "free" them. Binding theory thus goes hand-in-hand with Government; in large part, it has to do with the power of a governor to bind the reference of "anaphors" (words like *herself, himself, themselves*) to possible antecedents within the governed domain, and conversely to free the reference of "pronouns" (words like *she, he, they*) from possible antecedents within that same domain. Insights of this sort may well represent the most surprising discoveries of the new theory. Up until now, the governing laws and allowing conditions by which ordinary speakers and hearers determine which possible antecedent may be referred to by any given pronoun or anaphor have been one of the least clearly understood aspects of human language. Traditional grammarians, for instance, have often attempted to account for such referential connections purely in terms of a bipolar relation between the pronoun and antecedent in themselves, appealing to rather weak and often vague pragmatic factors like their "proximity" to each other. Apparently, no model of language before Government and Binding has even considered the startling possibility that pronoun-antecedent relations are controlled, at least in large part, by a third element—a governor that defines the syntactic domain within which a "pronominal" must (or may not) have an antecedent.

The reference of pronominals is by no means all there is to Binding theory, but people who take the time to read the Government and Binding literature are often struck with how much time and space is devoted to pronominals. Sometimes my students complain, in fact, that Chomsky seems to be interested only in pronouns nowadays. Most of them have learned not to make this particular complaint, however, because whenever they do, they are immediately subjected to my "barium milk shake" analogy. The reader may not yet have found cause to complain about Chomsky's apparent obsession with pronouns, but just in case, here is the medicine: If a team of medical doctors gives you a barium milk shake to drink and then takes an X-ray picture of the barium as it courses through your innards, this is not because they wish to make exotic photographs of barium. What really interests them of course is the internal configurations and convolutions of your particular viscera. Similarly, Chomsky explains his recently strong focus on pronouns and anaphors by saying that he has simply found them to be "extremely good probes" (*GenPrize,* 83). Because the referential behavior of these particular linguistic phenomena is channeled and driven by abstract grammatical structures and conditions that are seldom apparent at the surface level, they merely serve as very useful and powerful "trackers" of what Chomsky is indeed obsessed with—the inner workings of the human linguistic mind.

Another reason pronominals serve well as trackers, however, has to do with "Case Theory," in which the principles of Government also figure prominently. Students of Latin, or of the Romance languages derived from it, or of any other highly inflected language, will already be very familiar with the phenomenon of morphological case—the system of inflectional endings added to nouns, showing their grammatical function in the sentence (nominative = subject, accusative = object, genitive = possessor, etc.)—but students of English may not be aware that all Noun Phrases fulfilling a grammatical function in a sentence are assigned Case, in Chomsky's sense. The reason they may not be aware of this is the fact that English has long since lost its morphological case inflections for ordinary nouns; thus Case-assignment is not so apparent in English, and in Chomsky's work it is actually an abstract phenomenon that manifests itself, not so much at the morphological level, but in other, much more subtle ways. One area of English in which Case still has some readily apparent morphological realizations, however, is the English pronominal system. We still mark our personal pronouns, for instance, with morphological case: *she, he, they* are "nominative" or "subjective" (used in the subject position), whereas the "accusative" or "objective" (used for objects) appear as *her, him, them,* and so forth. Even here, morphological case in English seems to be fading (e.g., the *who/whom* distinction certainly ought to be on the endangered species list), and it is tempting to speculate that this trend in English might actually be explainable in terms of Chomsky's theories about abstract Case: English can "afford" to give up its inflectional case endings, perhaps, because the principles of (abstract) Case-assignment are realized or crystallized at other levels or in other aspects of the language. Be that as it may, pronouns in English may at least serve as fairly reliable trackers of Case-assignment. For instance, if the sentence "I believe Olivia is beautiful" leaves the linguist in any doubt as to whether *Olivia* is in fact assigned subjective Case, a convenient test is to substitute the appropriate pronoun; the standard form would be "I believe *she* [SUBJECTIVE] is beautiful," not "*I believe *her* [OBJECTIVE (or possessive)] is beautiful."

Observations of this sort seem rather trivial and obvious until one begins to seek an explanation. It is one thing merely to say that *Olivia* (as evidenced by *she*) "is assigned" subjective Case in a sentence like the one above, and quite another thing to ask why, to ask what mechanism or linguistic principle does the "assigning." Perhaps there is no mechanism or principle at stake; maybe we just have to "learn" a rule that says (as in many traditional grammars), "Use *she, he,* and *they* as the subject of a Verb." Then, of course, we should have to start learning all the exceptions to this rule. For instance, in the sentence

I believe *her* to be beautiful

surely *her* is in some obvious sense the subject of the Verb *to be*; then why is the form *her* instead of *she?* Well, that is an exception to the rule in traditional grammar, and it is usually stated as such: "Use *she, he,* and *they* as the subject of a Verb, except when the Verb is preceded by *to,* in which case use *her, him,* and *them.*" I distinctly remember being taught something of this very sort in "grammar" school, as a matter of fact; I had never heard of the rule before, and there were two things about it that puzzled me. The first was why the teacher was teaching me this—had I been doing it wrong? Once I was assured that I had in fact been doing just fine, I asked the teacher about the second puzzling thing: Why should the rule be this way in the first place? Why does a Verb with *to* in front of it require *her, him,* and *them,* whereas other Verbs take *she, he,* and *they?* As I recall, the teacher told me something to the effect that it was just one of those things about English that made no sense whatever, and that we all therefore just have to "learn the hard way"—by memorizing the rule, along with its exceptions. (Naturally, this made me wonder all over again about the first puzzling thing, since I could not remember ever having been taught such a rule before, let alone having memorized its exceptions.)

Of course we do have to learn certain things about language, but certainly not in just the hard way my teacher suggested. Surely Chomsky is right in thinking that language acquisition is manifestly "natural" (if not altogether easy or effortless) for children because of the deep regularities that govern language, regularities that "fit" the innate dispositions of the human mind with such felicity that no conscious attention or instruction at all is really required. Indeed, the regularities of language are often so deeply unconscious that the very evidence for them may at first seem more like irregularities or quirky exceptions, at least to the ordinary conscious mind. That is why it took such an extraordinary mind, with an exceptional gift for finding simple (albeit abstract) patterns in the complexity of apparent chaos, to begin uncovering the Governing regularities of Case.

To get a preliminary sense of how Government might explain some regularities "hidden" among the apparent irregularities of Case, look again at the two sentences above:

I believe *she* is beautiful

I believe *her* to be beautiful

She and *her* are both subjects of their respective embedded clauses at d-structure, but only *she* is in the subjective case at the surface level; *her* is in the objective case, which is normally reserved for the objects of Verbs or Prepositions, not for the subjects of clauses. Why should the subject of an embedded clause surface with the objective case instead of the subjective case? Of course it must have something to do with the inflectional form of the embedded clauses, for that is the only difference between the two sentences: The Verb *be* would appear in the d-structure of both embedded clauses, but in the first clause it surfaces in its "third-person-singular, present-tense" inflectional form (*is*); in the second clause, the *be* Verb surfaces with no number/tense inflection at all—it is still in its underlying "base" or "infinitive" form (*be*), preceded by the infinitive particle *to* (with which infinitives are usually announced in English).

Linguists capture this distinction by saying that the infinitive form (*be*) is "nonfinite" (with no limitations of number of "time," in the sense of tense), whereas any inflected form of *be* (*am, is, are, was, were*) is "finite"—with specific limitations on time and number. We can easily test this: In the test frame "She believes _____ am beautiful," we know the blank must be filled with *I* (first person singular); but in the frame "She believes _____ to be beautiful," the blank could be filled with a pronoun of any person or number (*me, you, him/her/it, us, them*).

In contemporary theory, this finite/nonfinite distinction between Verbs that do and do not carry tense-number-agreement information is handled by positing a d-structure node INFL (short for inflection), whose value can be either positive (finite), or negative (nonfinite). With this provision, we can now stipulate precisely how our two embedded clauses above are different, as well as how they are similar:

I believe [*she* + INFL be beautiful]   (finite)

I believe [*her* − INFL be beautiful]   (nonfinite)

This new INFL node handles some (though not all) of the matters that used to be handled under AUX in the old theory; specifically, if its value is positive, it contains a Tense marker (present or past) and may (optionally) contain a Modal (though there is no Modal in these two examples). In addition, if its value is positive, INFL also contains all the number-agreement information needed for the ultimate proper inflection of the Verb (first, second, or third; singular or plural). Thus, in the first sentence above, + INFL would contain the information "present tense, third person singular," which is exactly the information needed for the Verb to be properly inflected. In the second sentence, however, − INFL would contain no information of this sort; its value is negative (nonfinite); it is empty or neutralized; its only surface realization is the empty "infinitive particle" *to,* which is essentially the nonfinite counterpart of a finite (tense-marked) Modal (notice that we can have TO *be* or *shoulD be,* but not TO *should be* or *shoulD* TO *be*).

Now what does all of this have to do with Government and Case? First, consider some simple examples of how governors are identified and of how they assign Case. In the most typical situation of government, the Head (X) of any phrase (XP) is a governor that assigns Case to its Complement(s); identifying a governor and explaining Case assignment can thus be as simple as isolating a phrase and identifying its Head. If the XP happens to be a VP, for instance, the lexical Head—the V itself—is a governor; thus, in the VP *killed him,* the V *killed* governs *him,* assigning it objective case (notice that we do not say **killed he*). If the XP happens to be a Prepositional Phrase (PP), the P(reposition) is the Head X of this particular XP, so the P is a governor; in the Prepositional Phrase *with them,* the P *with* governs *them,* assigning it objective case (which of course explains why it is not **with they*). In short, the central, controlling Head or core "X-factor" of any XP is a governor, assigning Case to any of its Complements (projected constituents) within that XP.

What happens, though, if Move-α shifts a constituent from a domain governed by one Head to a domain governed by another? Does the moved constituent now come under the government of the new Head? Let us see what Case Theory—or more accurately, the interaction of Case Theory and Move-α—can tell us about this interesting question of Government. We have been considering the sentence, "I believe her to be beautiful," but suppose we go back to the level of d-structure and make some hypothetical changes that would trigger Move-α. Specifically, let us take the "I" out of the sentence, leaving an empty category in the main subject position, and change the main Verb morphology to passive (*is believed,* instead of *believe*). That would give us a hypothetical d-structure like the following, which (as we have seen) would trigger Move-α:

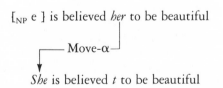

The d-structure above is hypothetical in the sense that it represents *her* as already being in the objective Case; the fact of the matter is that ordinary Case assignment happens only at s-structure, not at d-structure, as indeed the effect of Move-α in this very instance illustrates: When the NP represented by *her* in the hypothetical above is moved to the empty NP-subject position (*e*), it is assigned the SUBJECTIVE case ("*She* is believed [*t*] to be beautiful"). On the other hand, if the main Verb had been active (*believe*), and if the main subject position had already been filled (with *I*), then Move-α would have been blocked (if only because there would have been no open or empty "destinations"), and the NP represented by *her* would have had to remain in its original d-structure position, receiving the OBJECTIVE case ("I believed *her* to be beautiful"). The point is simply that moving a constituent can change what its ultimate Case assignment will be; since governors are what assign Case, a change in Case assignment suggests a change of governors. Governors can assign Case only within their own domains; if a constituent is moved from one domain to another, it must be assigned its Case by the governor of the new domain.

Thus far, however, we have not yet identified exactly what governors are involved in these examples; we only know they are not the same. That is, whatever Head governs (and assigns objective Case to) *her* in the sentence "I believe *her* to be beautiful" is obviously not the same Head that governs (and assigns subjective Case to) *she* in the sentence "*She* is believed to be beautiful"—even though *her/she* is understood as the underlying subject of the predication "be beautiful" in both instances. After the movement, what might have been *her* becomes *she,* so the governing Heads are clearly different, but what are these governing Heads? We know, for instance, that active Verbs govern their objects, assigning them objective Case (*killed her,* not **killed she*), but what Head governs (and assigns objective Case to) the SUBJECT of our "infinitive" example (". . . *her* to be beautiful")?

Perhaps the governing Head in question is the preceding Verb: ". . . BELIEVE *her* to be beautiful." On its surface, this explanation would seem to have some appeal, because notice that the Case of *her* stays the same (objective) even if we leave off the infinitive phrase altogether: "I believe *her.*" Here, there seems little room for doubt that *her* is in the objective Case because it is governed (as a direct object) by the Verb *believe.* Is *her* also a direct object of the Verb *believe* in the sentence "I believe *her* to be beautiful"? The only problem with that explanation is that it ignores the rather clear sense in which *her* is understood as the SUBJECT of the predicate *be beautiful.* Well, maybe *her* is, in one sense, the subject of *be beautiful* but, in another sense, the object of *believe.* This explanation in fact comes very close, but it also raises an even more interesting and difficult problem: If *her* is (in any sense) an object governed by the Verb *believe* in the sentence

I believe *her* to be beautiful

then we still must explain why *she* is not also governed as an object of the same Verb in the sentence

I believe *she* is beautiful

After all, *she* immediately follows *believe* in this sentence, just as surely as *her* follows *believe* in the other sentence; why is it *she* in this sentence instead of *her,* as in the other? Obviously, it has to be because the predication *she is beautiful* is a FINITE clause.

That of course brings us right back to +INFL. One of the most startling and provocative hypotheses of Government theory, in my opinion, is that +INFL is the governing Head of the "clause proper"— where clause proper refers to what in the old theory was called S(entence). Because whole clauses are now treated (in X-bar theory) as instances of the general pattern XP, and because +INFL Heads the clause proper in Government, you will often see what used to be called S represented in the current literature as IP (or I″—short for "INFL-double-bar"). In other words, +INFL is to S (or IP) what N is to NP, what P is to PP, what V is to VP, or what any X is to any XP— namely, the central, controlling Head, the governing core of its domain, from which the very identity and structural integrity of the domain itself is projected. Just as it is impossible to imagine an NP without a Head N of some sort, or a VP without a governing V, or any XP without its essential X-factor, so there is no clause (as clause proper) without +INFL.

Of course, a clause could have a negative inflectional value −INFL)—indeed, we have just been looking at an instance of this in the nonfinite clause *her to be beautiful*—but the point is that − INFL is not a viable governor. It is essentially an empty Head, a mere "figurehead," without any real power to govern. It exerts no real control over its own clausal subject and cannot make "dispensations"—it has no features (tense, person, number, or Case) to assign. Consequently, its domain has little or no integrity as a clause and is always vulnerable either to "invasion" by other would-be governors or to the "defection" of its subject to other domains.

Starting with the hypothesis, then, that +INFL Heads the clause and governs its subject (whereas − INFL is an empty figurehead that cannot govern), we now have a regular principle that can explain the apparent irregularities of Case we have been considering. That principle can be illustrated with a schema like the following:

NP◄——(subj)——+INFL   V——(obj)——►NP

which is simply to say that +INFL governs (and assigns subjective Case to) the subject of the clause, and that V governs (and assigns objective Case to) the object of the Verb Phrase. In terms of this schema, we then would have the following situation for the sentence "I believe *she* is beautiful":

I believe   [*she* ◄——(subj)——+INFL be beautiful]

where +INFL governs within the embedded clause, assigning subjective Case to the NP filled by *she*. Even though *she* immediately follows the main V *believe*, which might at first look like an instance of the schematic situation "V → (obj) → NP," the V *believe* cannot assign objective Case to *she* in this instance, for the simple reason that *she* is already "claimed," as it were, as a subject of the positive governor +INFL inside the embedded clause.

Now it would certainly be true, according to Government Theory, that the V *believe* in this sentence governs the whole construct [*she* ◄ +INFL be beautiful], but this construct is unified or solidified into a discrete, inviolable domain by the positive governing influence of +INFL. We might say that the main Verb *believe* cannot "get to" *she* (thus making it *her*) because the governing Head of the embedded clause (+INFL) is asserting the integrity of its own clausal "boundaries"; there is thus a "barrier" between *believe* and *she* that "shields" *she* from "invasive" assignment of the objective Case by *believe*. In short, even though *believe* governs the embedded clause as a whole, *she* takes its Case assignment from its "immediate superior"—the local governor +INFL.

In the sentence "I believe *her* to be beautiful," however, we have a rather different situation:

I believe   [*her*   −INFL   be beautiful]

where the boundaries that circumscribe the embedded clausal domain (*her . . . beautiful*) are now rather weak or tenuous ([]) as opposed to strong and definite ([ ]). This is of course because the clausal domain so circumscribed lacks a viable local governor. The negative Head (− INFL) of the embedded clause surfaces only as the empty infinitive function particle *to*. We say that − INFL is empty because it has no information or "features" to dispense to its clausal constituents—no tense, person, or number agreement factors to distribute between the Verb *be* and the subject *her* (contrast + INFL, which—being a real governor—essentially regulates subject/verb agreement or harmony). It is not surprising, then, to discover that − INFL cannot assign Case to its subject, either; having no real substance, it simply has no force or power to govern (*KnowLang,* 162–69). It seems rather logical that *her* must take its Case assignment, under these circumstances, from another governor—perhaps from the next highest governor, which (in this instance), just happens to be the Verb *believe.*

To some, postulating a category INFL and then attributing governing power to + INFL (while denying it to − INFL) will no doubt seem like an artificial reification of something too abstract to be real. There are many other motivations for the theory that INFL is in fact a real and independent constituent (not the least of which is the fact that it can move, as in questions), but the justification for INFL suggested just here is that it makes possible a principled account of what must otherwise seem a rather strange instance of chaotic irregularity in language. That is, the difference between "believe *she* is . . ." and "believe *her* to be . . ." is not a quirky idiosyncrasy of English after all. There is no such bizarre rule (except in traditional pedagogical grammars) stating that "SUBJECTS of infinitives take the OBJECTIVE Case." The better alternative of Government theory is simply to say that infinitive phrases have no governing Heads with the power to assign any Case at all; the subjects of infinitive clauses must therefore take their Case assignments, not from the infinitives per se, but from the next highest governor (in accordance with the same regular principle of government by which Case is assigned in every other instance). The reduction of irregularity via generalization to a single unifying abstract principle thus moves the theory closer to a solution for Plato's problem where language acquisition is concerned.

That single abstract principle is known in Government theory as the "Case Filter." It simply states that every phonetically realized NP must be assigned Case (*KnowLang,* 73–74). In many languages, this principle is consistently realized at the morphological level; in languages like

English, which is morphologically impoverished (marking inflectional case only for pronouns), the Case Filter has other important manifestations. Notice how this principle unifies the facts about pronoun-case assignment with the facts about syntactic movement in English, allowing us to reduce the seemingly large number of transformational operations to one: Move-α. One way to account for exactly what happens in the sentence "I believe *her* to be beautiful," for instance, is to say that the Case Filter triggers Move-α:

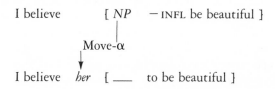

I believe   [*NP*   − INFL be beautiful]

Move-α

I believe   *her*   [___   to be beautiful]

The idea here is that the underlying *NP*, belonging as it does to a domain Headed by − INFL, is essentially ungoverned. Being ungoverned, it cannot be assigned Case in that position. But the Case Filter *requires* every lexical (phonetically realized) NP to be assigned Case. Thus, Move-α comes into play in order to solve the impasse. Triggered by the necessities of Case assignment, Move-α shifts the underlying *NP* into an s-structure position governed by the Verb *believe,* where it can indeed be assigned (abstract) Case. If the *NP* happens to surface as a pronoun, this Case-assignment will be reflected in its actual morphological form—*her,* as opposed to *she.*

The movement in the above example perhaps seems a bit vacuous, but there are many other situations in which the very same process— the Case Filter's triggering of Move-α—is much more apparently real. One is the example of the passive sentence "She is believed to be beautiful," which we have already examined but can now reexamine in terms of the facts about INFL and the Case Filter:

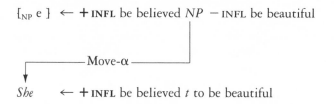

[NP e]   ← **+ INFL** be believed *NP* − INFL be beautiful

Move-α

She   ← **+ INFL** be believed *t* to be beautiful

This seems to give some real (and more natural) substance to the notion (suggested earlier) that passive Verb morphology also somehow triggers Move-α. Here is how it might work: Unlike active Verbs, which assign objective Case to any otherwise ungoverned NPs that follow them ("believe *her* to be . . ."), it is a characteristic of passive Verbs that they cannot assign objective Case to NPs that follow them, even if these NPs are otherwise ungoverned (e.g., "*It is believed *her* to be . . ."). Like −INFL, which cannot assign subjective Case, a passive Verb cannot assign objective Case; the passive morphology neutralizes it. While passive Verbs are still governors (*be believed* in fact governs the trace *t* in the s-structure above), we might wish to say that making a Verb passive somewhat vitiates its governing power, in the sense that its authority to assign objective Case is thereby neutralized. In any event, since the Case Filter requires that all lexical NPs must be assigned Case, it also requires that any NP in a position where it cannot receive Case must be moved to a new position, under a different governor that *can* assign it Case. In the example above, that new position where Case assignment is possible is of course the empty NP-subject position of the main clause. While the Verb of the main clause is passive, the INFL of the main clause is positive (+INFL). Thus the main-clause +INFL assigns subjective Case to *she* in this example, just as +INFL always assigns subjective Case to whatever NP ultimately fills the position governed by +INFL (namely, the NP-subject position).

Again, the real claim here is that children do not learn construction-specific transformations like passive; rather, what used to be called the passive transformation in the old theory is really just an instance of generalized movement motivated by very general principles of Government. Notice that the same principles that motivate grammatical passives, for instance, also automatically block ungrammatical passives. If children merely learn a passive transformation from hearing examples of it like

> *She* is believed ⎯⎯⎯ to be beautiful

we then must somehow explain why children *never* generate ungrammatical passives like the following:

> **She* is believed ⎯⎯⎯ is beautiful

If, on the other hand, Government theory is correct in saying that there is no passive rule to be learned, but only some abstract principles of Government that trigger generalized movement in some circumstances and "block" it in others, then we have a more feasible account of how children acquire grammatical constructions and naturally avoid the ungrammatical ones. Given the *INFL* conditions assumed in the above example, for instance, the ungrammatical sentence "*She is believed is beautiful" would have to be derived as follows:

$$[_{NP} \text{ e }] \ +\textsc{infl} \text{ be believed } [_{IP} \text{ NP}_{she} \ +\textsc{infl} \text{ be beautiful}]$$

$$*She \qquad +\textsc{infl} \text{ be believed } [_{IP} \underline{\hspace{1cm}} \ +\textsc{infl} \text{ be beautiful}]$$

But this movement would be *blocked,* please note, by the same general conditions of Government we have considered in the previous grammatical examples of Case and movement. Specifically, the NP represented by *she* (NP$_{she}$) is *not* free to move out of the embedded clause in this instance because the governor of that clause is + INFL. (If the Head of the clause had been − INFL, the NP not only would have been free to move, but in fact it would have *had* to move in order to receive Case, thereby satisfying the Case Filter.) In other words, + INFL—as a real governor—projects clausal boundaries that represent too much of a barrier for the governed subject (NP$_{she}$) to cross. This is related to what is called a "Bounding constraint" in current theory—a constraint on movement—and even though it is somewhat oversimplified here, I hope you can see that this is not an extra constraint or something new being added to the theory. Rather, it is a logical consequence of the very same general principles of Government that we have already seen regulate and motivate other aspects of movement, as well as the facts about Case assignment.

Given the level of abstraction in discussions of these general principles, the theory complicates matters for students of linguistics, but it characterizes the task of language acquisition as a radically simplified sort of task for the child: Instead of having to learn a plethora of complexities and eccentricities having to do with Case and inflection, as well as a whole catalogue of transformational rules (not to mention a whole series of construction-specific situations in which these rules may and may not be grammatically applied), the minds of children have only to develop an unconscious grasp of certain very general structural principles and patterns. These same principles and patterns have dramatic ramifications in many different and seemingly unrelated aspects of the language. The theory is thus attempting to depict the global complexity of language as the logical and deterministic but nonlinear result of several interacting subsystems, all of which are nonetheless governed by the same relatively small set of basic laws.

As one final illustration of this, I must say at least a little about how these same principles of Government we have been examining manifest themselves in yet another seemingly unrelated area of language—the phenomenon called Binding. Here, too, certain obvious facts that appear at first to be instances of some incorrigible quirkiness in language nevertheless yield with surprising clarity to the insights of Government theory. Consider the following two sentences:

Olivia believes *she* is beautiful

Olivia believes *her* to be beautiful

Examples of this sort are of interest in Binding theory because they raise quite interesting and surprising considerations having to do with pronoun reference: To whom can *she* and *her* possibly refer in these two sentences? As all competent speakers of English know (though we may have to think about it for a moment), in the first sentence ("Olivia believes *she* is beautiful"), *she* could refer to any female—including Olivia. But in the second sentence ("Olivia believes *her* to be beautiful"), the possible referents of *her* CANNOT include Olivia.

That is, notice that all of the following (subscripted) interpolations represent legitimate possible interpretations except for the last one:

Olivia believes she$_{(Martha)}$ is beautiful

Olivia believes she$_{(Olivia)}$ is beautiful

Olivia believes her$_{(Martha)}$ to be beautiful

*Olivia believes her$_{(Olivia)}$ to be beautiful

Assuming that there is only one person named Olivia under consideration, the last interpretation above is not legitimate. To express that meaning, we would have to say something like

Olivia believes herSELF to be beautiful

The question, then, is why *she* can refer either to Olivia herself or to someone else (e.g., Martha) in these examples, whereas *her must* refer to someone else besides Olivia herself. It will not do to fabricate some rule saying something like "*She* always refers back to the subject, whereas *her* always refers to some other person." For one thing, we have just observed that *she*—like *her*—can also refer to some other person (as in "Martha may be ugly, but Olivia believes she is beautiful," where *she* may legitimately refer to Martha); and for another thing, *her*—like *she*—can also refer back to the subject of a sentence, as in

Olivia lost the ring that Martha gave *her*

where *Olivia*—the subject of the main clause—*can* be the antecedent of *her.* Examples of this latter sort also clearly indicate that the rule of proximity cannot consistently predict pronoun reference: Here, *Martha* is closer to *her* than *Olivia* is, yet notice that the reference of the pronoun *must,* for some reason, completely "skip over" *Martha,* the closer Noun, and may refer all the way back to *Olivia*; it need not "stop" at *Olivia,* either, but can "reach" even further:

Tom lost Alice's purse, Jim lost her gloves, and Olivia lost the ring that Martha gave her!

where *her* could legitimately reach all the way back to *Alice* (or even further). Such facts about the reference of pronouns in English may seem trivially obvious to speakers of English, once pointed out, but sometimes the most obvious aspects of language are nevertheless the most surprising to anyone seeking a truly systematic explanation. As Chomsky has said, "The beginning of science is the recognition that the simplest phenomena of ordinary life raise quite serious problems" (*Managua,* 43).

Binding Theory sheds light on problems and apparent oddities of pronoun reference by appealing to the principles of Government—the very same principles that we have already observed can explain certain peculiarities in the (seemingly unrelated) phenomena of Case and transformational movement. Specifically, the same general concept of "governing domain" that is systematically related to certain peculiar Bounding constraints on NP-movement, and that accounts for certain apparent anomalies of Case assignment, also figures prominently in the phenomenon of Binding.

To see how this might work, consider the relevant elements of d-structure as these would be defined for our first example/problem above ("Olivia believes she is beautiful"):

Olivia believes $[_{IP}$ NP$_{she}$ $\leftarrow$ $+$INFL be beautiful $_{IP}]$

As noted in earlier discussions, $+$INFL is a governor. Within its "local domain" ($[_{IP} \ldots _{IP}]$), $+$INFL governs the NP represented by *she* (NP$_{she}$) as the subject of a fully viable finite clause, which explains why this NP is ultimately assigned subjective Case *(she)*. The "integrity" of this local domain thus explains why NP$_{she}$ is shielded from invasive Case-assignment by another would-be governor, say the Verb *believes* (which of course would tend to turn NP$_{she}$ into *her*); or, if you prefer, the same basic principle can be expressed as a Bounding constraint on movement: NP$_{she}$ is not free to move outside its local domain (thus becoming an object of *believes*) because NP$_{she}$ is being governed by a positive Head, $+$INFL. The barriers circumscribing this local domain governed by $+$INFL are in fact so formidable that NP$_{she}$ could not "escape" even if the main Verb were passive *(is believed)*, with an empty category needing to be filled in the main subject position, as shown in the following hypothetical:

$[_{NP}$ e $]$ is believed $[_{IP}$ NP$_{she}$ $\leftarrow$ $+$INFL be beautiful $_{IP}]$

In this situation, the empty NP category would need to be filled with something (recall that English, unlike Spanish, does not allow the null subject—in other words, does not allow a subject position to be left empty at s-structure). We might imagine, therefore, that this empty NP-subject-category is trying to "pull" or "draw" (as if into its "vacuum") the only substantive NP in the sentence—NP$_{she}$. But NP$_{she}$ cannot "break loose" from its own local domain; it is not free to move forward and fill the empty subject position of the main clause, because it is being forced (by its own local governor, $+$INFL) to fill the subject position of the embedded clause *(she is beautiful)*. In such a situation, then, the surface form would probably turn out to be

IT is believed (that) [she is beautiful]

where IT is the "pleonastic" (empty or superfluous) IT (an English construction not unlike certain constructions in Spanish, interestingly enough). The point is simply that NP$_{she}$ is so forcefully bound to the subject-position of the embedded clause (governed, as it is, by a + INFL) that even the main clause would have to look "elsewhere" (namely, to pleonastic IT) in order to fill its own empty subject position.

Now it is remarkable that these facts of Bounding (having to do with NP-*movement*) represent something of a complementary mirror-image pattern to the parallel facts about Binding (having to do with NP-*reference*). That is, while the Bounding constraints related to Government mean that NP$_{she}$ is not free to *move* outside its local domain (IP):

Olivia believes [$_{IP}$ NP$_{she}$ ← + INFL be beautiful $_{IP}$]

the complementary principle of Binding requires that NP$_{she}$ must be free to *refer* outside this very same local domain. This may sound rather cryptic, but it simply means that a pronoun may not have an antecedent inside its own local domain (*KnowLang*, 60); it must be free of any reference inside its local domain, which of course means that it must refer to an antecedent or referent *outside* its local domain. The same structural barriers that deny freedom of movement to NP$_{she}$, in our example, categorically assure its freedom of reference: *she* is free to refer to *Olivia* because *Olivia* is outside the local domain of *she* (namely, IP); by the same token, *she* is free to refer to any other Noun or person (named or otherwise), just so long as that Noun or person is outside the local domain of *she*, as defined in Government.

Admittedly, these principles of Government and Binding hardly seem to explain very much about pronoun reference until we apply them to the parallel (but converse) example

Olivia believes [NP$_{her}$ − INFL (to) be beautiful]

where the NP represented by *her*, please note, *cannot* refer to *Olivia*. In terms of Government (as we have already seen is true in matters of Case-assignment and movement), changing the inflectional value of the embedded clause to − INFL, as above, effectively neutralizes the governing power of INFL; as a collateral consequence, we might say, the integrity of the clausal boundaries is undermined. With no real clausal governor, the embedded clause is "reduced" to the status of a mere "infinitive phrase," only to be subsumed as a part of the larger clause—the main clause, or whole sentence. The local domain of NP_{her} (as far as the Binding principle is concerned) is now the whole sentence, whose subject is *Olivia*. In short, *her* and *Olivia* now belong to the same domain, which would explain why *her* cannot refer to *Olivia*: A pronoun must be free of any (otherwise possible) antecedent within its own domain. To put it the other way around, because a pronoun must refer to something outside its own domain, and because the domain of *her* in this case is now the whole sentence, *her* must refer to something outside the whole sentence—namely, something besides *Olivia*.

This discussion of Government, Binding, Bounding, and Case Theory is certainly oversimplified in many respects. The primary technical literature, while sometimes difficult, contains a wealth of much richer and more provocative examples, as well as a much greater depth of analysis. I can only hope that this brief sampling will pique your curiosity about the kinds of questions raised in Chomsky's new theory. The questions, after all, are much more important than the tentative answers offered at the present stage of development in this new theory, for they are questions that cut right to the heart of Plato's problem. Surely there is no form of human knowledge that poses this problem more clearly or dramatically than does the complexity of human linguistic knowledge. And surely there is presently no approach to human language that offers a better hope of solving Plato's problem—at least where language is concerned—than Chomsky's approach, for it is an approach that fully appreciates the complexity and diversity of human language at the same time it conceives of this complexity and diversity as the global, nonlinear effects of interacting subsystems—subsystems whose foundation is ultimately physical, and whose fundamental laws are relatively few and simple.

Nevertheless, among the many problems Chomsky himself thinks we may simply not be equipped by our own physical nature to solve—ever—is Descartes' problem, that age-old paradox between the human mind's creative freedom, on the one hand, and its rational lawfulness, on the other (e.g., *LangResp*, 66–69; 96–97; *Kyoto*, 5; 35; *Managua*, 138–52). Perhaps Chomsky's assimilation of linguistic mind-study into the physical sciences offers some hope of understanding many aspects of language and mind in terms of human biology; it does not, however, imply that some future understanding of the mind's freedom and creativity in these terms is now necessarily inevitable. Perhaps modern physics—a physics concerned with the unpredictable and yet strangely patterned chaotic effects of self-organizing systems—may now verge on the new conceptions about physical cause and effect that are needed in order for scientists to understand the human brain's remarkable powers of choice and novelty as purely physical processes. But perhaps not. After all, even supposing that free will and human abductive creativity properly belong to biophysics as opposed to metaphysics, why should we necessarily believe that we will ever understand such phenomena? It is a shallow epistemology that supposes everything physical—and nothing metaphysical—is ultimately knowable.

As Chomsky has now clearly reformulated the central problem of what is knowable and of how it is knowable for us, then, it is initially Plato's problem but ultimately Descartes' problem, recast in the light of modern science—the problem of reconciling human free will and creativity with our growing understanding of the human mind as the abstract function of a physical brain. If that old door to the mind can ever be unlocked at all, the key may very well lie hidden right before our eyes, in those ordinary mysteries of human language to which Noam Chomsky has called the world's attention.

Chapter Five

Chomsky's Linguistic and Political Thought: The Underlying Connections

Although Chomsky's contributions to modern linguistics certainly warrant his inclusion in the Twayne series, he has not devoted all of his time and energies to the field. During the last twenty-five years, he has published twenty books and numerous journal articles and essays on various political topics.

When considering Chomsky's prolific political commentary, one of the first questions that arises is what, if any, connection there is between his linguistic and political writings. Various critics have offered thoughts on this matter. Chomsky himself has been outspoken on this issue, for example in *Language and Responsibility,* where he argues that "The social sciences generally, and above all the analysis of contemporary affairs, are quite accessible to anyone who wants to take an interest in these matters" (*LangResp,* 4). He further says that he does not want to claim any connection between politics and linguistics, since he does not want to give in to the mentality that one needs some type of expertise to enter this discussion. Despite the fact that much of his political discussion is flavored with semantic twists, Chomsky argues that there is no reason to assume a specific connection between politics and linguistics. According to Chomsky, any intelligent observer should be able to see the ways dishonest people use language to hide their misdeeds.

Chomsky is certainly right. There is no inherent connection between linguistics and politics, but that does not imply that there are no parallels to be drawn between his work in these two areas. Certain parallels do exist—parallels that likely would exist had Chomsky devoted his life's work to biology or archeology, or any other scientific endeavor. They arise from Chomsky's way of thinking, rather than from the disciplines themselves.

In this chapter I do not propose to give a complete analysis of the various national and international political events that Chomsky has treated. To do so would require much more space than I have here, and is made unnecessary by various existing critiques. Rather, I will offer a brief overview of the political issues that Chomsky has treated and move quickly from this overview to some discussion of connections I see between his ways of thinking about linguistics and politics.

Basic Principles of Chomsky's Political Thought

Let us begin with some basic beliefs that Noam Chomsky brings to his political writings. First, he believes that human beings know the difference between good and evil, and that as a rule they attempt to do that which is good. This basically optimistic view of human nature is tempered by his distrust of the effect that various institutions have upon human action. As noted in chapter one, Chomsky distrusts authority. He chooses to call it a distrust of "arbitrary power and hierarchy and authority," (Interview2), though one wonders exactly what forms of nonarbitrary authority there might be and how Chomsky would react to this authority.

Although it might not be inevitable, depending upon how one understands Chomsky's use of "arbitrary" above, it seems to be the case that Chomsky distrusts all governments. One searches his work in vain for an example of good government. That is not to say that there are no differences among various governments in regard to the evil they do. These differences, however, seem to reflect their differing opportunities more than their basic character as social institutions.

It follows, then, that the U.S. government does not escape criticism from Chomsky. Far from it. As the largest and most powerful nation in the world, the United States is portrayed as the chief villain. When asked why he is so vocal in his criticism of his own country, Chomsky answers that it is his duty as a citizen to be especially critical of his government. If he lived in a communist or a fascist state, he would be especially critical (if given the opportunity) of the evils of that society. As a U.S. citizen, he says, he cannot be silent about the atrocities he contends this government is responsible for.

Chomsky sees U.S. society as deceptively repressive and undemocratic. Given what most of us know, or think we know, about democracy and freedom in the United States, especially in light of the lack of freedom and democracy in many parts of the world, it is necessary to explain how Chomsky can make these claims without entirely losing his credibility. First, Chomsky admits that the United States is a democratic society, but he qualifies, and thereby undercuts, that admission by calling it a "ratified" democracy. He argues that the two major political parties (in conjunction with the so-called free press) completely control the political agenda for the citizens. By the time the people have the opportunity to vote, everything has basically been decided, and the people thus are reduced to ratifying the choices that have been made for them.

Chomsky also admits that American society is free in important ways. That is, individuals are free to come and go as they please, and to say what they please, so long as they do not overstep the bounds guaranteed by freedom of speech. The government does not exercise control over dissidents; it does not have to, he argues. The society that has created this government, and been created by it, will do so. The press is certainly free from direct government intervention, but it is not free, he contends, from the ideological constraints placed on it by the big business interests that run it—and the country. These interests ensure that there is, in the press, the appearance of dissent, but that, in reality, there is no dissent.

As a case in point, Chomsky cites the so-called dissent that arose during the Vietnam war. Hawks and doves clashed over whether the United States should continue to prosecute this war. All discussions of the matter, however, were carried out within the framework laid down by those in charge. The disagreement between hawks and doves concerned only the question of whether U.S. intervention in Vietnam was "working." One could argue that we should not be in Vietnam, so long as one assumed that the U.S. had the right, morally, to intervene in other countries. According to Chomsky, it is not possible to question that assumption.

In fact, he believes it is not possible for U.S. citizens or the press to question the motives of the U.S. government at all. It is quite permissible for critics of U.S. policy to point to cases in which attempts to do good have not turned out as they should; it is also possible to suggest that at times the U.S. government is bungling or clumsy. No one, however, is allowed to question the basic altruistic motives of our government. But Chomsky believes that no such motives exist.

This is not to suggest that an individual could not attempt to question the assumption. Certainly Chomsky did, and still does. Individual members of the press would also be "free" to make the attempt, but they should understand the consequences entailed, for there are consequences. For example, a reporter assigned to political stories might find it more and more difficult to get access to certain politicians, who find his or her point of view "bizarre." That employer will then have to decide whether it wants a reporter who cannot seem to "get along" with politicians and other influential persons well enough to get first-hand stories from them. Or, a journalist may find himself or herself working for a paper that is owned by a corporation with interests in parts of the world that the reporter is suggesting the United States has no business tampering with. Such a reporter may be asked to sell his or her services elsewhere. After all, this is a *free* country, and an employer has a right to say who works for it.

In still another case, a member of the press may be dealt with in an entirely different manner. He or she might be allowed to advocate so-called bizarre points of view to a public that has been conditioned by the major purveyors of information so well that it knows bizarre reporting when it sees it. After he or she is labeled by the public, the journalist may well not be fired but will be relegated to a position reserved for the kooks and misfits in our society.

As he reflects on the powerful way this kind of control works, Chomsky is led to conclude that "if a rational Fascist dictatorship were to exist, then it would choose the American system. State censorship is not necessary, or even very efficient, in comparison to the ideological controls exercised by systems that are more complex and more decentralized" (*LangResp,* 20).

If the U.S. government, with the aid of the press, exercises such control over its citizenry, for what purposes does it do so? Chomsky states categorically that the U.S. government's intentions are evil. His indictment is nowhere harsher than in the preface to a book coauthored with Edward Herman, *The Washington Connection and Third World Fascism:*[1] "The basic fact is that the United States has organized under its sponsorship and protection a neo-colonial system of client states ruled mainly by terror and serving the interests of a small local and foreign business and military elite. The fundamental belief, or ideological pretense, is that the United States is dedicated to furthering the cause of democracy and human rights throughout the world, though it may occasionally err in the pursuit of this objective" (ix).

Elsewhere, Chomsky summarizes all U.S. policy with reference to what he calls the Fifth Freedom. To the Four Freedoms enunciated by

President Franklin D. Roosevelt during World War II—freedom of speech, freedom of worship, freedom from want, and freedom from fear—Chomsky adds a fifth: freedom to rob and exploit.[2] He elaborates in saying that all of Roosevelt's and the United States' fine rhetoric in defense of our four freedoms should be seen for what it is, ". . . a means to gain public support for crusades in defense of the Fifth Freedom, the one that really counts" (*PowerIdeol*, 7).

Vietnam as a Model.   Chomsky began to attract some attention from the U.S. media during the Vietnam conflict. But as I have suggested above, his is not a popular dissent that suggests we have merely veered from our true and right course. Such criticisms could be heard and understood by U.S. citizens. Instead Chomsky calls into question basic U.S. motives and actions, even those actions that led to World War II. In *American Power and the New Mandarins,* he offers a revisionist view of U.S. and Japanese relations before the war. In discussing the events of the 1920s and 1930s, Chomsky argues that the United States was to a large extent forcing Japan's hand. From 1928 on, there was a debate within Japan between the Japanese civilian government and the Kwantung Army as to whether Japan should take over Manchuria, as it ultimately did in 1931. According to Chomsky, it is an open question whether a more conciliatory American diplomacy might have helped the civilian government's anti-imperialistic agenda prevail. Instead, what the United States did—curtailing Japan's world markets and cutting it off from raw materials it badly needed—virtually forced Japan to join the imperialistic game. Just as it did so, however, the United States declared the day of imperialism over, suggesting that Japan keep what it had (not very much) and that the United States, having won its acquisitions "fair and square," during the time when imperialism was permitted, keep its acquisitions. Everyone would hold the cards they came to the table with. When Japan no longer could accept the economic squeeze the United States was administering, Chomsky argues, it attacked Pearl Harbor, not in an attempt to conquer the United States and take over the world, but in hopes that it could force the Americans to allow Japan to exercise more control in its own sphere of the world.[3]

Chomsky is not arguing that the United States was, or is, attempting to rule the world militarily or politically. In pre-World War II interventionist forays (into Cuba and the Philippines, for example), the U.S. goal was to see that the "correct" indigenous forces were in control. And by correct, Chomsky contends, the United States meant those that would allow the native resources to be robbed and plundered by U.S. economic interests. U.S. foreign policy goals remained the same during the Vietnam conflict. Our actions there were consistent with the pursuit of the Fifth Freedom, the freedom to rob and exploit.

Chomsky's comments on U.S. involvement in Vietnam embody his basic criticism of U.S. actions on the world stage. It is worth noting that his criticism begins with the imperialistic tradition brought to America by Europeans. According to Chomsky, Columbus's "discovery" of America "launched, in terms of scale, the major act of genocide in world history," the decimation of the native American population (Interview2). The pattern simply repeated itself in another venue in Vietnam.

Chomsky's explanation of what really happened in Vietnam takes into account the reasons proffered for U.S. involvement there: preventing the spread of Communism. According to Chomsky, this argument was patently false. The so-called rotten apple theory was a strategy first employed by Dean Acheson in the late 1940s to incite the world against the USSR. In reality, the Soviet Union was no threat to do any of the things Acheson alleged (*PowerIdeol,* 32). But the ploy was effective, Chomsky asserts. Acheson's success in using this strategy taught U.S. political leaders an important lesson: "When the U.S. political leadership wants to drum up support for intervention and aggression, it need only shout the Russians are coming" (*PowerIdeol,* 32).

While he did not discount the possibility of a nuclear war between the United States and the USSR—he felt the danger was particularly imminent during the Cuban Missile Crisis (1962)—Chomsky offers us a different way of looking at the Cold War. In a sense it was a tool that both powers used to their advantage: "The actual events of the Cold War illustrate the fact that the Cold War is in effect a 'system of joint global management, a system with a certain functional utility for the superpowers, one reason why it persists.'" (*PowerIdeol,* 41). If the real reason for intervening in Vietnam was not to prevent the spread of Communism, then why did the U.S. spend so much money and so many lives there? Like so many countries before and after it, Vietnam was endangering the Fifth Freedom. Its people had the audacity to think that Vietnam should manage its own resources, that it should create an environment that would not be conducive to business interests in the United States. Thus, it was the U.S. duty to "save" the Southeast Asian country from itself by setting up a puppet government friendly to the United States.

Chomsky has charged repeatedly that the United States "invaded" South Vietnam. (He is often bemused by the inability of the U.S. citizenry to make any meaning of the word *invasion* in this context.) He bases his claim on a straightforward argument. In the first place, the United States signed the Geneva Agreement of 1954, calling for a unified Vietnam and for national elections. But when it became clear to the U.S. government that such elections would be won by the communists, it violated its agreement to abide by the results of free elections. Instead the United States put in place its own dictator, Diem, who lacked the support of the indigenous population and who could be counted on to keep Vietnam open to U.S. business interests.

It is important to understand that Chomsky regards U.S. actions in Vietnam as prototypical. The United States contended that it wished to save the indigenous population from Communism and help keep the world safe for democracy. But in fact, he says, the United States wanted to be sure that no true democracy developed. As defined by U.S. leaders, communists are "those who attempt to use their resources for their own purpose, thus interfering with the right to rob and to exploit, the central doctrine of foreign policy. Naturally, the U.S. is consistently 'anti-Communist,' while only selectively anti-fascist" (*PowerIdeol,* 10).

In fact, Chomsky maintains, its record in world affairs would suggest that the United States, the leader of the free world, has been responsible for placing and keeping in power numerous dictators and fascists, who have themselves been responsible for untold crimes against humanity within the countries they terrorize. Chomsky calls these governments "client states" and "subfascists." They are clients of U.S. business interests, and they are subfascists because they lack the popular support that a real fascist state would enjoy.

In a particularly stinging indictment of these policies, Chomsky charges that the "torturers in the client states [the heads of state] are functionaries of IBM, Citibank, Allis Chalmers and the U.S. Government, . . ." (*WashConn,* X). He asserts that the United States has sponsored such governments in Brazil, Chile, Uruguay, Paraguay, Guatemala, Nicaragua, Indonesia, U.S. occupied South Vietnam up to 1975, and Iran (*WashConn,* 10).

It would take much more space than allotted here to detail Chomsky's charges in regard to each of the aforementioned countries. And the list here is not all inclusive. Other states could be added, among them Puerto Rico, El Salvador, Honduras, Libya, the Philippines, and Cuba. Chomsky's criticism of U.S. intervention in the affairs of other nations extends to our recent dealings with Iraq. Iraqi leader Saddam Hussein is another dictator who enjoyed the support of the U.S. government because he served American policy in the Persian Gulf. Throughout the 1980s his regime was valued by Washington as a counterforce in the region to Iran. Because he was useful, Hussein received U.S. support despite the atrocities he perpetrated in his own country. He made a crucial mistake, however, when he threatened U.S. economic interests by invading neighboring Kuwait in 1990. Chomsky contends that the purpose of Operation Desert Storm, the U.S.–led military response to the Iraqi incursion, was never to bring true democracy to Kuwait, or even to free the Mideast of the terror of Hussein. The U.S. purpose was achieved when it put the repressive pro–U.S. government back in place in Kuwait. Soon after that was accomplished, Hussein returned to terrorizing the defenseless and unimportant (from the standpoint of U.S. economic interests) Kurds and Iraqis who had opposed his dictatorship. The United States had secured its cheap Mideast oil supply—and all was right with the world.

Chomsky's Analysis of U.S. Policy Toward Israel

Chomsky's critique of Israel illustrates his refusal to spare any government condemnation for its purported evils. Few Jewish historians or political scientists of any nationality have been as hard hitting in their criticism of Israel as Chomsky.

Although he is extremely critical of Israeli policies, Chomsky does not see himself as antisemitic, or even anti-Israeli. He argues that "Israel within its internationally recognized borders should be accorded the rights of any state in the international system, no more, no less, and that discriminatory institutional structures that in law and practice assign a special status to one category of citizens (Jews, Whites, Christians, etc.), granting them rights denied to others, should be dismantled."[4] Chomsky is not antisemitic, but he is anti-Zionist. This was not always the case. In his youth, Chomsky considered himself a Zionist, very much interested in the well-being of the Zionist state and in a peaceful co-existence with its Arab neighbors (*Reader*, 7, 11, 14). When the Zionist movement was founded in the late 1800s, its express purpose was the establishment of a Jewish state in Palestine. More recently, however, according to Chomsky, Zionism has come to be "the doctrine that Israel must be accorded rights beyond those of any other state" (*PirEmpers*, 29). This doctrine has led Israel to a "commitment to discriminatory practice . . . so profound that the issue cannot even be addressed in Parliament . . ." (*PirEmpers*, 30). Given what he believes is this shift in the term's meaning, Chomsky is most definitely anti-Zionist.

Chomsky is especially critical of Israel's political dealings with its neighboring states. In case after case, he portrays Israel as so committed to its Zionist view that it can neither admit its own culpability nor accept the compromises necessary for peace. As an example, Chomsky tells the story of an incident between Israel and Lebanese guerrilla fighters. The event "entered historical memory" in an account by Edward Haley, who recounted an attack on Israel by guerrilla soldiers in Lebanon on 6 November, 1977. Since three Israeli soldiers were killed in this incident, the Israeli government responded by attacking Tyre, Lebanon, killing 70 people, most of them Lebanese. But according to Chomsky, that is not the whole story. It seems that two Israeli journalists (employed by the *Jerusalem Post*) happened to discover while touring southern Lebanon that the guerrilla attacks on 6 November, 1977, were in fact responses to an Israeli attack on Nabatiya on 4 and 5 November that killed three women. The 6 November attack with which Haley's report begins was, in fact, a counterattack rather than an unprovoked attack as implied in Haley's telling. If this type of misrepresentation happened only once or twice, it might be seen as natural confusion in describing complicated events. But according to Chomsky this is a consistent pattern of Israeli distortion. As Chomsky puts it, "in properly sanitized history Palestinians carry out terrorism, Israel then retaliates . . ." (*PirEmpers*, 62).

Chomsky goes so far as to call Israel a terrorist state that engages in murder, hijackings, and mistreatment of hostages. And these attacks are "directed against those who are vulnerable, not the perpetrators of atrocities" (*PirEmpers*, 52). Anyone who dares to call Israel accountable for its actions, Chomsky asserts, is labeled antisemitic (*PirEmpers*, 3).

Why is Chomsky so harsh in dealing with Israel? One reason may be Israel's close relationship historically with the United States. As Chomsky sees it, the United States has supported Israel against all other Mideast countries and kept Israel totally dependent upon U.S. backing so that the United States could keep its hand in this all-important oil-rich part of the world. Israel has, thus, become an accomplice to the United States in pursuing its "freedom to exploit" the rest of the world. At one point, Chomsky referred to President Ronald Reagan and Israeli Prime Minister Shimon Peres as "two of the world's leading terrorist commanders . . ." (*PirEmpers, 46*).

Language and Politics: The Underlying Connections

As I mentioned earlier in this chapter, other writers have commented on the connections between Chomsky's linguistic and political thought. Most of these analyses deal with language as somehow central to what it means to be human. Many refer to the influence of Descartes and Humboldt on Chomsky's thought. Chomsky credits a good many others with helping shape his philosophy: "My own personal commitments and hopes are . . . based on the ideas of libertarian socialism, that is, rooted in some of the ideas of Rousseau, Humboldt, Marx, Bakunin, and others, with a crucial concern for the opportunity for meaningful creative work under the control of the worker" (*Managua,* 195). Seizing on the word *creative* and on the fact that Humboldt's theories of language inspired Chomsky's work on linguistic creativity, commentators have forged connections between his linguistic and political work. Language is taken to be emblematic of what it means to be human.

When asked about the connection between his linguistics and his political thought, Chomsky responded that if "there is a connection, it is on a rather abstract level" (*LangResp,* 3). I would argue that the kinds of connections usually offered are not abstract enough, or more precisely, that they are abstract in the wrong directions. Rather than looking at linguistics and politics, we should focus on Chomsky, on his way of thinking.

As noted in chapter one, a salient characteristic of Chomsky's thought is his belief in the concept of "abduction." Chomsky finds this concept in the work of Charles Sanders Peirce, the 19th-century American philosopher who pioneered the study of signs that led to development of the field of semiotics. Peirce is also known as a proponent of Realism, a philosophical approach that postulates the existence of phenomena independent of the mind of the perceiver. (As I shall argue below, Chomsky is also a realist.) Chomsky talked about abduction in one of his interviews with us.

HALEY: I'm really intrigued about your concept of abduction.

CHOMSKY: Abduction? Well, Peirce had this one very stimulating essay, which I don't think he ever pursued further, called—when it was reprinted in the fifties, it was called—"The Logic of Abduction." I don't remember what he called it; I think that was the first time it ever appeared, actually—when the Peirce stuff started coming out in the fifties—but it was about the turn of the century. He began by saying that you can't—he's talking really about theory construction in the sciences, but the same would be true in any kind of learning whatever, and he made that clear—he said that you can't get anywhere by association, you can't get anywhere by induction; induction is not a method of acquiring any knowledge. He said that induction and confirmation, and so on, may be ways of checking out what you've discovered, and clarifying it and filling out the details, and so on, but there's something else going on. And the other thing that's going on is what he called abduction. He didn't tell you much about what it was, which is not so surprising, but he said whatever it is, it's instinctive. He's said it's on a par with a chicken pecking at grain, so there's some instinctive mechanism we have that is a kind of a theory construction module of the brain, to put it in contemporary terms. And that maps—that constructs—theoretical interpretation from scattered data. And we do it instinctively. And then we check it out by induction and methodology of science and all that kind of stuff. And he said if you really want to understand what happens in science—or what happens in ordinary life when people gain a conception of the world—why, you have to understand this instinctive process. And I think that's exactly right. (Interview 1)

As Chomsky indicates, Peirce's abduction is quite different from traditional induction. Induction depends on a mass of observed data, from which the reasoner gradually builds up generalizations. Conversely, Peirce's abduction rapidly constructs theoretical interpretations from only minimal or scattered data; it thus depends much more on the instinctive hunches of the reasoner than on observable fact. Chomsky believes that just as we as native speakers are born with certain structures in the brain that constrain and allow us to learn language, we are born with structures that constrain and allow us to construct theories about how we learn language. These abductive processes are not limited to theory construction about language, however; they extend to all theory construction, even to knowledge about human behavior.

In his interview with us, Chomsky made it clear that this concept of abduction had relevance for the ways humans deal with each other politically.

LUNSFORD: I'm intrigued by that [abduction] and I was wondering if there is any sense in which you feel that there's any kind of abductive process at work in your political thought, just as there is—

CHOMSKY: Sure, and there is in everything you do. I mean, forget political thought. Take something even simpler. How do you place yourself in a social structure? Plainly, you do. You interact with other people in a way which relates to their expectations. Sometimes we make mistakes and get into trouble, but there's a tremendous amount of adaptation in complex social situations, which by and large works. And that must mean that you have in your head, somehow, a theory of society, a theory of personality, and when things go wrong, you notice it and try to adjust. How did that get there? Well, it got there by animal instinct again, by abduction. It is a theory that we don't know much about, but if we could figure out what it was, we would doubtless find that it's extremely refined in comparison with the crude evidence on which it was constructed, that it's pretty much uniform in basic respects across the species because it reflects species characteristics. And in fact that's kind of like language.

And what one calls political thought is just a conscious part of this, dealing with problems that are somewhat remote from direct, immediate experience—problems of power and decision-making and control in the broader social world, beyond those of the world in which you are directly interacting. So everybody has a theory about their school, let's say, and that's a system of power; they have a politics of their school. If you want

HALEY:

CHOMSKY:

to think beyond, you'll also get a politics of your city, or of your government, or of the world, or of your history. But it's not different in essentials; it's just different in the limits to which you push your thinking and reasoning. Maybe you do it somewhat more consciously when you get beyond immediate circumstances, but everyone is doing it all the time, just in order to live in the world.

Is this a Cartesian "common sense morality" with which you approach the facts of the world political situation, or is that something that comes from your early training, your early environment?

I'm not sure exactly what it comes from. It's a little tricky to dig out influences in your early childhood. I can think of things that might have been significant, but I don't think there's anything very profound going on here. I think that political issues and moral issues are rather generally accessible to common sense, Cartesian common sense, if you like. There are cases which are difficult and require thought, undoubtedly, but I don't know of anything that's beyond the scope of ordinary reasoning. I also suspect that moral values are pretty much shared across the species. To the extent that they seem to be different, it's because we're missing the uniformities and only observing the differences, or because you get cases in which society distorts and modifies, in a way which really is counter to fundamental human needs and concerns—that plainly happens. (Interview2)

As I indicated above, Chomsky's thoughts on the role that abduction plays in human reason are tied to his philosophical attachment to Realism. To understand what Realism has to do with his approach to linguistics, one only has to compare some of Chomsky's statements about the science of linguistics with those of a scientific "relativist" such as Thomas Kuhn. In *The Structure of Scientific Revolutions*, Kuhn suggests that historians of science may "have to relinquish the notion, explicit or implicit, that changes of paradigm carry scientists and those who learn from them closer and closer to the truth" (Kuhn, 170). Kuhn elaborates on this point in his Postscript to the 1970 edition: "There is, I think, no theory-independent way to reconstruct phrases like 'really there'; the notion of a match between ontology of a theory and its 'real' counterpart in nature now seems to me illusive in principle" (206).

As a realist, Chomsky has no aversion to talking about what is "really there." Although he concedes that, by definition, scientific theories are underdetermined (*RuleRep,* 15), and although he admits that "no empirical evidence can be conclusive . . ." (*RuleRep,* 190), Chomsky approaches science as a search for the Truth. His language often contains words suggestive of this mindset. In discussing the concept of grammar in *Language and Mind,* for example, he asserts that "The problem of determining the character of such grammars and the principles that govern them is a typical problem of science, perhaps very difficult, but in principle admitting of definite answers that are *right* or *wrong* as they do or do not correspond to the mental *reality*" (*LangMind,* 18; emphasis added). In *Rules and Representations,* he talks about the work of Jiels Kaj Jerne as indicative of the role that "learning" plays in cell immunology. Although it has long been thought that cells learn to be immune, Jerne's works suggest that "An animal cannot be stimulated to make antibodies of this specificity before the antigen arrives. Thus, when an outside agent seems to be teaching cells to make antibodies, it is *really* triggering them to do what they were genetically coded to do" (*RuleRep,* 137; emphasis added).

A third example also comes from *Rules and Representations,* where Chomsky is talking about progress in recent linguistic theory: "I think we may now be at the stage where, for the first time *really,* we can propose systems of universal grammar that at least have the *right* properties" (*RuleRep,* 68; emphasis added). In a more recent statement illustrating his approach to scientific inquiry, Chomsky talks about the concept of a language module: "It is an empirical matter, so of course there is room for doubt, but it seems to me that the facts lead us to the conclusion that the structure of mind is *in fact* modular, which shouldn't be terribly surprising despite the common assumption to the contrary."[5]

This last example brings us to a pivotal issue in Chomsky's linguistic inquiry of the last thirty years: the question of "psychological reality." At the moment he rejected the "discovery procedures" of the Structuralists, Chomsky committed himself to psychological reality. He is not content to deal in analogies, metaphors, or models that may provide insight into (but not necessarily get at the reality of) linguistic competence. Rather, linguistic research must always be getting us closer to understanding the structure of the human brain. He continually makes this claim in language such as the following: "When should we be willing to say that we are presenting psychological hypotheses and describing 'inner psychological mechanisms'? As far as I can see, we should be willing to say at every stage that we are presenting psychological hypotheses and presenting conditions that the 'inner mechanisms' are alleged to meet . . ." (*RuleRep,* 112).

There can be no doubt that Chomsky's Realism also permeates his political thought. Unlike many of the leading philosophers of the twentieth century (Camus, Sartre, Lacan, Derrida, and Kenneth Burke—to name a few whose theories suggest that language helps humans create the worlds in which they live and that values are relative), Chomsky believes in the concepts of "good" and "evil." They are real.

This is not to say that the human mind does not play a role in recognizing good and evil. As explained above, the abductive processes in the human brain allow it to recognize—as opposed to create—these concepts. In talking about humankind's ability to deal with morality, Chomsky argues that moral judgment "is rooted in fundamental human nature. It cannot be merely a matter of convention that we find some things to be right, others wrong. . . . As in the case of language, the environment is far too impoverished and indeterminate to provide this system to the child, in its full richness and applicability. Knowing little about the matter, we are compelled to speculate; but it certainly seems reasonable to speculate that the moral and ethical system acquired by the child owes much to some innate human faculty" (*Managua,* 152, 153).

At first glance, this passage might seem to make Chomsky an adherent of George Berkeley's Idealism. Put simply, Berkeley argued that the entire physical world exists only in the minds that perceive it. In Berkeley's philosophy, ideas themselves have no existence apart from the minds in which they are perceived. There is a sense in which Chomsky's theory of language might seem to lend itself to Idealism, as opposed to Realism. After all, it is Chomsky who introduces "I" language as opposed to "E" language, and in doing so defines language as abstract knowledge in the speaker's mind, rather than as the material utterances of the speakers of a language. However, it is important to realize that Chomsky does not accept the Cartesian duality of mind and body that is necessary if one is to espouse Idealism. When Chomsky talks of mind, he is talking about the material world, as he makes clear in the following passage: "We can, and I think should, continue to use mentalistic terminology, . . . But we do not see ourselves as investigating the properties of some 'second substance,' something crucially distinct from body that interacts with body in some mysterious way, perhaps through divine intervention. Rather, we are studying the properties of the material world at a level of abstraction at which we believe, rightly or wrongly, that a genuine explanatory theory can be constructed, a theory that provides genuine insight into the nature of the phenomena that concern us" (*Managua*, 145).

Taking about what is going on here is complicated (in something of the fashion of an M. C. Escher painting). Let's look into this complexity a little. The phenomena that concern Chomsky here happen to be the workings of the human brain. And Chomsky argues, of course, that the human brain itself may be constructed in a fashion that makes it possible for it to discover things about itself—through abductive processes. But since the investigating tool here (the brain) is material, we are not able to differentiate between mind and matter in the fashion required in Idealism. The structures in the human brain (both the tool and object of investigation) are real.

There is no reason, then, to see Chomsky's political thought as Idealism, even though he does talk about the innate principles in the mind that allow humans to discover moral principles. Just as Berkeley did not deny the reality of the physical world, so long as one granted him that it could not be known without a "mind," Chomsky will not deny the essential role that the mind plays in "knowing," so long as one grants him the material nature of mind. Once this is granted, then moral concepts become real.

Chomsky's stance as a realist accounts for the uncompromising way he presents political judgments such as the following:

What must be obvious to a person with a grain of political intelligence: that the present world problem is not "containing China" but containing the United States. (*AmerPower*, 378)

It turns out, therefore, that if we cut through the propaganda barrage, Washington has become the torture and political murder capital of the world. (*WashConn*, 16)

If the facts [of our involvement in Vietnam] were faced, and international law and elementary morality were operative, thousands of U.S. politicians and military planners would be regarded as candidates for Nuremberg-type trials. (*WashConn*, 30)

Chomsky's political assessments are seldom qualified. He does not say, "if the facts are as they seem, Washington is the torture and murder capital"; or, "seen from one perspective, Washington is the torture and murder capital." In the same way that the human brain is (or is not) structured in a given way—and scientific analysis should help us determine whether it is—political realities are as they are. We can pretend otherwise, but pretending changes nothing.

Before leaving this brief discussion of similarities between Chomsky's linguistic and political thought, it is worth noting one other theme that runs throughout his political commentary and plays a significant role in his thinking about language: his distrust of authority. It is abundantly clear that Chomsky distrusts all authority in the political arena. In talking with us, Chomsky expressed his misgivings about all arbitrary authority (Interview2). It is not clear exactly what would constitute nonarbitrary authority, but I would guess that Chomsky would say that true authority comes from the worth of the cause one is exerting authority in behalf of. That is, the authority that Chomsky might be willing to recognize is "moral" authority. A government's authority to take any action should be equated with the justness of the actions it proposes to take.

Despite his many assaults on governments in general, and the U.S. government in particular, Chomsky does not rule out the possibility that a government should have the authority to take decisive actions, even military actions. In *American Power and the New Mandarins,* Chomsky says that he sees no reason to believe that "kindness will beget kindness" (*AmerPower,* 162), and so he reasons there are times when peaceful settlements may not be possible. In a specific (and recent instance), while Chomsky does not think the U.S. was justified in going to war against Iraq in the winter of 1991, he does believe that there was a moral reason for the world community to take some action against Saddam Hussein's government.[6] To anyone able to analyze the situation correctly, it is obvious that Hussein was (and is) a threat to world peace.

In order to come by their authority naturally, however, Chomsky believes governments must be in the right. They cannot claim authority because they are powerful, because they are duly elected, or because they are ours. If they are right in their actions, they have authority. If not, they do not, or should not. And, as should be clear by now, Chomsky assumes all rational and clear-thinking parties should be able to discern whether they are right.

Authority is also an important concept in the history of linguistic thought. Julie Tetel Andresen provides insight into the role of authority in her review of American linguistics, *Linguistics in America 1779–1924: A Critical History*.[7] Andresen divides linguistic approaches into two types: political and autonomous. She traces the history of American linguistic thought showing that, until the advent of Structuralism, it was basically political. Two of America's most important early philologists, Noah Webster and William Whitney, saw language as the sum total of the society and beliefs of its speakers (*LingAmer*, 33, 154). According to Whitney, "No item of existing language is the work of an individual, for what we may severally choose to say is not language until it be accepted and employed by our fellows. The whole development of speech, though imitated by the acts of individuals, is wrought out by the community."[8] This essentially democratic view of language gave way in the later part of the nineteenth century to pseudophilologists of the ilk of Thomas Sheridan, who saw language as the property of an aristocratic elite.

The opposite to the political approach to language study is autonomous linguists. Rooted firmly in the autonomous linguistic tradition, Chomsky traces his heritage back to the Neogrammarians, and before them, to Wilhelm von Humboldt. Chomsky speaks of Humboldt's contributions in *Cartesian Linguistics*: "In developing the notion of 'forms of language' as a generative principle, fixed and unchanging, determining the scope and providing the means for the unbounded set of individual 'creative' acts that constitute normal language use, Humboldt makes an original and significant contribution to linguistic theory—a contribution that unfortunately remained unrecognized and unexploited until fairly recently" (*Cartesian*, 22).

In the autonomous view of language, then, the "forms of language" are within the brain of the native speaker rather than in some body politic, or social, outside the speaker. Thus, a speaker of the language, and one who studies the native speaker's abilities, need appeal to no authority outside that "natural" authority responsible for the structure of the human brain.

Chomsky would argue that if linguistics is to be a science, such basic principles are unavoidable. For the most part, his predecessors in American language studies would not have agreed. They did not see language study as a science, at least not a natural science. Given his basic way of thinking, Chomsky would not be interested in it if it were not.

Chomsky's Contributions: An Assessment

Chomsky's contribution to linguistic science is, in one sense, very simple: he created it. It is true, of course, that there were those who referred to themselves as linguists before Chomsky. Many people trace the beginnings of the word *linguistics* to the systematic approach of Whitney, others to Sir William Jones; still others to Boas. Each of these men moved the study of language forward to the place at which it could become a science, but it was up to Chomsky to ask the questions that would signal the birth of this new science.

Of course, not everyone agrees that linguistics is a science. Ian Robinson in *The New Grammarians' Funeral* argues shrilly that it is not, that it is really a "sham science" (12). In the tradition of Harvard philosopher Willard V. Quine, Robinson refuses to accept Chomsky's definition of language as the native speaker's competence. As Robinson puts it: "He [Chomsky] wants to locate language in 'competence,' the set of rules that will describe the sentences of the language. I believe on the contrary that language is found (always and only) in use by human beings" (56).

Robinson is certainly correct in saying that linguistics, as he envisions it, is not a science. His viewpoint has much more in common with those of Whitney or Webster than that of Chomsky. Robinson is not the only contemporary linguist who questions the autonomy of linguistics and, thereby, its status as science. After reviewing the history of American linguistic thought, Andresen concludes that "many linguists have already turned away from rationalist and autonomous interpretations of the syntactic regularities of the last thirty years and have returned to the study of language as human behavior in both the cognitive and social settings" (*LingAmer,* 248). In support of her position, Andresen quotes Michael Studdert-Kennedy, who objects to autonomous linguistics in saying:

As soon as we consider how such formally distinct processes might be instantiated in the nervous system, the sharp distinctions begin to blur . . . this does not mean that separable subsystems within language do not exist; it means only that they are not readily isolated in practice. This serves to emphasize that all studies of brain activity in language function will be of dubious value until we can increase our knowledge of neural circuitry. . . . Systems are conceptually recalcitrant because, by definition, they consist of parts that are both separable and connected. In other words, full autonomy of language, or its subsystems, is neurologically implausible. (*The Psychobiology of Language,* 224)

The principal objection raised above (and encapsulated in the passage by Studdert-Kennedy) represents a crucial misunderstanding of what Chomsky means by psychological reality. When Chomsky argues that, as a scientist, the linguist is making predictions about the human brain, he is not saying that the linguist is describing the actual wiring of the human brain. In postulating that the linguistic module of the human brain contains certain semantic concepts, or certain principles of government and binding, he does not assume that he has said anything specific about the actual way in which this information is "wired in."

In fact, it might be argued that the linguist's assertion that there is something like a linguistic module does not imply that the mechanisms that carry out the functions of this "system" are wired separately from other systems in the brain.[9] This would be like saying that the various components in a modern information system are all discrete. They are not, since all come in over telephone wires. However, there are discrete components, such as voice transmission, facsimile operations, even cable television reception, all intertwined in this one mechanism. To say that they are not mechanistically separate is not to say that there is no such thing as a cable component (as separate from a telephone component) in this configuration.

Once we cut through such misunderstandings as this one, we can ask a relatively straightforward question that makes clear Chomsky's contribution to linguistics. Is the study of language the study of human behavior in the context of various sociological and political forces within various cultures? Or is it an investigation of part of the natural world?

Chomsky's great contribution is to see linguistics as the scientific study of a natural phenomenon: that part of the human brain involved in human language. He could not be content with earlier definitions of the discipline that labeled linguistics a branch of the moral sciences[10] or as a political or social science. In the final analysis, and even though he tried for some time, he could not be content with structuralist discovery procedures and the inductive method they implied. Victoria Fromkin captures Chomsky's contributions to modern linguistics in saying that "because of him, 'it [linguistics] passed beyond the stage of stamp collecting' and has become a theoretical science" ("Language and Brain" *The Chomskyan Turn,* 99).

Chomsky's effect on political thought of our time is not so dramatic. There is a sense in which his critique of political events suffers from the characteristic that proves so valuable to his linguistic work: his unfailing idealism. As Fromkin noted, Chomsky, the linguist, is not content with cataloguing data. Rather, he must bring the scientific method to bear on that data, which entails abstracting away from the miscues and false starts in language (performance) and studying language competence in the ideal (competence). Translated to the political arena, this same idealism tends to make him uninterested in the pragmatic concerns that may, in part, account for the actions of human institutions. He seems to expect human institutions to run by the same logic that governs the working of natural science. Jay Parini notes this characteristic in saying that "Chomsky's great strength is that he places so much faith in the persuasiveness of intricately constructed reason. It is his vulnerability as well" ("Noam is an Island" *Mother Jones,* 38).

Chomsky's political thought can be questioned from various perspectives. Ironically, one of Chomsky's own tactics can be turned on him with rather damaging results to his position. In his linguistic analyses, he continually challenges those who object to his "mentalistic" approach (e.g., Quine) to come up with a model of their own that will account for the data. Those world leaders whom Chomsky is so critical of might ask him to do the same. That is, if communism, fascism, and capitalism are such terrible forms of government, what exactly would he recommend? It is never clear. His language in response to this question resembles the language of scientific behaviorists, who talk in general terms about a system for learning, but never describe that system in any way that would make it vulnerable to scientific investigation. When Chomsky tells us that he favors a libertarian government that does not take for itself arbitrary authority and that respects the individual freedoms and creativity of its citizens, we can nod approvingly, but we cannot "imagine" this government. It is not clear that Chomsky has a vision for what this government would look like.

Chomsky may be even more vulnerable in a second respect. As I noted at the beginning of this chapter, he operates on an assumption that individual human beings know the difference between good and bad and that they attempt to do good where possible. He offers no support for these assumptions. His tactic here may be compared with his reliance on intuition in his linguistic theory. As we have noted in earlier chapters, one of Chomsky's greatest contributions to linguistics is to remove the empiricist limitations of the structuralists. As a native speaker, Chomsky felt that his intuitions about grammaticality were perfectly good data for research. Although linguistic research has developed in many different ways, some of them inimical to Chomsky's thought, there can be no doubt that Chomsky's redefinition of data has changed linguistics forever.

His tacit appeal to intuition in sociopolitical thought has had much less impact. Many people question Chomsky's assumption that humans have an inborn knowledge (or faculty for finding knowledge) about right and wrong. Still more, I would imagine, find it hard to believe that given the choice between doing right and wrong, humans will do the right thing. Chomsky is correct, I suspect, in assuming that this is not a case that lends itself to any kind of empirical investigation. For every famous televangelist who bilks an innocent widow of her life's savings, we can find an example of a widow who is willing to give her money to help feed and save the poor. So whom do we fix our attention on: the sleazy evangelist or the generous widow?

As one reads Chomsky, one gets the feeling that he is always fixing his gaze on the widow. But that may not be the case. He may see the evangelist, but believe that he has gotten caught up in the web of a human institution that has taken arbitrary authority. Having been trapped in this institution, the evangelist has begun to act in the customary way for humans to act in such institutions. This line of thought would make Chomsky sound much more like a behaviorist than he (or I) would like.

A more plausible answer is to say that Chomsky does here exactly what he does in his linguistic analyses: he looks inside. And what he finds is a basic intention to do good, an intention he generalizes to the human race—in individual cases, of course. Who is to say whether he is right or wrong? We can only say that the institutions that these individuals comprise do much evil, as Chomsky continually points out.

In critiquing Chomsky's political analyses, it is tempting to charge him with not being able to make distinctions among various levels of evil. Most Americans, I suspect, would be willing to admit that their government does some harm—perhaps in taxing its citizens more than necessary, in not providing as well as it might for the underclass, and so forth. However, when they compare the evils of the American government with the atrocities perpetrated by communism and various fascist states, they find the United States to be comparatively benign— or, at least, less evil. Chomsky's analysis of U.S. actions, domestically and internationally, rips this safe ground from under those who would support the government. He does so when he talks about the CIA-sponsored terrorism of members of the Black Panthers in Chicago

(*LangResp*, 20). He does so when he refers to the United States as the state that has "sponsored and supported the Somoza family, the Shah, Marcos, Park, Pinochet, Suharto, Mobutu, the Brazilian generals, and their many confederates in repression and violence, . . ." (*WashConn*, 42). These and many other such charges, ranging from genocide of Native Americans to collusion with Saddam Hussein, suggest that Chomsky is some sort of madman—or that the United States is no better than the worst terrorist governments it stands so self-righteously against in its public rhetoric.

Although Chomsky continually asserts an affinity with the average person, I do not think he can make such a claim. In fact, I would argue that the average person listening to his political views for very long will be more willing to believe that Chomsky is a madman than to believe that the United States government is morally no better than the communist government of the former Soviet Union. Chomsky's attempt to reduce the workings of nations to reasonable equations just does not take into account how much of our lives, political and otherwise, are not controlled by, or evaluated by, reason.

We found one exchange in our second interview with Chomsky particularly telling on this point. Michael Haley had asked Chomsky to talk about his feelings regarding competition, and in doing so, Chomsky made some comments on loyalties in sports. This passage caused Haley to probe further regarding an individual's ability to delude himself/herself about certain matters.

CHOMSKY: Oh, I don't think competition is a good thing anyway. Take sports, which doesn't lead to much in the way of hierarchy and domination—some, but not much. But I think especially professional sports brings out just the worst instincts in people. I mean it brings out gladiatorial instincts. First of all, it enhances blind and foolish loyalty. Why should you be loyal to your home team? What do you know about those guys? Do I ever meet anybody out of the [New England] Patriots? I remember when I was in high school, and I was all excited, passionate, about the high school football team. And I remember asking myself, Why do I care? I couldn't say one word to any of these guys. And I don't want to sit at the same table with them, and they don't want to sit at the same table with me, and they're no different than the guys at the other school, and what do I care whether they win a game or they lose a game? All that this does is enhance blind and foolish loyalties, which is extremely dangerous, because that carries over into chauvinism for the state and others; it's extremely dangerous. And in things like, say, professional football and professional boxing, it's really horrifying. It's like gladiatorial contests. You know, you're watching people kill each other—and cheering. So that kind of stuff is extremely dangerous.

HALEY: You just raised a point there that reminds me of another question. Some studies in clinical psychology have indicated that a certain amount of self-deception is necessary for a person to function. Those who suffer continual or enervating depression are sometimes the most uncompromisingly realistic. Is a certain amount of self-sanitizing also necessary for a healthy national ethos? For instance, is it healthy and natural for a nation, perhaps even necessary to a nation's survival, for it to mythologize its own history and behavior to a certain extent? Where do we draw the line between a healthy national ethos and "manufactured consent"?

CHOMSKY: Well, I would think it's worth raising the prior question, too, about individuals. I mean it's certainly true, and I think we all know it, that a certain amount of self-deception is helpful for getting around in the world, but that doesn't mean it's *healthy*. Maybe it's better to face reality. I think it probably is. If you face reality, you're going to find a lot to be depressed about. But the question is whether it's better to be honestly depressed or falsely euphoric. I don't know what the clinical psychologists you're talking about are saying, but if people would ask me for advice, I'd say be honestly depressed. Face reality and try to deal with it. And come to terms with it, and recognize that there are things that are not the way you want them, rather than pretending that they're not there. I think you're probably better off that way. So I don't even accept the prior assumption about people.

As far as nations are concerned, it's even worse. A national ethos is not something that's of very much value. Here we're back to the original question about patriotism. When you talk about the national ethos, which of those two nations are you talking about—the state that we're supposed to serve, or the people who we're supposed to be for? Now if you're talking about the people, most of them suffered under the nation. The slaves suffered, the poor immigrants suffered, the work force suffered. There's a tremendous amount of suffering in our national ethos. That's how the industrial system got built up. So when you care about our history, who are you caring for? The people who were working in the sweat shops? Well if you are, you aren't going to create any illusions about our great magnificence. Or do you care about the roughly ten million Native Americans who lived here before the European colonists took it away from them? Why not? Of course, they're not around anymore—they're all dead. But that's part of the national ethos. Do you care about what was really going on, let's say, in New England in the 17th century when Cotton Mather was talking about how we should "cleanse the forest of this pernicious growth" by wiping out the native peoples who are "infesting" it and getting in our way? I think we should care about that; I think we should recognize what the national ethos was: It was destruction of the native population, destruction of the environment, blind pursuit of gain, exploitation, rapaciousness, and so on. Those things are in fact a very substantial part of the national ethos. And if you ask me if it is healthy to recognize that, I'd say that it is *extremely* healthy to recognize it—healthy for ourselves, to try to compensate for much of what is done, and healthy for potential victims.

This sense of American innocence has cost millions and millions of people their lives. They're the ones who have to suffer that burden of our innocence. So we should divest ourselves of it and face reality—face reality about what the nation was and what the state was and who suffered internally and externally and who benefited internally and externally. (Interview2)

When I listen to Chomsky talk about false loyalties to sports teams, it is impossible to disagree with the logic of his argument. Why should it matter to me that the Atlanta Braves finally rose from the cellar to be National League Champions last year? It is thoroughly illogical for me to care one way or the other. But I seem to be unable not to, for a host of emotional reasons.

I do not mean, here, to be arguing that Chomsky is wrong. Quite the contrary. It seems that he is absolutely right—in theory. However, it seems just as obvious that humans, even intellectual humans—or as Chomsky would have it, most especially intellectual humans—do not rule their lives by reason.

When we say this, we should differentiate between two different areas in which we fail to use our reason. The first has to do with matters that can be argued, but that do not seem to lend themselves to resolution by reason, questions such as abortion, capital punishment and so forth. Human beings decide these issues on an emotional basis— and then construct rational arguments in support of their positions. Of course, their arguments are enthymemic: Abortion should be illegal because humans do not have the right to commit murder. Although the framers of such arguments may offer proof that abortion is murder, they cannot hope to convince their opponents of the validity of this proof.

But there are other arenas in which we do not, or cannot, even rationalize our positions. If we are forced to admit that we have taken a position in these matters, we are forced to admit our failure to live up to certain "ideal" principles. In such a situation, we may try some far-reaching rationalization, but we are not even fooling ourselves in these situations. A particularly troublesome example comes to mind from my own experience. As a chair of a rather large department of English, I was recently face to face with a part-time teacher who wanted to argue the merits of the way the university was treating part-time employees—the heavy workloads given them, the low pay, the lack of medical coverage. I was forced to admit, at the outset, that I could offer no rationalization for the treatment of part-time faculty. It is patently unfair. Yet I knew the condition existed when I became chair. And I knew that while I might have the opportunity to make some things slightly better for part-time teachers, I would not, as a member of this system, be in a position to right this wrong. The legislators (and the taxpayers) of this state are wrong—and I am wrong in aiding and abetting the abusive system we work in. I might argue that my refusal to participate in this system would not change it. However, I know that if all tenured faculty members in the system wanted badly enough to change it, there might be a chance to effect some change.

This is but one of a hundred moral dilemmas that each of us in a society such as that of the United States could put ourselves in on a daily basis if we chose to do so. Most of us give a token, from our affluence, to some charitable organization such as a church, the United Way, or the Salvation Army. But it is just a token. Knowing, as we do, that there are people in our own city, let alone in the world community, who do not have enough to eat, how do we justify using the extra funds we have for a new boat, a sports car, or a trip to Europe? The answer, of course, is that we do not. We do not want to subject such matters to reason because they do not lend themselves to rationalizations. If we are forced to face the fact that we are not living up to our principles, we are made uncomfortable. But we do not change our behavior.

At this point in his life, it would seem to be obvious to Chomsky that his political commentary seems to be much madness to most people.[11] One might think that this realization would embitter Chomsky. Indeed there is an edge to his writings that reminds one of the later writings of Mark Twain.

It is worth citing a few examples for those who have read only Chomsky's linguistic works and think his prose laborious. In noting that some people say that the U.S. policy of defoliation in Vietnam did some good, that it made it easier to get at timber, Chomsky quipped: "By the same logic, we must praise Hitler for his contributions to city planning in Rotterdam."[12] In talking about the famous Fifth Freedom, Chomsky notes that "In the perception of U.S. planners, which is not inaccurate, the world is peopled with enemies of the Fifth Freedom, who seek to impede the free exercise of our fundamental right to rob and to exploit" (*PowerIdeol*, 7). A couple of pages later he adds that "The major enemy, however, is always the indigenous population, which has the unfortunate tendency to succumb to strange and unacceptable ideas about using their resources for their own purposes" (*PowerIdeol* 9).

In these and many other passages like them, Chomsky's irony is reminiscent of the irony Twain uses in "To the Person Sitting in Darkness." Although their commentaries are separated by almost one hundred years, the situations they address do not seem to be much changed. There is this powerful and, supposedly, civilized nation that many underdeveloped, uncivilized nations are depending upon to bring civilization to them. But what the underdeveloped countries find is that when the United States decides to play the role of the barbarian, as it often does, the backward countries cannot hold a candle to the civilized country for evil.[13]

One other example should help make it clear to any reader of Twain just how much similarity there is between Twain's style and Chomsky's. One of the most telling marks of Twain's style is the aside, in which he explains, in the person of a huckster using language to hide the truth, differences in appearances and realities. Another salient characteristic is his tendency to make his villains so stupid as to be more laughable than frightening. We see both of these devices used expertly in the following passage, in which Chomsky is lampooning Hans Morganthau, a noted academic authority on U.S. foreign policy:

> . . . and to his credit [Morganthau] noticed this difference [between what the U.S. says and what it does]. . . . The United States, he said, has a transcendent purpose to pursue and bring about justice and freedom and all good things, but remember he's a realist, which means he pays attention to the historical record, and he observed that the historical record deviates rather sharply from this picture . . . and he then goes on to say that if we look at the difference between the American transcendent purpose, justice, freedom and so on, on the one hand, and the historical record on the other, that might lead us to question whether, in fact, the United States is pursuing the transcendent purpose of achieving peace and justice and freedom. But he points out that to draw that conclusion would be a logical error. Now here you've got to think carefully so follow the reasoning closely. The reason why it could be a logical error is this, we have to distinguish, he says, between reality and the abuse of reality. Reality is the actual history as it's interpreted through our perceptions and our self-image, that is, reality is what we prefer to see and what we would like to believe. Abuse of reality is the actual history. [laughter] As I said it's a fairly subtle point so you want to make sure you master it. [14]

Chomsky is incensed not only because Morganthau is putting forth a fallacious view of U.S. actions, but also because he is doing so in the name of "reality." As a realist, Chomsky knows what is going on and it is his duty to get that message across, even though doing so will damage the self-image of U.S. citizens.

When asked if he is conscious of the similarities between his and Twain's ironic styles, Chomsky made the following remarks:

> CHOMSKY: I think I've always been inclined to people who are unwilling to accept conventional pieties. Usually they're driven out of the society; in fact, that goes right back to the Bible.
>
> HALEY: Jeremiah?
>
> CHOMSKY: Yeah. I mean, the people WE honor are the people who were practically killed; the people THEY honored at the

time are the ones we call the false prophets. That's the
way it is. If anybody tells the truth, they're going to be
hated. (Interview2)

I mentioned above that Chomsky is aware that his political commentary is often thought to be madness. His comments above suggest
that he would expect this reception. To the extent that he sees himself
as a true prophet, he would seem to be predicting that he cannot be
heard. One question that arises in looking at Chomsky's comments
above is whether he is talking about human nature at this stage of its
evolution or whether he sees human nature as inherently flawed in ways
that make it impossible for true prophets to be heard. Chomsky never
answers this question for us. Chomsky's place in the history of ideas
very much depends on the answer history provides to this question.

Notes and References

Chapter One

1. G. A. Miller, "A Very Personal History," Talk to Cognitive Science Workshop, MIT, Cambridge, Mass., 1 June 1979, as cited in Howard Gardner, *The Mind's New Science: A History of the Cognitive Revolution* (New York: Basic Books, 1985), 28; Gardner's book supplies excellent background and analysis of this whole period; hereafter cited in text. See also G. A. Miller, *Language and Communication* (New York: McGraw-Hill, 1951) for more on the intellectual atmosphere of the "cognitive revolution."

2. Noam Chomsky, "Three Models for the Description of Language," *IRE Transactions on Information Theory* IT-2.3 (September 1956):113–24; reprinted in *Readings in Mathematical Psychology*, edited by R. D. Luce, R. Bush, and E. Galanter, vol. II (New York: John Wiley & Sons, 1965), 105–24; hereafter cited in text as "Three Models." Chomsky's own view of the cognitive revolution, incidentally, is that it should be understood as having independently replicated certain historical insights, going in fact all the way back to the Cartesians, as he says in *Generative Grammar: Its Basis, Development and Prospects,* Studies in English Linguistics and Literature, Special Issue (Kyoto, Japan: Kyoto University of Foreign Studies, 1987), 8; hereafter cited in text as *Kyoto.*

3. A preliminary definition: A "generative" grammar is an explicit, formal model that actually "generates" linguistic structures (sequences of sounds, words, or phrases); a grammar that is (additionally) "transformational" is one that contains formal devices for "transforming" already-generated structures into different structures. See chapter two for a more thorough definition and discussion of these concepts.

4. It should be noted that Chomsky himself thinks all this talk about a so-called revolution in linguistics—and most especially a "Chomskyan revolution"—is considerably overblown, at least in comparison to those true and rare conceptual revolutions in the natural sciences. The main difference, however, seems to be his feeling that the approach he has proposed (which I will continue to call revolutionary, with apologies to Chomsky) still represents a minority view, rather than a new (postrevolutionary) norm in linguistic science. See *Noam Chomsky on the Generative Enterprise, a Discussion with Riny Huybregts and Henk van Riemsdijk,* (Dordrecht, Neth.: Foris Publications, 1982), 40–43; hereafter cited in text as *GenPrize.* For an insightful comparison of the Chomskyan revolution in linguistics to the Einsteinian revolution in physics, see Justin Leiber, *Noam Chomsky: A Philosophic Overview* (New York: St. Martin's Press, 1975), 19–23, 69, 107; hereafter cited in text.

5. Noam Chomsky, interview with Ronald Lunsford and Michael Haley at MIT on 1 December 1989, unpublished; hereafter cited in text as "Interview1."

6. C. F. Hockett, *A Manual of Phonology—Memoir 11, Indiana University Publications in Anthropology and Linguistics* (Baltimore, 1955). A Markov finite-state machine is a formal device that, when applied to language, might produce a sentence in linear fashion from left to right, with the choice of each new element (sound or word) being governed by the identity of the immediately preceding element.

7. William Chomsky's work included a book entitled *David Kimhi's Hebrew Grammar* (New York: Bloch, 1952).

8. Noam Chomsky, *The Chomsky Reader,* edited by James Peck (New York: Pantheon Books, 1987), 5–6; hereafter cited in text as *Reader.*

9. Noam Chomsky, interview with Ronald Lunsford and Michael Haley at MIT on 4 December 1989, unpublished; hereafter cited in text as "Interview2."

10. Zellig Harris, *Methods in Structural Linguistics* (Chicago: University of Chicago Press, 1951); hereafter cited in text as *Methods.*

11. For a more complete explanation of the relation between synchronic and diachronic principles in Chomsky's thought, see Noam Chomsky, *The Logical Structure of Linguistic Theory* (New York: Plenum Press, 1975), 25–26; hereafter cited in text as *LSLT.*

12. Noam Chomsky, *Morphophonemics of Modern Hebrew,* Outstanding Dissertations in Linguistics, J. Hankamer, ed. (New York and London: Garland Publishing, 1979).

13. Most notably, Morris Halle and Noam Chomsky, *Sound Pattern of English* (New York: Harper and Row, 1968).

14. In our first interview, Chomsky told us that he first became aware of Peirce's "abduction" in the 1960s, when a biologist friend, noticing the similarity between Chomsky's notion of discovery and Peirce's, called his attention to an essay on the logic of abduction in *Peirce's Essays in the Philosophy of Science,* ed. by Vincent Tomas (New York: Liberal Arts Press, 1957).

15. Noam Chomsky, *Language and Mind,* enlarged edition (New York: Harcourt Brace Jovanovich, 1972), 93; hereafter cited in text as *LangMind.*

16. For more (including important provisos) on this analogy between language acquisition and scientific theory construction see Noam Chomsky, *Language and Problems of Knowledge: The Managua Lectures* (Cambridge, Mass.: MIT Press, 1988), 157; hereafter cited in text as *Managua.* See also *LangMind,* 90, 171; *LSLT,* 11; and Noam Chomsky, *Language and Responsibility* (New York: Pantheon, 1979), 69–70, 75; hereafter cited in text as *LangResp.* In his *Rules and Representations* (New York: Columbia University Press, 1980), 250–54, hereafter cited in text as *RuleRep,* Chomsky provides what may be his most provocative exploration of this analogy, extending it even into the do-

main of theory construction in the arts; however, elsewhere in this same work he also discusses appropriate cautions about the analogy (136–40).

17. Dean Elton Cook, *Chomsky: Towards a Rationalist Philosophy of Science,* (Ph. D. dissertation, University of Missouri, Columbia, 1981), 205.

18. Noam Chomsky, "Systems of Syntactic Analysis," *Journal of Symbolic Logic* 18.3 (September 1953): 242–56.

19. Noam Chomsky, *Knowledge of Language: Its Nature, Origin, and Use,* Convergence: A Series Founded, Planned and Edited by Ruth Nanda Anshen (New York: Praeger, 1986), 49, note 17; hereafter cited in text as *KnowLang.*

20. Noam Chomsky, *Syntactic Structures* (The Hague: Mouton, 1957); all citations are from the book's sixth printing (The Hague and Paris: Mouton, 1966) and are hereafter given in text as *SS.*

21. Robert Lees, "Review of Noam Chomsky's *Syntactic Structures,*" *Language* 33.3 (1957): 375–407.

Chapter Two

1. Noam Chomsky, *Aspects of the Theory of Syntax* (Cambridge, Mass.: MIT Press, 1965); all citations are from the book's fifteenth printing (1988); hereafter given in text as *Aspects.*

2. Noam Chomsky et al., *Language and Learning: The Debate between Jean Piaget and Noam Chomsky,* edited by Massimo Piattelli-Palmarini (Cambridge, Mass.: Harvard University Press, 1980), 73–75; hereafter cited in text as *Debate.*

3. Fractals are shapes in nature (e.g., snowflakes) or geometric designs (e.g., a Mandelbrot set) that exhibit "self-similarity" at all different scales or levels of magnification. See Benoit Mandelbrot, *The Fractal Geometry of Nature* (New York: Freeman, 1977) or James Gleick, *Chaos* (New York: Penguin Books, 1987); hereafter cited in text. Chaos theory, in which fractals figure prominently, seems to have an interesting connection to Chomsky's thought, by the way; it is intriguing that he cited some of Mandelbrot's earlier work on language in *Syntactic Structures* (*SS,* 17, 116). For some interesting remarks Chomsky made about the possible relevance of fractals to the evolution of the language faculty itself, see *GenPrize* 23.

4. Wilhelm von Humboldt (1767–1835) was a German linguist and diplomat to whom Chomsky often alludes, particularly for his early generative concept of language as a system that makes "infinite use of finite means." It is interesting that Chomsky admired Humboldt for his libertarian social theory, as well (e.g., see *Managua,* 154–55, 195). For a more thorough discussion of Humboldt's linguistic theory and its relevance to Chomsky's, see Noam Chomsky, *Current Issues in Linguistic Theory* (The Hague: Mouton, 1964).

5. Noam Chomsky, interview with Ronald Lunsford and Michael Haley at MIT on 7 December 1989, unpublished; hereafter cited in text as "Interview3."

6. The classic text is Claude E. Shannon and Warren Weaver, *The Mathematical Theory of Communication* (Urbana: University of Illinois Press, 1963); in *Syntactic Structures*, Chomsky cites the 1949 edition of this work (*SS*, 19). See Gleick, 255–62, for a brief but lucid discussion of information theory.

7. John Lyons, *Noam Chomsky* (New York: The Viking Press, 1970), 7; hereafter cited in text.

8. For example, Noam Chomsky and M. P. Schützenberger, "The Algebraic Theory of Context-Free Languages," in P. Braffort and D. Hirschberg, eds., *Computer Programming and Formal Systems: Studies in Logic* (Amsterdam: North Holland, 1963); see also Noam Chomsky, "Formal Properties of Grammar," and George Miller with Noam Chomsky, "Finitary Models of Language Users," both in R. D. Luce, R. Bush, and E. Galanter, eds., *Handbook of Mathematical Psychology*, vol. II (New York: John Wiley & Sons, 1963). See Lyons, 69–70, for a general assessment of Chomsky's work in this area.

9. Noam Chomsky, *Reflections on Language* (New York: Pantheon, 1975), 133; hereafter cited in text as *Reflections*.

10. Noam Chomsky, *Language in a Psychological Setting*, Sophia Linguistica, Working Papers in Linguistics, Number 22 (Tokyo: Sophia University, 1987), 16–17; hereafter cited in text as *Sophia*; see also *GenPrize*, 20–23.

11. Note that we do not necessarily mean "time" by "tense"; in Chomsky's use of the term, "past tense" merely refers to the form of the verb or auxiliary verb—the way it is spelled—when a past-tense suffix is added to it. The past-tense suffix is usually-ED; when it is added to *will*, for instance, we get *woul*D. But *would*, while it is past-tense in form, might be used in a sentence referring to the future, as in "Would you call me tomorrow?" Verb tense is indeed one device by which languages can indicate time, but there is no one-to-one correspondence between tense and time. Present tense, for instance, is often used to indicate present time, but not always; in "The train leaves at six tonight," the verb is in the present tense form (with the present-tense suffix -s), even though the sentence refers to future time.

12. We are assuming, here, the "ideal" of a homogenous speech community in which the (arbitrary) standard past-tense form of *take* is *took*; thus *took* = *take* + *past* at the abstract level at which Chomsky's Aux rule operates, even though its ultimate form is not **take*D (except, interestingly enough, in the dialect of some children at a certain stage of language acquisition—and perhaps Chomsky's rule explains why). Thus the irregular forms of some verbs should be no cause for concern at this level; Chomsky has another level in his grammar, the "morphophonemic" level, to handle these considerations (*SS*, 32–33). In some perfectly legitimate dialects, for instance, *take* + *past* may = *taken* or just *take*, much as in standard English *hit* + *past* = just *hit*.

13. Robert A. Hall, Jr., in a letter to the editor (under the heading "Language") in the Book Review section of the *New York Times,* 22 April 1979.

14. B. F. Skinner, *Verbal Behavior* (New York: Appleton-Century-Crofts, 1957).

15. The review first appeared in *Language* 35 (1959): 26–58; it is reprinted in *The Structure of Language: Readings in the Philosophy of Language,* edited by J. A. Fodor and J. J. Katz (Englewood Cliffs, N.J.: Prentice-Hall, 1964).

16. See, for example, Noam Chomsky, *Cartesian Linguistics: A Chapter in the History of Rationalist Thought* (New York: Harper and Row, 1966); hereafter cited in text as *Cartesian.*

17. Stephen Weinberg, "The Forces of Nature," *Bulletin of the American Academy of Arts and Sciences* 29.4 (January 1976): 28–29.

Chapter Three

1. Chomsky published some of this new work on a generative phonology of English in "The Morphophonemics of English" with Morris Halle, MIT *RLE Quarterly Progress Report* 68 (1960): 275–81, and presented some of his findings in a paper at the 1959 Fourth Texas Conference on Problems of Linguistic Analysis in English, to which he was invited back after his stormy appearance at the Third Texas Conference in 1958. The 1959 paper on the generative phonology of English was never published, but Chomsky continued this important line of work for several years; later he and Morris Halle published "Some Controversial Questions in Phonological Theory," *Journal of Linguistics* 1.2 (1965): 97–138, and ultimately their masterpiece in this area— *The Sound Pattern of English* (New York: Harper and Row, 1968). Chomsky made a conscious decision during the 1960s, however, to abandon further work on phonology to make time for his growing commitment to political activism (*GenPrize,* 57); in fact, he went on to say that his work in phonology was "one of the very minor casualties of the Vietnam war" (*GenPrize,* 98).

2. Noam Chomsky, "A Transformational Approach to Syntax," *Proceedings of the Third Texas Conference on Problems of Linguistic Analysis in English* (May 9–12, 1958), ed. by A. A. Hill (Austin: University of Texas Press, 1962), 124–58; reprinted in *The Structure of Language: Readings in the Philosophy of Language,* ed. by J. A. Fodor and J. Katz (Englewood Cliffs, NJ: Prentice Hall, 1964), 211–45, as well as in *Classics in Linguistics,* ed. by Donald E. Hayden, E. Paul Alworth, and Gary Tate (New York: Philosophical Library, 1967), 337–71.

3. In 1966, for instance, Chomsky was named Ferrari P. Ward Professor of Modern Languages and Linguistics at MIT, and in 1976 he was appointed Institute Professor.

4. Noam Chomsky, *Current Issues in Linguistic Theory* (The Hague: Mouton, 1964); a slightly earlier version appears in Fodor and Katz (1964,

cited above), and the original version was published under the session title, "The Logical Basis of Linguistic Theory," in *Proceedings of the Ninth International Congress of Linguists,* ed. by H. Lunt (The Hague: Mouton, 1964), 914–78.

5. In addition to the D.H.L., University of Chicago (1967), and the D.Litt., University of London (1967), a partial list of Chomsky's other honorary doctorates include the following: D.H.L., Loyola University of Chicago (1970); D.H.L., Swarthmore College (1970); D.H.L., Bard College (1971); D.Litt., Delhi University of India (1972); D.H.L., University of Massachusetts (1973); D.Litt., Visva-Bharati University, Santiniketan, West Bengal (1980); and D.H.L., University of Pennsylvania (1984)—his alma mater. We stopped counting after this.

6. Noam Chomsky, *Topics in the Theory of Generative Grammar* (The Hague: Mouton, 1966).

7. See P. Grice, "Logic and Conversation," in *Syntax and Semantics,* P. Cole and J. L. Morgan, eds. (New York: Academic Press, 1975), 41–58; Chomsky also cites L. Wittgenstein, *Philosophical Investigations* (London: Blackwell, 1953); J. Austin, *How to Do Things with Words* (Oxford: Oxford University Press, 1962); and J. Searle, *Speech Acts* (London: Cambridge University Press, 1969).

8. David Hume, *An Enquiry Concerning Human Understanding* (1748), Section IX, in *The Empiricists* (New York: Dolphin Books, [nd]), 386.

9. G. W. Leibniz, *New Essays Concerning Human Understanding,* translated by A. G. Langley (LaSalle, Ill.: Open Court, 1949), 45–46.

10. See V. J. Cook, *Chomsky's Universal Grammar* (Oxford: Basil Blackwell, 1988), 167–69, for discussion; hereafter cited in text.

11. In the interest of absolute accuracy, it should be noted that the *Aspects* model actually provides for slightly different deep structures for these two sentences. Specifically, the "passive" version ("I expected John to be examined by a specialist") would have the "dummy element" (BY PASSIVE) in the embedded clause at deep structure, like this:

I expected [a specialist to examine John—BY PASSIVE]

It is this (BY PASSIVE) marker that triggers the passive transformation, which means that the passive construction is not a stylistic option in the *Aspects* model, as it was in the model of *Syntactic Structures.* The implications of this will be pursued further in chapter four, but it is really without any significant consequence for the discussion of this chapter; after all, (BY PASSIVE) is, as Chomsky says, only a "dummy element" (see *Aspects,* 103–6)—a technical provision that does not materially affect the meaning or nature of the underlying logical relations of deep structure as represented in this discussion.

12. In the *Aspects* model, deep structure fully determines meaning "in some important sense of this notion" (*LSLT,* 22), though it is worth noting that the slight role of surface structure in semantic interpretation was also noted in *Aspects* (221, 224–25)—a point that is often overlooked in the controversy that ensued over this important issue of deep-structure vs surface-structure meaning.

It is also important to note that Chomsky does not elaborate, in his model of deep structure, the details of the semantic interpretation component itself (the book is, after all, *Aspects of the Theory of Syntax,* not of *Semantics*), for it had already been elaborated in some detail by his young colleagues at MIT, Jerrold Katz and Jerry Fodor. See J. J. Katz and J. A. Fodor, "The Structure of a Semantic Theory" *Language* 39.2 (1963): 170–210; reprinted in Fodor & Katz, eds., *The Structure of Language: Readings in the Philosophy of Language* (Englewood Cliffs, N.J.: Prentice Hall, 1964). What Chomsky did in *Aspects* (at the suggestion of Katz and Fodor, in fact) was to formulate his syntactic model of deep structure in such a way that it *could* be read directly by a semantic component like that of Fodor and Katz.

13. Michael C. Haley, *The Semeiosis of Poetic Metaphor* (Bloomington: Indiana University Press, 1988), 102.

14. See Robert J. Matthews, "Concerning a 'Linguistic Theory' of Metaphor," *Foundations of Language* 7 (1971), 413–25; reprinted in *Linguistic Perspectives on Literature,* ed. by Marvin K. L. Ching, Michael C. Haley, and Ronald F. Lunsford (London: Routledge & Kegan Paul, 1980), 76–90.

15. See J. J. Katz and P. M. Postal, *An Integrated Theory of Linguistic Descriptions* (Cambridge, Mass.: MIT Press, 1964).

16. See R. S. Jackendoff, *Semantic Interpretation in Generative Grammar* (Cambridge, Mass.: MIT Press, 1972).

17. See Noam Chomsky, *Studies on Semantics in Generative Grammar* (The Hague: Mouton, 1972).

18. See, for example, George Lakoff, "On Generative Semantics" in D. Steinberg and L. Jacobovits, eds., *Semantics: An Interdisciplinary Reader* (Cambridge, Mass.: MIT Press, 1971). Other instigators or proponents of this approach, according to Chomsky, include a variety of his former students and/or colleagues: Paul Postal, James McCawley, John Ross, Charles Fillmore, Thomas Bever, and Peter Rosenbaum (*LangResp,* 148, 151).

19. Noam Chomsky, *Language and Politics,* ed. by C. P. Otero (Montreal: Black Rose Books, 1988), 264; hereafter cited in text as *LangPol.*

Chapter Four

1. See Robert Bieber, ed., *Dialogues on the Psychology of Language and Thought* (New York: Plenum Press, 1983), 61; Thomas S. Kuhn, *The Structure of Scientific Revolutions* (Chicago: University of Chicago Press, 1962); hereafter cited in text.

2. Kurt Gödel (1906–1978) was an Austrian-born mathematician associated with the development of recursive function theory, whose principles and notation Chomsky adapted in his early formulation of phrase-structure rules. British mathematician Alan Turing, a pioneer in the fields of computing and artificial intelligence, is perhaps best known as the inventor of the so-called Turing test of machine intelligence. The test involves submitting to a machine (e.g., a programmed computer) a series of questions and then asking whether the machine's responses might fool a human observer into believing that the responses could be those of another human being; if so, the machine is judged as having intelligence like our own. In Chomsky's view, this is merely a modern formulation of the old Cartesian mind/machine distinction; see *Managua*, 141; *KnowLang*, 234; and *Sophia*, 18.

3. Noam Chomsky, *Lectures on Government and Binding* (Dordrecht: Foris, 1981), 4; hereafter cited in text as *GovBind*. This book (which is rather difficult for nonlinguists) represented something of an opening proclamation for the second conceptual shift in Chomsky's work, although the movement itself had actually begun much earlier—surprisingly, perhaps as early as the 1960s, as Chomsky seems to indicate below.

4. Chomsky has in mind his important lectures of 1987 at Kyoto University (cited in text as *Kyoto*) and at Sophia University of Tokyo (cited in text as *Sophia*).

5. Chomsky here refers to the cognitive revolution of the 1950s as the "second" such revolution because he believes it merely recovered the revolutionary insights of philosophers like Descartes and Humboldt from the seventeenth and eighteenth centuries. Thus Chomsky is saying that what I have been calling the first revolution (of the 1950s) is really the second—which of course would make the second conceptual shift of this chapter into the third. This difficulty in numbering all the revolutions perhaps gives some credence to Chomsky's view that such talk is rather inflated.

6. As we will see later in this chapter, structural conditions of government can bind the reference of pronouns to certain antecedents or, alternatively, can dictate that such reference must be free within certain specific syntactic domains. These structural conditions that govern pronoun reference—the facts of which are often quite surprising—represent a crucial topic in Chomsky's new Government and Binding approach. It is thus natural that the label Government and Binding should often be used to designate the new theory resulting from the second conceptual shift of the 1980s, especially since the seminal publication was Chomsky's *Lectures on Government and Binding* (*GovBind*); it is nonetheless a somewhat misleading label for the new theory as a whole, inasmuch as government and binding constitute only one major complex of topics in the new theory. See the relevant section later in this chapter.

7. Among the developments leading to the second conceptual shift, Chomsky attaches considerable importance to island theory, a discovery he

attributes to one of his students, John Ross (*GenPrize* 74, 80). Basically, an island is a syntactic structure within which a given constituent is marooned (as if on an island), and from which it therefore cannot be extracted and moved by a transformation. Subject-NPs, for instance, are islands; Object-NPs are not. Thus, a WH-question transformation can extract and move a WH-word from an Object-NP, as in the following example:

Who(m) did he cause [obj-NP the downfall of ____]?

If the same NP were in the Subject position, however, applying the transformation to extract and move the WH-word from it would produce an ungrammatical sentence:

**Who(m)* did subj-NP the downfall of ____] cause concern?

This constraint on WH-movement is thus called an island constraint—*Who* is marooned (in the example above) on the island of the Subject-NP, from which it cannot be moved. Such colorful metaphors for syntactic phenomena, by the way, are rather typical of Ross. See J. R. Ross, *Constraints on Variables in Syntax,* Ph.D. dissertation (Cambridge, Mass.: MIT, 1967); published as *Infinite Syntax!* (Norwood, N.J.: Ablex Publishing, 1986). Chomsky has shown how island constraints are largely a special case of certain more general principles in his new theory (*Kyoto,* 65); for a technical discussion, see Noam Chomsky, *Barriers* (Cambridge, Mass.: MIT Press, 1986), 31–42; hereafter cited in text as *Barriers.*

    8. This is a slightly more complex example illustrating a transformational constraint somewhat like those discussed and annotated above. The ungrammatical question, "Who did you read the book that wrote?" would presumably have resulted from an illegal WH-question movement like the following:

*Who did you read the book that ____ wrote?

Chomsky's point is simply that children never make this sort of mistake, despite the fact that they often hear WH-questions that extract and move WH-words from other complex structures, as for example:

Who(m) did you read a book about ____?

    9. The A over A condition is yet another constraint on transformations. According to this general principle, if there is a constituent of type A (A =

arbitrary, or any type) that happens to contain a smaller constituent of the
same type (i.e., a smaller constituent of type A), then any transformation that
applies to a constituent of type A would have to apply to the *larger* (matrix)
A—not to the smaller A it contains. For instance, the whole phrase *a picture
of the boat* is an NP that happens to contain a smaller np (*the boat*):

[$_{NP}$ a picture of [$_{np}$ the boat $_{np}$] $_{NP}$]

According to the A-over-A constraint, the whole NP (*a picture of the boat*)
would be subject to an indirect question transformation, for instance, but not
the smaller np (*the boat*). Thus, assuming an underlying structure like:

I wonder   [*a picture of the boat* is on the table]

we could have a transformation that foregrounds the entire larger NP (*a picture
of the boat*) for interrogation:

I wonder *what* [_____ is on the table]

but not a transformation that foregrounds only the smaller np (*the boat*):

*I wonder *what* [a picture of _____ is on the table]

The status of this A-over-A principle, however, has been subject to much
debate. For more discussion, see *LangMind,* 50–56 and *KnowLang,* 71.

    10. These lectures were in fact published as *Lectures on Government and
Binding* (*GovBind*).

    11. GLOW stands for Generative Linguists in the Old Worlds (see
GenPrize, 47).

    12. The Empty Category Principle (often abbreviated in the literature
as ECP) is an important general principle of Chomsky's new Government and
Binding theory. It stipulates that an empty category (e.g., a sentence slot
vacated by a movement transformation) must be properly governed. Space
does not permit a thorough explication of the notion proper government; one
example will have to suffice for the moment. In the structure

John is likely [_____ to win]

John is understood as the NP-subject of *to win,* even though *John* has obviously
been moved out of that slot, leaving an empty category to mark its underlying
(understood) position (compare the paraphrase, "It is likely that *John* will
win"). This is possible only because *likely* happens to be a proper governor—

it governs the empty category vacated by *John,* thus trace-marking *John's* original or underlying position. However, compare the following ungrammatical sentence:

*John is probable [_____ to win]

Here, the movement of *John* out of the NP-subject position of *to win* is illegal (the grammatical form would have to be something like, "It is probable that *John* will *win,*" which keeps *John* in its underlying position). In Government and Binding theory, the explanation is simply that *probable* (in contrast to *likely*) does not happen to be a proper governor. Thus the movement of *John* in this case leaves behind an empty category that is *not* properly governed—a violation of the Empty Category Principle. Other factors besides such lexical idiosyncrasies of the sort illustrated by the difference between *likely* and *probable* enter into proper government, but the basic principle of the ECP is always the same: In order for a constituent to be moved from its underlying position to a different surface position, some governor is needed to control or place-mark the original (vacated) position, so that the underlying connections can be reconstructed by the hearer. A properly governed or place-marked empty category is called a trace in the technical literature. See Noam Chomsky, *Some Concepts and Consequences of the Theory of Government and Binding* (Cambridge, Mass.: MIT Press, 1982), 21–22; hereafter cited in text as *Concepts.* For a much more technical account, see *Barriers,* 16–21; 87–89.

13. Note that Complements and Adjuncts differ in the degree of closeness to the lexical Head (X). In the NP *a student of physics,* for instance, *of physics* is a Complement—it completes or complements the lexical idea of a student by telling what is studied. In the NP *a student with long hair,* however, *with long hair* is only an Adjunct—it only supplies additional (modifying) information about the student and does not supply anything necessary to the idea of being a student. The intimate relationship between a Head and its Complements, as opposed to the much looser or more distant relation between a Head and its Adjuncts, explains why the Adjunct must remain outside the Head-Complement relation; we can have

the student *of physics*(COMP) *with long hair*(ADJUNCT)

but not

*the student *with long hair*(ADJUNCT) *of physics*(COMP)

14. D-structure is the new theory's counterpart of the old deep structure, but there are some differences. As you will recall from chapter 3, the deep structure of *Aspects* was formed by first applying the Phrase Structure

Rules to generate an underlying tree structure and then inserting the lexical items into it. In the new theory, Phrase Structure Rules have been all but abolished in favor of the general structural principles of X-bar theory, and the Lexicon now plays a much bigger role. Basically, the words now come first: Lexical Heads project a syntactic (Complement) structure for other words to plug into, the overall configuration being formed in accordance with the general principles of X-bar theory. Thus, while words were inserted into structures in the old deep structure model, structures are projected from words in the new d-structure model. In the new theory, children are therefore acquiring structure at the very same time they are acquiring words.

15. It is for this reason, by the way, that s-structure in the new theory is not quite the same as surface structure in the old theory; s-structure is a trace-enriched version of surface structure—a version of surface structure that retains a record (in the form of traces) marking the original d-structure positions of all elements that have been moved, thus allowing the reconstruction or recovery of the underlying grammatical relations necessary to semantic interpretation. This also of course explains why semantic interpretation is now possible at the level of s-structure in the new model (in contrast to the old model, where semantic interpretation had to take place at the level of deep structure). This solves a host of problems related to semantic interpretation; see the concluding sections of Chapter 3.

Chapter Five

1. Noam Chomsky and Edward Herman, *The Washington Connection and Third World Fascism*: Volume 1 of *Political Economy of Human Rights*. (Nottingham, Eng.: Spokesman, 1979), ix; hereafter cited in text as *WashConn*.

2. Noam Chomsky, *On Power and Ideology* (Boston: South End Press, 1987), 7; hereafter cited in text as *PowerIdeol*.

3. Noam Chomsky, *American Power and the New Mandarins* (New York: Pantheon, 1969), 179; hereafter cited in text as *AmerPower*.

4. Noam Chomsky, *Pirates and Emperors* (Brattleboro, Vermont: Amana Books, 1986), 29; hereafter cited in text as *PirEmpers*.

5. Noam Chomsky, *Modular Approaches to the Study of the Mind* (San Diego: San Diego State University Press, 1984), 16; emphasis added.

6. Chomsky made statements to this effect during an appearance on the MacNeil/Lehrer Newshour on PBS prior to the Gulf War.

7. Julie Tetel Andresen, *Linguistics in America 1769–1924: A Critical History* (New York: Routledge, 1990); hereafter cited in text as *LingAmer*.

8. William Dwight Whitney, *Language and the Study of Language. Twelve Lectures on the Principles of Linguistic Science*, 5th edition (New York: Charles Scribner's, 1887 [1867]), 404.

9. Chomsky makes this point very clear in *Sophia*: "We might refer to

such systems [as the language facility] as 'mental organs,' again, *not supposing that the physical realizations are literally separable*" [emphasis added] (2).

10. Andresen, *Linguistics in America 1769–1924: A Critical History*, asserts that "Whitney views linguistic science to be a branch of the moral sciences and not the physical sciences."

11. The language here may remind the reader of Emily Dickinson's poem "Much Madness":

> Much Madness is divinest sense
> To a discerning eye;
> Much sense the starkest madness
> 'T is the majority
> In this, as all, prevails.
> Assent, and you are sane;
> Demur,—you're straightway dangerous,
> And handled with a chain.

The parallels between Dickinson's "discerning eye" and Chomsky's are striking.

12. Noam Chomsky, *Problems of Knowledge and Freedom: The Russell Lectures* (New York: Pantheon Books, 1971), 94.

13. Walter Blair, ed., *Selected Shorter Writings of Mark Twain* (Boston: Houghton Mifflin, 1962). See, for example, p. 293: "Sometimes an ordained minister sets out to be blasphemous. When this happens, the layman is out of the running; he doesn't stand a chance."

14. Noam Chomsky, speaking at a benefit for the Middle East Children's Alliance (president, Barbara Lubin) and KPFA radio (manager, Pat Scott) at the University of California at Berkeley on Saturday, 16 March 1991. Topic: The New World Order.

Selected Bibliography

PRIMARY SOURCES

Books

American Power and the New Mandarins. New York: Pantheon, 1969.
Aspects of the Theory of Syntax. Cambridge, Mass.: MIT Press, 1965.
Barriers. Cambridge, Mass.: MIT Press, 1986.
Cartesian Linguistics: A Chapter in the History of Rationalist Thought. New York: Harper and Row, 1966.
The Chomsky Reader (James Peck, ed.). New York: Pantheon Books, 1987.
Current Issues in Linguistic Theory. The Hague: Mouton, 1964.
Generative Grammar: Its Basis, Development and Prospects. Kyoto, Japan: Kyoto University of Foreign Studies, 1987.
Knowledge of Language: Its Nature, Origin, and Use. New York: Praeger, 1986.
Language and Learning: The Debate between Jean Piaget and Noam Chomsky (edited by Massimo Piattelli-Palmarini). Cambridge, Mass.: Harvard University Press, 1980.
Language and Mind (enlarged edition). New York: Harcourt Brace Jovanovich, 1972.
Language and Politics (C. P. Otero, ed.). Montreal: Black Rose Books, 1988.
Language and Problems of Knowledge: The Managua Lectures. Cambridge, Mass.: MIT Press, 1988.
Language and Responsibility (Mitsou Ronat, ed.). New York: Pantheon, 1979.
Language in a Psychological Setting. Tokyo: Sophia University, 1987.
Lectures on Government and Binding. Dordrecht, Neth.: Foris, 1981.
The Logical Structure of Linguistic Theory. New York: Plenum Press, 1975.
Modular Approaches to the Study of The Mind. San Diego: San Diego State University Press, 1984.
Morphophonemics of Modern Hebrew. New York and London: Garland Publishing, 1979.
Noam Chomsky on the Generative Enterprise, a Discussion with Riny Huybregts and Henk van Riemsdijk. Dordrecht, Neth.: Foris, 1982.
On Power and Ideology. Boston: South End Press, 1987.
Pirates and Emperors. Brattleboro, Vermont: Amana Books, 1986.
Problems of Knowledge and Freedom: The Russell Lectures. New York: Pantheon Books, 1971.

Reflections on Language. New York: Pantheon, 1975.
Rules and Representations. New York: Columbia University Press, 1980.
Some Concepts and Consequences of the Theory of Government and Binding. Cambridge, Mass.: MIT Press, 1982.
Sound Pattern of English (with Morris Halle). New York: Harper and Row, 1968.
Studies on Semantics in Generative Grammar. The Hague: Mouton, 1972.
Syntactic Structures. The Hague: Mouton, 1957.
Topics in the Theory of Generative Grammar. The Hague: Mouton, 1966.
The Washington Connection and Third World Fascism (with Edward Herman). Nottingham, Eng.: Spokesman, 1979.

Papers and Articles

"The Algebraic Theory of Context-Free Languages" (with M. P. Schützenberger). In P. Braffort and D. Hirschberg, eds., *Computer Programming and Formal Systems: Studies in Logic* (Amsterdam: North Holland, 1963).
"Finitary Models of Language Users" (with George Miller). In R. D. Luce, R. Bush, and E. Galanter, eds., *Handbook of Mathematical Psychology,* vol. II (New York: Wiley, 1963).
"Formal Properties of Grammar." In R. D. Luce, R. Bush, and E. Galanter, eds., *Handbook of Mathematical Psychology,* vol. II (New York: Wiley, 1963).
"The Logical Basis of Linguistic Theory." In *Proceedings of the Ninth International Congress of Linguists,* ed. by H. Lunt (The Hague: Mouton, 1964), 914–78.
"The Morphophonemics of English" (with Morris Halle). *RLE Quarterly Progress Report* 68 (1960): 275–81.
"Some Controversial Questions in Phonological Theory" (with Morris Halle). *Journal of Linguistics* 1.2 (1965): 97–138.
"Systems of Syntactic Analysis." *Journal of Symbolic Logic* 18.3 (September 1953): 242–56.
"Three Models for the Description of Language." *IRE Transactions on Information Theory* IT-2.3 (September 1956):113–24. Reprinted in *Readings in Mathematical Psychology,* ed. by Luce, Bush, and Galanter, vol. II (New York: John Wiley & Sons, 1965), 105–24.
"A Transformational Approach to Syntax." *Proceedings of the Third Texas Conference on Problems of Linguistic Analysis in English* (May 9–12, 1958), ed. by A. A. Hill (Austin: University of Texas Press, 1962), 124–58. Reprinted in *The Structure of Language: Readings in the Philosophy of Language,* ed. by J. A. Fodor and J. Katz (Englewood Cliffs, NJ: Prentice Hall, 1964), 211–45, as well as in *Classics in Linguists,* ed. by Hayden, Alworth, and Tate (New York: Philosophical Library, 1967), 337–71.

Unpublished Material

Tapes and transcripts of three interviews with Noam Chomsky conducted by Michael C. Haley and Ronald F. Lunsford at MIT on 1 December 1989, 4 December 1989, and 7 December 1989.

SECONDARY SOURCES

Ching, Marvin K. L., Michael C. Haley, and Ronald F. Lunsford, eds. *Linguistic Perspectives on Literature.* London: Routledge & Kegan Paul, 1980. A collection of essays using Chomsky's model of language as a tool for investigation of style and figurative language in literature.

Cook, Dean Elton. *Chomsky: Towards a Rationalist Philosophy of Science.* Ph.D. dissertation, University of Missouri, Columbia, 1981. Good analysis of Chomsky's theories of knowledge and scientific discovery, especially as they relate to Peirce's theory of "abduction."

Cook, V. J. *Chomsky's Universal Grammar.* Oxford: Basil Blackwell, 1988. Clear and readable introduction to Chomsky's latest theories on Universal Grammar, Government and Binding, X-bar theory, Case Theory, and so forth; particularly good on the relevance of Chomsky's recent work to language instruction and first and second language acquisition.

Gardner, Howard. *The Mind's New Science: A History of the Cognitive Revolution.* New York: Basic Books, 1985. Excellent intellectual history of the cognitive revolution in which Chomsky participated during the 1950s and following.

Gleick, James. *Chaos.* New York: Penguin Books, 1987. Fascinating and easy-to-read introduction to modern chaos theory that seems influential in Chomsky's most recent work.

Harris, Zellig. *Methods of Structural Linguistics.* Chicago: University of Chicago Press, 1951. This is the book that Chomsky cites as having provided his formal introduction to structural linguistics; Harris was Chomsky's teacher.

Kuhn, Thomas S. *The Structure of Scientific Revolutions.* Chicago: University of Chicago Press, 1962. The standard work describing Kuhn's theories on how and why "paradigm shifts" occur in the history of science.

Lees, Robert. "Review of Noam Chomsky's *Syntactic Structures,*" *Language* 33.3 (1957):375–407. Chomsky credits this review by his student, Robert Lees, with having drawn the attention of the linguistic community to *Syntactic Structures.*

Leiber, Justin. *Noam Chomsky: A Philosophic Overview.* New York: St. Martin's Press, 1975. Readable and helpful introduction to and assessment of Chomsky's theories from a philosopher's point of view.

Lyons, John. *Noam Chomsky*. New York: The Viking Press, 1970. Lucid and helpful introduction to Chomsky's early theories (up through *Aspects of the Theory of Syntax*).

Tomas, Vincent, ed. *Peirce's Essays in the Philosophy of Science*. New York: Liberal Arts Press, 1957. A collection of essays on epistemology by the American semiotician and philosopher Charles Sanders Peirce, whose theory of "abduction" was influential in Chomsky's work.

Index

The Authors

Michael C. Haley is professor of English at the University of Alaska Anchorage, where he teaches general linguistics, transformational grammar, and linguistic/semiotic approaches to literature. His other works include *The Semeiosis of Poetic Metaphor* (Bloomington: Indiana University Press, 1989), and he is the managing editor of *The Peirce Seminar Papers* (Berg, forthcoming).

Ronald F. Lunsford is professor of English and chair of the English department at the University of North Carolina at Charlotte, where he teaches courses in language, composition theory, and rhetoric. His other works include (with Michael Moran) *Research in Composition and Rhetoric* (Westport, Conn.: Greenwood Press, 1984) and (with Richard Straub) *Twelve Readers Reading: Responding to Student Writing* (New York: McGraw-Hill, forthcoming).

Lunsford and Haley studied linguistics together in graduate school at Florida State University, and they have collaborated on other works, including *Linguistic Perspectives on Literature* (London: Routledge & Kegan Paul, 1980), for which they were contributing coeditors with Marvin K. L. Ching.